QUEER
Allusion

POETIC
CONNECTIONS
from WILDE
to GINSBERG

FLORIAN
GARGAILLO

Louisiana State University Press
BATON ROUGE

Published by Louisiana State University Press
lsupress.org

Designer: Kaelin Chappell Broaddus
Typefaces: Fournier MT Std, text; Bodoni Classic, display

Cover illustrations: paper card, Adobe Stock / Sociologas;
marbled paper background, Adobe Stock / alexlibris.

Cataloging-in-Publication Data are available from the Library of Congress.

ISBN 978-0-8071-8473-8 (cloth: alk. paper) —
ISBN 978-0-8071-8556-8 (pdf) — ISBN 978-0-8071-8555-1 (epub)

CONTENTS

QUEER
ALLUSION

Introduction

If you had leafed through the British journal *Academy* in July 1887, you would likely have come across a love poem by Amy Levy titled "London in July." At this point in her life, Levy had enjoyed moderate success as an author. She had already published two volumes of poetry, *Xantippe* (1881) and *A Minor Poet* (1884), but she had yet to release her first novel, *The Romance of a Shop* (1888), or the collection *A London-Plane Tree* (1889), which would feature her best-known verse. As a love poem, "London in July" is elusive as much as it is ardent. The speaker is described winding through the busy city streets, haunted by the memory of an unnamed lover. The beloved's gender is made clear in the first stanza, when we are told that all the people in the street "wear one woman's face." The pronoun *she* in the following stanza settles the matter.[1] Strikingly, though, Levy never discloses the *speaker's* gender. Most readers in 1887 would have assumed that the poet had adopted a man's perspective and that the speaker is a fictional mask, distinct from Levy herself. But others would have been alert to a second possibility. This smaller circle of readers may have been familiar with the particulars of Levy's life. For example, all of Levy's affections had been for other women. During her student days at the Brighton High School for Girls, she wrote letters about her "grand passion" for the headmistress. Later, at Newnham College, she developed feelings for fellow student Helen Gladstone and lovingly sketched her profile in correspondence. In 1886, one year before the publication of this poem, she met the novelist Vernon Lee while visiting Florence and fell in love.[2] Certainly, Levy's closest friends would have known these details from her letters or conversations and so identified the homoerotic potential of "London in July." But the poem's omission of gender would also have been discernible to a larger audience of queer readers, eager to discover in literature traces of same-sex love and clues that the author shared their own experience.

Four decades later, Valentine Ackland alluded to "London in July" in her own poem "The Eyes of the Body," inspired by her love for fellow poet Sylvia Townsend Warner. Ackland had been introduced to Warner in 1927, and while their first meeting was rather stilted, they felt immediately attracted to one another. Three years later, Warner bought a cottage in Chaldon and asked Ackland to look after it when she was in London. As they grew closer, they decided to cohabitate, sleeping in separate rooms until one night in 1931, when they first made love. They became lifelong partners after that point.[3] Written during the first few months of their relationship, "The Eyes of the Body" later appeared in *Whether a Dove or a Seagull* (1933), a book combining pieces by both Ackland and Warner. The poem borrows extensively from Levy's language, drawing out the eroticism that had remained implicit there. Consider the climax of "London in July," in which the speaker imagines the possibility of a reunion:

> O various and intricate maze,
>   Wide waste of square and street
> Where, missing through unnumbered days,
>   We twain at last may meet![4]

And compare it to the following lines by Ackland:

> Thus and by these ordered ways
> I come at you—Hand deft and delicate
> To trace the suavely laid and intricate
> Route of your body's maze.

The rhythm and tone are entirely different. Levy's stanza is notable for its clarity. Three of the four lines end with a pause for breath, thanks to a comma or an exclamation mark. Levy also reinforces the sense of directness by only using stressed monosyllables as rhyming words: *maze, street, days, meet*. By contrast, Ackland allows herself to meander. There are enjambments throughout the stanza, even an awkward split between noun ("maze") and adjective ("intricate"). Moreover, the middle rhyme is based not on stressed monosyllables but on three-syllable words ending in unstressed syllables. The resulting tone is still firm, at least in the first line and a half: "I come *at* you," not *to* you. But after the dash in particular, the tone grows more sensuous, luxuriating, as "deft and delicate" as the hand that it describes.

The most important change, however, occurs with the poem's imagery. Ackland takes the labyrinthine city of "London in July" and turns it into a metaphor for the lover's body. In Levy, the city is a psychological landscape that absorbs and reflects the speaker's longing. In Ackland, the body itself becomes a world for the poet to explore. The metamorphosis not only makes desire explicit but also satisfies through poetry the lust that remains unfulfilled in Levy. While the latter does express joy at the thought of finding her lover in the mazelike streets of London, she says that the two "*may* meet," not that they "*will* meet." In the last stanza, she claims to be satisfied by "The summer in the city's heart— / That is enough for me." Because their reunion will likely not come to pass, she must content herself with the summer heat. In "The Eyes of the Body," however, the poet touches the beloved directly: "I come at you—Hand deft and delicate." The speaker also exerts far more control. Whereas Levy's speaker roams the maze, lost like the beloved but still separated from her, this poet stands above the "maze" of the lover's body, able to view and caress her as she pleases. The poem ends dramatically with sexual contact, which she describes like an aircraft strike:

> My hand, being deft and delicate, displays
> Unerring judgment; cleaves between your thighs
> Clean, as a ray-directed airplane flies.[5]

The boldness of this poem's sexual expression is partly an attempt to disturb the timidity of Levy's writing, to coax its buried impulses into the light. But the attitude is not corrective. "The Eyes of the Body" is generous in its effort to grant Levy what she did not feel she could grant herself. Ackland recognizes the desires that Levy could only write about indirectly, and by making them explicit, she affirms their validity.

This book argues for the importance of allusion for LGBTQ poets, particularly during the pre-Stonewall era, when the obliqueness—but not total obscurity—of allusion granted writers much-needed protection. These references are distinct enough in their function and sensibility to warrant a distinct category: what I call "queer allusion." The purpose of this poetic tool is manifold. On a personal level, queer allusion enables LGBTQ poets to make virtual connections with authors who share similar experiences. The pleasure of allusion for these poets stems from the realization that they are not alone, that others have felt the same desires, and that their emotions are not deviant but part of a longer history. In other words, their lives are vindicated by being reflected in some of the most canonical works of literature. By weighing their experiences against those of their predecessors, queer authors can seek to better understand themselves. On a public level, queer allusion makes it possible for poets to establish an alternative literary canon, distinct from the canon established by critics, scholars, and institutions. By claiming a prior text, the poet recodes it as queer, no matter if its author is known to be queer or merely suspected of such. In turn, the writer can assert their own position within that alternative literary tradition, making themself a part of that which they help to build. This is not to say that queer allusion is merely self-serving. It also extends a hand to LGBTQ readers who are eager to find signs of kinship in poetry. For these individuals as well, queer allusion offers an opportunity for reassurance, self-affirmation, and companionship.

Queer allusion is a historical phenomenon originating in the late nineteenth century, along with a broader cultural shift in the understanding of sexuality. As Michel Foucault and Eve Sedgwick both famously demonstrated, the invention of "homosexuality" as a word and a concept led sexuality to be viewed in terms of identity rather than action.[6] A person did not simply perform a sexual act with another man or woman; they *were* homosexual. It was now said that same-sex desires reflected a distinct identity, which "the homosexual" needed to conceal. Queer allusion emerged in this context as a way for LGBTQ poets to understand themselves and their experiences. Because homosexuality carried with it significant risks to one's reputation and safety, allusion provided a useful, and partial, cover.

The special appeal of allusion to queer poets lies in its peculiar mix of openness and secrecy. Allusion requires the reader not just to identify the text that is being referenced but also to make sense of the connection. This poses a challenge no matter how explicit the allusion may be. As William Irwin points out, a line such as T. S. Eliot's "No! I am not Prince Hamlet," which goes so far as to give us a name, still requires the reader to decide which aspects of Shakespeare's character Eliot invokes and which he excludes. Besides, allusions are typically more discreet than this, relying not on names and titles but on verbal echoes that readers will recognize only if they are intimately familiar with the source text. Irwin takes this further and says that allusions "are often covert; they may even be concealed."[7] Yet allusions are also there to be identified by readers able to trace the lineage of a given phrase or line and puzzle through its significance to the new work. Queer allusions function like open secrets, revealing just enough for interested parties to recognize their meaning but also withholding enough to afford the poet protection from readers who may be hostile to their experience.

The double nature of allusion resonated deeply with a culture that depended on codes—be it a gesture, a glance, a choice of dress and accessory, or a fixed phrase ("Do you have the time?")—to connect. Graham Robb has described several examples in his book on gay life in nineteenth-century England: "Certain expressions and gestures were almost universally understood: slightly prolonged eye contact, a flick of the tongue, a particular way of smoking a cigarette or offering a light, a style of dress."[8] Granted, the immediate purpose of allusion differs from the social codes described here. By evoking other texts, poets do not seek to identify potential sexual or romantic interest. Instead, they wish to engage with oblique expressions of desire, to explore and understand their own experiences, and to enable future readers to do the same as well. They do, however, share a broader impulse and motivation: a desire to connect.

Queer allusion presents us with a different way of thinking about poetry's relationship to the literature of the past. Influence has usually been discussed according to one of two models. The first is Walter Jackson Bate's notion of literary history as a "debt" or "burden." According to this model, the poet feels powerfully their tininess in relation to the achievements of their forebears. Since the Renaissance, in fact, artists have suffered a "remorseless deepening of self-consciousness, before the rich and intimidating legacy of the past," which seemed to be expanding constantly. But the pressure has also fostered a "search for difference," a desire to "contribute in some respect, however small."[9] For Bate, influence is a form of tribute but one that ultimately positions the new poet as inferior and beholden to their predecessor. The second, much-cited model is Harold Bloom's "anxiety of influence." Borrowing from Freud's theory of Oedipal struggle, Bloom has argued that poets find themselves locked in a masculinist competition for dominance with their predecessors. The literary antecedent is cast as the father, while the younger poet assumes the role of the son. As in Bate, the past is a burden, but it is not a positive force inspiring the author to make a modest contribution, "however small." Rather, the specter of prior achievements creates considerable stress for the young artist. The only way that they can achieve dominance over their predecessor and figuratively "kill the father" is to perform what Bloom calls "creative misprision," willfully and creatively distorting the source text to produce a radically new work.[10] For Bloom, very few writers achieve this supremacy to become "strong poets." Most remain "weak poets," feebly reflecting their influences but never innovating upon them.

Both models are deeply hierarchical. The poet is always hyperaware of their status in relation to their predecessor, whether that awareness proves enabling or disabling. Queer allusion expresses a different sensibility. This is not to say queer allusion is always free of friction, be it envy or a feeling of inadequacy. But the emotions underlying this mode of reference extend beyond gratitude and hostility to longing, titillation, excitement, and sympathy. When queer poets look to other poems for parallels to their experience, literary history ceases to be a distant, intimidating monolith. Because it is immediately and personally relevant, the canon also becomes malleable. The new poet enjoys far more freedom to play around with the material once they have established a personal connection. They no longer view their predecessor as an abstract force, an overbearing parent, or a relentless competitor, but as kin. Of course, queer allusion cannot erase hierarchical relations entirely, but it can bring poets past and present closer to equal footing. The idea proposed by Christopher Ricks, that poets allude to prior works to come to terms with their loneliness, better reflects the sensibility of queer allusion than the theories of Bate and Bloom.[11] Ultimately, all queer allusions are motivated by a common desire: to see oneself in poetry and thereby to feel a little less alone. The relationship that LGBTQ poets seek through their antecedents is not competition but companionship.

At this juncture, it may be useful to further narrow the definition of queer allusion as I use it throughout the book. Importantly, queer allusion does not encompass all allusions by or to queer-identifying poets. The term refers to a specific *use* of allusion, rather than simply the sexuality of the poet performing the allusion or the poet being referenced. For instance, I would not discuss under this rubric W. H. Auden's allusions to the Bible ("A prophet is not without honor, save in his own country, and in his own house" [Matthew 13:57]) in "Adolescence" ("this prophet, homing the day is ended, / Receives odd welcome from the country he so defended"). The unnamed figure in Auden represents the entirety of English youth, whose ambitious desire for rebellion is thwarted by social constraint and family influence, rather than the gay teenager specifically. For similar reasons, I would not include Philip Larkin's allusion to Auden's "New Year Letter" ("the abyss / That always lies just underneath") in "Ambulances" ("the solving emptiness / That lies just under all we do"), since both passages are concerned with existentialism, not any of the particularities of gay life.[12] By queer allusion, I have in mind passages in which a queer author, in alluding to a prior text, apprehends that text as reflecting issues connected to queer experiences—from gender expression and closeted desire to social alienation—either because the author believes their predecessor to have been LGBTQ themself or because they are choosing to recode the source text through allusion so that it can speak to those experiences.

It is more difficult to determine the intended audience for queer allusion. In making use of this technique, were poets writing for their immediate contemporaries or for readers in the future? Did they envision their audience as an elite subset with a specialized knowledge of Anglo-American poetry, or is queer allusion more democratic in its reach? Readership is largely a matter of speculation, except in rare cases in which the poet addresses or evokes an audience directly. However, it is possible to make some tentative generalizations based on the distinctiveness of this poetic tool. First, queer allusions can reach both contemporary and future readers. They operate like proverbial messages in a bottle: missives to be read by whoever chances to find them and understand them, be it on the year of the poem's publication or at a later point in time. The issue of specialization is far stickier. Granted, a reader does need some knowledge of Anglo-American poetic history to identify Adrienne Rich's allusion to Christina Rossetti's "Goblin Market" in "Holiday" or Countee Cullen's evocation of A. E. Housman's love poems in "Advice to Youth" and "To a Brown Boy." One could say that the price of admission to these allusions is relatively high: not just a solid literary education but time and leisure to read widely. However, the same could be said of all forms of allusion, so that familiarity with the canon, and the social privileges this requires, is not the determining characteristic of queer allusion. During the period discussed in this book (the 1890s to the 1960s), such advantages were complicated by the hostility of a dominant heterosexual culture to queer experiences at every level of society. The more important feature of queer allusion's intended audience is the reader's alienation from the mainstream and their willingness to reconstruct a history that has been quietly, and in many cases intentionally, buried.

This book contributes to recent studies of how LGBTQ authors have sought to create an alternative history. For instance, Christopher Nealon's *Foundlings: Lesbian and Gay Historical Emotion before Stonewall* (2001) examines queer authors' complex relationship to the past, arguing that many view themselves as "foundlings," alienated from traditional structures of family and nation.[13] At the same time, Nealon shows that this sense of exile has led LGBTQ authors to envision their own lineages and communities. Likewise, Kevin Ohi, in *Dead Letters Sent: Queer Literary Transmission* (2015), considers how queer authors have tried to pass down "a minority queer culture . . . from generation to generation" by encoding "queer meaning in contexts that often forbid explicit mention of queer concerns."[14] He reflects on how LGBTQ readers have recognized these codes and established an alternative ancestry, standing apart from the domains of mainstream culture and the biological family that have often proved so inhospitable. My book continues that line of inquiry by looking closely at a major, yet under-discussed, technique that queer poets have used to form virtual communities and lineages.

Queer Allusion spans roughly eight decades, from the trial of Oscar Wilde (which made that new idea "homosexuality" the subject of much public discussion) to the late 1960s and the LGBTQ rights movement that followed the Stonewall Riots. The term *queer* that I lean on throughout this book is, of course, anachronistic when dealing with the late nineteenth and early twentieth centuries. I use it not to elide the difficult history of terminology surrounding same-sex affection but merely out of convenience. This period witnessed radical transformations in how gender and sexuality were understood, both within scientific circles and among the broader public. It would be impossible to provide a satisfactory account of these changes here, since any such summary would doubtless feel shallow. However, the readings in this book will collectively provide an overview of the evolving ideas surrounding gender and sexuality through specific examples. By studying how poets engaged with prior texts, *Queer Allusion* considers how the poems reflect LGBTQ culture at the time, the poet's own self-development, as well as the public understanding of sexuality.

Readers looking for queer allusions will discover unusual pairings between poets who are rarely considered together. Because these authors sought antecedents to their lived experiences, oblique expressions of queerness became more important than other, expected affinities based on style, movement, or artistic principles. Poets as different as Charlotte

Mew, Amy Lowell, and Adrienne Rich all engaged with Christina Rossetti. A. E. Housman (the Victorian poet whose popularity rested, at least
in part, on his quintessential "Englishness") keeps company with Countee
Cullen (one of the most important figures of the Harlem Renaissance).
It is here that the promise of an alternative canon bears fruit. For queer
allusion brought together poets who would otherwise appear in different segments of literary history. Indeed, they *have* been separated by the
structure of academic criticism, which requires scholars to delimit their
field according to a specific era or movement. Queer allusion forces us to
think beyond the usual categories of literary studies.

To show the unique conversations made possible by queer allusion
and to demonstrate the nuances and complexities of this method in action, I will consider here an example of Elizabeth Bishop alluding to Amy
Lowell. These writers are almost never considered together. Amy Lowell
is one of the founding members of Imagism, a movement committed to
austere simplicity and purity of diction. Elizabeth Bishop, meanwhile,
eschews simplicity for a more challenging style marked by unusual shifts
in perspective and associative descriptions. It is not surprising, then, that
Lowell has never been identified as an influence on her. Yet Bishop did
allude to Lowell in the most sensual piece she ever published: "The Shampoo," from *A Cold Spring* (1955), inspired by her partner, Lota de Macedo
Soares. Bishop first got to know Lota deeply in 1951, when she moved to
Brazil on a traveling fellowship awarded by Bryn Mawr College. Lota
served as her host, and the two women lived together in a top-floor apartment with beautiful views of Rio. When Bishop fell in love with Lota,
she decided to stay in Brazil even beyond the end of her fellowship. "The
Shampoo" is based on the first blissful weeks of their relationship. The
hair-washing scene was especially significant to Bishop because of its association with intimacy and caretaking but also because (as she reported
in a letter to May Swenson) it was Lota's "straight long black hair" that
struck her most intensely during their first meeting in Rio.[15]

Fittingly, the two poems that Bishop evokes in "The Shampoo"—
"Bright Sunlight" and "Merchandise"—are love poems as well, based
on Lowell's relationship with the actress Ada Dwyer Russell, whom she

met in Boston in 1909. It took longer for the two to settle down together, Russell repeatedly turning down Lowell's invitations to move in with her permanently. Still, they eventually became life partners, until Lowell's passing in 1925 (more on their story later).[16] In "Bright Sunlight," Lowell describes Ada standing by a fountain, so distracted by the clouds that she fails to notice the corner of her shawl blowing into the water. In "Merchandise," Lowell adopts the persona of a singer who once performed a beautiful song for their lover and who offers to sing it again in exchange for a silver shilling. Both poems appeared in the same book, *Pictures of the Floating World* (1919), so their reunion in a single poem by Bishop is even more appropriate. But while "The Shampoo" builds upon a series of images in Lowell, the context, narrative, and sensibility are quite different. Bishop allows herself the freedom to reimagine Lowell's poetry for her own purposes.

In "The Shampoo," Bishop describes the intense pleasure she feels washing her lover's hair, so that the environment surrounding her becomes wondrous. In the first stanza, she writes:

> The still explosions on the rocks,
> the lichens grow
> by spreading, gray, concentric shocks.
> They have arranged
> to meet the rings around the moon, although
> within our memories they have not changed.

She goes on to describe the "shooting stars" in her beloved's hair, until she finally interrupts herself to make a direct plea: "—Come, let me wash it in this big tin basin, / battered and shiny like the moon."[17] The first way that Bishop engages with Lowell is by borrowing the circular imagery from her poems. In "Bright Sunlight," Lowell describes her lover so: "Your fingers pick at the lichens / On the stone edge of the basin." These two line-ending words supply the first object of "The Shampoo" (the "lichens" growing like "still explosions on the rocks") as well as its last ("this big tin basin" in which the speaker is about to wash their lover's hair). The ending of "The Shampoo" also evokes a specific line from the second stanza of "Merchandise," in which the singer requests a shilling for their song.

> Would you like to hear my song?
> I will play it to you
> As I did that evening to my Beloved,
> Standing on the moon-bright cobbles
> Underneath her window.
> But you are not my Beloved,
> You must give me a silver shilling,
> Round and glittering like the moon.[18]

Bishop's "battered and shiny like the moon" closely echoes Lowell's own "Round and glittering like the moon." Yet Bishop does not simply copy the circular images in Lowell's poems: she expands on them. The "lichens" are said to be "spreading" in "gray, concentric shocks" like "explosions," while the "moon" ripples outward, forming multiple "rings." Lowell's imagery finds itself multiplied and magnified—a fitting metaphor for the process of allusion itself.

Despite these parallels, Bishop might appear to change the tone and significance of Lowell's images. In "Merchandise," the singer requires a silver shilling as payment for song because their love is so precious that anything cheaper would devalue it:

> Copper I will not take
> How should copper pay for a song
> All made out of nothing,
> And so beautiful!

In Bishop, by contrast, the shilling "round and glittering like the moon" becomes a basin "battered and shiny like the moon," a far less immaculate object than Lowell's. The oxymoronic description, of a thing that was damaged and yet continues to shine, fits nicely with Bishop's aesthetic sensibility, her attraction to things that have weathered much but can still impress. (One close analogue is the titular subject of "The Fish," "battered and venerable / and homely.")[19] Bishop captures a deeper quality in Lowell's tone than the expected Imagist traits of simplicity and directness. The speaker of "Merchandise" is weary because their beloved is no longer with them; their performance must be a pale copy to some extent. Yet it still holds tremendous value because of the love that it evokes. That paradox gets carried over to Bishop's "battered and shiny" basin—which, like Lowell's song, is "so beautiful" even though it is "all made out of nothing." Granted, the paradox in "The Shampoo" stems from a different emotional situation: settled domestic love. The poet and the beloved are well past the first blush of passion. Bishop conveys this through the cool, formal, evaluative quality of words like *precipitate, pragmatical,* and *amenable,* which invoke the mind rather than the heart. In this context, the phrase *dear friend* functions less as a euphemism meant to disguise the romantic nature of the relationship (though it does serve that end to some degree) and more as an accurate reflection of the companionship they have achieved over time. The fact that they share a history is made clear by the reference to "our memories" at the end of the first stanza. However, their comfort does not prevent her from enjoying occasional moments of wonder. As the speaker washes their beloved's hair, the whole basin becomes luminous and celestial, as shiny as the moon that hangs above their heads. The paradoxes in "Shampoo" dovetail with those in "Merchandise." By alluding to Lowell, Bishop draws on certain poetic qualities that other poets and critics, focused on the literary movement that Lowell is known for, may have overlooked.

Bishop's reimagining of lines from "Merchandise" and "Bright Sunlight" shows the complex process of queer allusion. Bishop identified the homoeroticism that was implicit in Lowell and used her poems as a starting point for her own work. Through allusion, she transformed Lowell's imagery to fit the specific emotional situation that she wanted to represent. Bishop does not approach Lowell as a burden who will always overshadow her. Nor is her attitude competitive: she does not distort Lowell's verse to show that she can be the stronger, more dominant poet. Instead, her allusions build creatively on Lowell's poetry. Bishop finds comfort in, and expresses appreciation for, a poet who wrote about same-sex love in a partly open, partly covert fashion before her. At the same time, she also feels free to play around with Lowell's poetry and use it for her own purposes, to describe a different emotional situation. Lowell is not a relic of the past that must be preserved at all cost, nor must she be dominated to make way for the new. She is an active voice that Bishop can engage with in the present. This attitude is the dominant mode of queer allusion as it emerged in the late nineteenth century and as it continues to this day.

This book is divided into two parts, each focused on a different subtype of queer allusion. The first, titled "Fellowships," considers two pairs of poets who shared a close personal connection for several years and who used allusion to reflect on that connection while retaining some degree of privacy. The nature of the relationship varied considerably. Oscar Wilde and Lord Alfred Douglas had a tempestuous romantic and sexual affair that lasted nearly ten years. By alluding to lines from Wilde's *Poems* (1881), published a decade before their first meeting, Douglas sought to articulate his feelings about Wilde and present his own view of their relationship. He drew from *Poems* for thirty years, well beyond his companion's death in 1900. When read in sequence, Douglas's poems reveal his shifting emotions about Wilde, from the affection and longing of their early years together to his deep pain upon Wilde's passing and later his renunciation of homosexuality during the 1910s, after converting to Roman Catholicism. W. H. Auden and Stephen Spender, the second pair of poets, were not involved sexually or romantically. Instead, their friendship was founded on creative mentorship. When the two met at Oxford in the summer of 1928, Auden had established himself as the leader of a group of aspiring writers. Spender, timid and in search of a guide, found himself swept up into Auden's orbit. Like many young poets in the decade that followed, Spender imitated general features of Auden's style, like his impersonal tone and his aerial, eagle-like point of view. Yet surprisingly, he rarely echoed specific lines or phrases. Instead, it was Auden who alluded to Spender repeatedly throughout his career. Allusion enabled him not only to acknowledge his influence on Spender but also to think through the differences between them and defend his own approach. At times, he even used allusion to school Spender—for example, by taking his friend's thinly veiled love poems, which he deemed too adolescent, and revising these into works of political commentary, politics being, to his mind, a more appropriate subject for the modern poet to take up. But his allusions also tell a sadder story of lost friendship. As Spender abandoned gay love and focused his affections on women, Auden turned to poetry to mourn a profound shift in their relationship. Although the two remained friends for the remainder of Auden's life, his allusions to Spender suggest that he felt an important aspect of their connection—a common experience of sexuality—had been lost. His final allusions to Spender serve as an act of leave-taking and an attempt to hold on to the memory of their relationship through the medium of poetry.

The second part of this book, titled "Lineages," focuses on cases in which a poem or book is alluded to by multiple writers across time. These examples show the capacity of allusion to build an alternative literary canon. The third chapter traces the history of queer responses to Christina Rossetti's "Goblin Market" (1862). While biographers deem it unlikely that Rossetti was queer, many LGBTQ poets have detected the potential for coded queerness in the sensual description of physical touch between the sisters Laura and Lizzie. The remarkable thing about these responses is their diversity of theme, tone, and style. For A. E. Housman, "Goblin Market" became a resource to think about the pain and pleasure of unrequited love. Charlotte Mew saw in Rossetti's poem a welcome depiction of queer solitude as a shelter from the world that must be preserved no matter the cost. To Amy Lowell's ear, "Goblin Market" expressed the joys of sensuality at a time when physical pleasure was viewed with condemnation, specifically for women and even more so for lesbians. Finally, Adrienne Rich saw in the poem a daring representation of the ephemerality of same-sex romance in a hostile culture.

The fourth chapter considers poetic allusions to A. E. Housman's *A Shropshire Lad* (1896), a volume that has mattered to many queer readers, particularly gay men, for its coded homoeroticism. Several of the love lyrics in the book are inspired by his unrequited love for his college friend Moses Jackson. Housman uses several tricks to obscure the nature of the affection expressed: for example, making explicit the beloved's gender (who is usually referred to as "lad") but omitting any reference to the speaker's gender. Fittingly, many poetic responses to *A Shropshire Lad* reflect on the topic of concealment: the security afforded by being in the closet and the desire to free oneself of it. For a writer like Countee Cullen, who did not feel safe disclosing his attraction for other men, Housman served as a model for exploring his sexuality in art while retaining some degree of privacy. But he also alluded to poems that push back against the idea that queer people should feel shame at all. In one poem, he expands his references to Housman beyond the topic of sexuality to race and writes about the necessity of Black pride as a counterforce to white supremacy. Auden displays an equally complex attitude to the issue of concealment, even as his experiences differed considerably. Unlike Cullen, Auden had little doubt about his sexuality. To some extent, he used allusion to draw out the latent homoeroticism in Housman's poetry and coax the *Shropshire* poet further out of the closet. At the same time, Auden hesitated to openly address his own sexuality in poetry and so refrained from making Housman's desires explicit either, no doubt recognizing a degree of hypocrisy in his wish to publicly expose Housman. By writing through *A Shropshire Lad*, then, Auden confronted the mixed emotions he felt about his own sexuality and the issue of coming, or being, out.

My final example, Walt Whitman's *Leaves of Grass* (1855–1892), stands out because the queer allusions to the book present a radically different understanding of its philosophy than the scholarly consensus. Whitman is typically described as a poet of connection, be it to the environment, to the United States, or to the people whom he meets. It is also said that the book has mattered to LGBTQ readers in particular for its praise of same-sex camaraderie and its depiction of physical, emotional, and spiritual connections between men—including between his lyric persona and the male figures who populate his poetry. Complicating this standard reading, I argue that many queer poets saw Whitman as a poet of solitude. Their allusions to *Leaves of Grass* echo passages that either deal with the subject of loneliness or depict Whitman himself as a solitary figure seeking and failing to connect. This pattern is evident in the best-known apostrophes to Whitman by gay poets, such as Hart Crane and Allen Ginsberg. For these authors, Whitman represented the isolation that many queer people experience and that the poets feared for themselves. At the same time, allusion gave them a chance to enjoy a virtual form of companionship on the page. Even if it did not resolve the problem entirely, alluding to Whitman could provide a temporary stay against loneliness within the fictional realm of a poem.

While it is useful to acknowledge the differences between the two subtypes of queer allusion discussed here, it would be wrong to separate them entirely. Granted, the dynamics differ up to a point. Douglas and Auden used allusion to reflect on their personal and creative relationships as they were unfolding off the page, whereas the poets collected under "Lineages" engaged with the canon to find evidence of queerness in the literature of the past. But in the end, all these writers share a set of common purposes: to better understand themselves, to make connections in a society largely hostile to them, and to extend a hand to queer readers longing for poetry that speaks to their experiences. This is a book about what queer allusion has achieved for well over a century and what it can still provide.

I

Fellowships

ONE

Oscar Wilde *and* Alfred Douglas

To begin, I will take up contemporaneous poets who alluded to each other's work repeatedly across several decades. My first case study is Oscar Wilde and Alfred Douglas. Their romantic and sexual bond has long been the subject of extensive discussion—from journalists covering Wilde's trial to biographers and filmmakers in the twentieth century. Still, little attention has been paid to the many textual crossings between Wilde and Douglas and, more specifically, Douglas's many allusions to his friend and lover. The fact that Douglas alluded to Wilde more than Wilde alluded to Douglas is not surprising. After all, Wilde was already a well-established author when the two met, Douglas being a younger man and a less experienced writer. But Douglas did not use allusion for aesthetic mentorship, as one might have expected. Instead, his references were far more personal. Allusion enabled him to express what he felt about the affair, from desire and pleasure to pain and frustration, including emotions that he likely had difficulty voicing off the page. This is not to say that his allusions were monologic. By writing through his companion's language, Douglas fostered a virtual dialogue that could stand parallel to their correspondences and conversations.

The question of *whom* the references were intended for is especially complex in this opening chapter, for Douglas's allusions had several distinct audiences. The first was Douglas himself. Evoking Wilde in verse served partly as an act of self-reflection: a way for him to think through his feelings about the relationship. The second was Wilde, as allusion gave Douglas another medium through which to convey his emotions. The fact that Douglas showed Wilde his poems-in-progress reinforces the notion that he used allusion to communicate with his lover indirectly.[1] The third and fourth audiences represent different parts of his public readership: the queer readers eager to identify allusions to Wilde and same-sex love generally; and straight readers less likely to catch the references and their significance. This third category matters since it doubtless influenced what Douglas chose to include and omit. The poems reflect not the author's most private thoughts and statements but what he chose to put on display for those able to catch the meaning of his allusions. In sum, they do not present an objective record of what occurred between Wilde and Douglas but, rather, a curated account of how Douglas wanted others to perceive him.

Even if they do not provide a wholly reliable narrative, the poems deepen and complicate the biographical record, which has long tended to be partisan. The earliest biographies typically ascribed blame to one party while voiding the other of responsibility. In his 1916 book on Wilde, Frank Harris depicts the older poet as an unwitting victim of Douglas's corruption. He frames the lovers as opposites, always praising one to condemn the other: "Oscar was as yielding and amiable in character as the boy was self-willed, reckless, obstinate and imperious." And again: "Oscar always enjoyed good living; but for years he had had to earn his bread. He knew the value of money; he didn't like to throw it away; he was accustomed to lunch or dine at a cheap Italian restaurant for a few shillings. But to Lord Alfred Douglas money was only a counter and the most luxurious living a necessity." Harris faults Douglas with spoiling Wilde's character ("Douglas' boldness gave Oscar *outrecuidance,* an insolent arrogance"), his finances ("As soon as Oscar Wilde began to entertain him, he was led to the dearest hotels and restaurants; his expenses became formidable and soon outran his large earnings"), and his reputation among polite society ("Again and again Lord Alfred Douglas flaunted acquaintance with youths of the lowest class . . . From this time on the rumors about Oscar took definite form and shaped themselves in specific accusations; his enemies began triumphantly to predict his ruin and disgrace"). In a telling slip, he resorts to misogynous language when describing Douglas, as though the young author's perceived femininity were a mark of villainy. For example, he writes that the young man is "articulate as a woman" and that he possesses "feminine cunning."[2]

Other biographers reversed this attitude and positioned Douglas as the victim of Wilde's corruption. Rupert Croft-Cooke, in *Bosie: The Story of Lord Alfred Douglas, His Friends, and Enemies* (1963), describes Wilde as the reckless party: "In his private life Wilde was indiscreet to a point of imbecility. He wrote, behaved and talked as a homosexual till his 'dining-out connection' became almost a chore from which he escaped to his circle of admirers with relief." Furthermore, it is he who gets the blame for debasing his own social status by mixing with the wrong crowd: "Wilde, as can be gathered from the evidence against him in court, was addicted to roughs, criminals and male prostitutes, and though his promiscuous nature admitted at times affairs with young men of some refinement he felt a distaste, very common among intelligent homosexuals, for sexual relations with those of his own class or education." Here as well, Wilde and Douglas appear as opposites, but this time Douglas receives the kinder light. Assuming that queer desire is a knock against one's moral character, Croft-Cooke excuses Douglas's sexuality away by describing it as a youthful mistake that he needed to outgrow: "Bosie's homosexuality, while it lasted, was reckless and irresponsible, with no sense of sin or twinge of conscience . . . It was one of his many phases and he was to grow out of it, but at this time he was frankly pleasure-loving, perhaps somewhat licentious." The account of Douglas's time in London after the death of Wilde is especially sentimental: "He has described some of the snubs he received in those years, but there must have been countless other small humiliations of which we cannot know, countless mean little slights and hypocritical turnings away which, by accumulative slow degrees, wore down his natural amiability and that trust in the general friendliness of the world which had characterized his youth." In Croft-Cooke's hands, then, Douglas becomes a figure fit for tragedy. By contrast, Wilde cuts a devilish figure, aware of his corruption and delighting in it: "Theatrical to the last flick of his gloves, [Wilde] saw in these 'strange sins' the fulfillment of a macabre destiny. He was conscious of the danger and delighted in it."[3] In particular, the image of the gloves evokes the stock villains of melodrama.

More recent accounts—by Barbara Belford, Trevor Fisher, Douglas Murray, and Matthew Sturgis, to name a few examples—have worked to establish a more balanced view of Douglas and Wilde's relationship. But the temptation to sensationalize remains hard to resist. Trevor Fisher, for instance, regrets that "much of the writing about the two men is markedly partisan" and asserts that "their human frailties and follies were more complex than the legends allow."[4] Yet his narrative still contains more than a few traces of melodrama: "In the final analysis, the relationship of Oscar Wilde and Lord Alfred Douglas was a true Fatal Passion . . . Wilde sought as his life's goal an idyll of Greek Love, as once revealed to him by a schoolmaster. His relationship with Bosie Douglas, however, produced a tragedy the Ancients would have understood."

To be sure, the truth of their relationship probably lay between the two extremes presented in the earliest biographies on the two men, even if it is difficult to parse the facts of their affair from their radically different interpretations of it and the gossip that surrounded them both. For example, there is some disagreement as to who initiated the affair. We know that the two were introduced by Douglas's cousin Lionel Johnson in the summer of 1891. While they both felt an immediate spark, they saw each other only sporadically in the first few months of their acquaintance, and it was only in 1892 that their commitment to one another deepened. Douglas later maintained that Wilde had pursued him aggressively, though Wilde insisted that Douglas took the initiative. As they became inseparable, they were subject to increasing scrutiny from their families and wider London society. Wilde's mother warned her son against Douglas's "vanity and extravagant habits," and to be sure, Douglas loved to live large and spend lavishly. But so, too, did Wilde. And while Douglas required many gifts and enjoyed being kept, it is undeniable that Wilde found pleasure in the arrangement as well. After all, Wilde generally pursued younger men of lesser means because he liked the role of benefactor. Granted, as time wore on, their relationship grew increasingly stormy. Douglas had a temper, and his mood could change drastically and suddenly. The two men often fought, as when Wilde critiqued the translation of his French play *Salomé* that he had commissioned from Douglas. Still, Wilde did not doubt Douglas's love. On the contrary, he saw that love as a saving grace, even as its discovery by Douglas's father, the marquess of Queensberry, proved to be his unmaking.[5]

The poems that Douglas alluded to are all drawn from a single volume, *Poems* (1881), that Wilde published a decade before the start of their love affair. The collection, intended to establish Wilde's literary reputation, proved to be a commercial success, despite receiving a tepid response from critics. The first edition sold out quickly, leading the press to order a second edition of 250 copies.[6] Significantly, Wilde gifted Douglas a copy in 1892 as they were growing more committed to one another. The book was inscribed:

> From Oscar
> To the Gilt-mailed
> Boy
> at Oxford
> in the heart
> of June
> OSCAR WILDE.[7]

By alluding to this volume, Douglas was responding to poems that had been—symbolically and retroactively—addressed to him. If the allusions have not been discussed before, it is no doubt because scholarship on Douglas's poetry remains quite thin. To this day, he remains a subject of interest for biographers rather than critics. Moreover, Wilde scholars tend to gravitate to his plays more than to his poetry. But a close look at Douglas's poetry reveals a series of allusions over the course of more than two decades.

Douglas's allusions can be divided into three distinct periods. First, there are the poems that he wrote during the first four years of their relationship, from their first meeting in 1891 to Wilde's trial in 1895. These references afford us a unique perspective on their time together: a glimpse into his day-to-day experiences and how he wanted these experiences to be perceived by others. Allusion, at this stage, enabled Douglas to reflect on his ever-changing feelings about his companion, ranging from affection and sympathy to frustration and resentment, and to communicate those emotions obliquely to Wilde. Second, there are the three years that followed Wilde's release from prison in 1897. At this point, Douglas's allusions grew more public in nature, as he attempted to defend his companion in verse after enduring the shame of a gross indecency trial. Finally, in the two decades that followed Wilde's death, Douglas used allusion to reframe both their relationship and his own queer past for the record: first to mourn Wilde, then to distance himself, and finally to attempt some reconciliation. I will address each of these periods in turn, beginning with the poems of 1891–1895.

Douglas first alluded to Wilde's verse in "A Summer Storm" (1891), written the summer that the two men were introduced.[8] The poem expresses the turbulent feelings experienced by Douglas in the early days of their acquaintance. The speaker laments the perceived slights and disagreements of an unnamed (and ungendered) beloved. Fittingly, Douglas does not include any concrete details that might capture a real, lived relationship, so the sonnet reflects the misunderstandings typical of unconsummated infatuations:

> Alas! how frail and weak a little boat
> I have sailed in. I call it Happiness,
> And I had thought there was not storm nor stress
> Of wind so masterful but it would float
> Blithely in their despite; but lo! one note
> Of harsh discord, one word of bitterness,
> And a fierce overwhelming wilderness
> Of angry waters chokes my gasping throat.
>
> I am near drowned in this unhappy sea,
> I will not strive, let me lie still and sink,
> I have no joy to live. Oh! unkind love!

Why have you wounded me so bitterly?
That am as easily wounded as a dove
Who has a silver throat and feet of pink.[9]

Douglas weaves in multiple allusions to a passage from Wilde's "Athanasia" about the discovery of an Egyptian girl's body in "the dim womb
of some black pyramid." A seed is found in her hand and subsequently
planted in English soil. The flowers that grow as a result become a center
of gravity for the natural world, attracting birds that circle out of adoration for the seed:

For love of it the passionate nightingale
  Forgot the hills of Thrace, the cruel king,
And the pale dove no longer cared to sail
  Through the wet woods at time of blossoming,
But round this flower of Egypt sought to float,
With silvered wing and amethystine throat.[10]

Douglas borrows from "Athanasia" the image of a flying dove with
"silvered wing and amethystine throat." Wilde imagines the bird as a
boat, thanks to the verbs *sail* and *float*. Douglas divides the two halves
of this metaphor into distinct images: he starts the poem by comparing
his happiness to a fragile "little boat," which he believed would "float"
despite the gathering storms, and he ends by comparing himself to an
"easily wounded . . . dove / Who has a silver throat and feet of pink."
The very image intended to convey solidity and permanence in Wilde—
the bird becomes a boat, rotating around the central hub—has become
in Douglas an emblem of the poet's fragility. The "silvered wing and
amethystine throat" in Wilde gets carried over, in a reduced form, to the
"silver throat" in Douglas, but even that phrase finds itself undermined
by association with the end of the octave: "a fierce overwhelming wilderness / Of angry waters chokes my gasping throat." The dove's throat
no longer represents beauty but, rather, pain and distress. Moreover,
both the bird and the ship have lost their center of gravity. Rather than

sailing around a point, the boat is tossed about on stormy seas until it is wrecked, no longer able to float, and the dove is too "easily wounded" to be shown flying at all.

Tellingly, the speaker of "A Summer Storm" sets the blame at the feet of an "unkind love": "Why have *you* wounded me so bitterly?" By absorbing and transforming Wilde's imagery, Douglas also turns that language against its author, identifying Wilde as the cause of the lover's unhappiness. The reversal has an accusatory edge, as if the young poet wished to correct a fallacious record. Of course, Wilde wrote "Athanasia" long before the two met, but Douglas is content to pretend that "Athanasia" is somehow about him, so that "A Summer Storm" can serve as a direct response. The sonnet shows Douglas at a low point, before he gained a sense of security in his relationship with Wilde.

Consider, by contrast, the sonnet "Amoris Vincula," which Douglas first published in the undergraduate magazine the *Spirit Lamp* in 1893.[11] By this point, Douglas had become the focus of Wilde's love, and his allusions reflect a far happier and more benevolent attitude than "A Summer Storm." "Amoris Vincula" calls back to Wilde's "Silentium Amoris." The parallel between that title and the title of his sonnet makes the connection between the two explicit. Moreover, as indicated by the pairing of "Silentium" (silence) and "Vincula" (link), Douglas's sonnet functions as an imaginary sequel, offering a happy resolution that evades the speaker of Wilde's poem. In the first two stanzas of "Silentium Amoris," the speaker laments his inability to give love a voice, since the strength of his passion has overwhelmed his capacity for speech. In the last stanza, he expresses hope that his beloved will have understood the true cause of his silence:

> But surely unto Thee mine eyes did show
> Why I am silent, and my lute unstrung;
> Else it were better we should part, and go,
> Thou to some lips of sweeter melody,
> And I to nurse the barren memory
> Of unkissed kisses, and songs never sung.[12]

Whatever optimism this stanza might have expressed is dimmed by the fact that most of the lines (four out of six) focus on an unhappy alternative: the lover does not understand, and so the two must part. The poet imagines himself alone while the lover seeks out another companion. The final line, with its regretful evocation of "unkissed kisses" and "songs never sung," makes its way into the final line of Douglas's "Amoris Vincula":

> As a white dove that, in a cage of gold,
>   Is prisoned from the air, and yet more bound
> By love than bars, and will not wings unfold
>   To fly away, though every gate be found
> Unlocked and open; so my heart was caught,
>   And linked to thine with triple links of love.
> But soon, a dove grown wanton, false it sought
>   To break its chain, and faithless quite to rove
> Where thou wouldst not; and with a painted bird
>   Fluttered far off. But when a moon was past,
> Grown sick with longing for a voice unheard
>   And lips unkissed, spread wings and home flew fast.
> And lo! what seemed a sword to cleave its chain,
>   Was but a link to rivet it again.[13]

Douglas's sonnet reads as a direct response to Wilde, the beloved of "Silentium Amoris" addressing the speaker in turn, and giving his version of the events. Wilde's speaker fears that his passion has proved so strong he will be unable to confess his feelings, thus pushing his beloved into the arms of another. Meanwhile, Douglas's speaker compares himself to a dove "bound" in a "cage of gold" by his love. When he does manage to escape, his flight feels more like a betrayal than a liberation. He berates himself for having grown "wanton" and "faithless," dismissing his new lover as a mere "painted bird" of no real substance. Whereas Wilde concludes by imagining the lovers' separation, Douglas ends his poem by describing their reunion in the past tense, as something that has already been achieved.

The touching thing about Douglas's allusion is that it serves as a cure for the pain suffered in "Silentium Amoris." Wilde's speaker is alone at the end of the poem, with only "the barren memory / Of unkissed kisses, and songs never sung" to keep him company. Douglas's speaker, after fleeing his cage, also grows "sick with longing for a voice unheard / And lips unkissed." When the poems are set side by side, Douglas's allusion turns Wilde's lament into an image of unity. The lovers may have been separated, yet they share the same pain and the same desire. Even though one lover may have been too overwhelmed with emotion to express his feelings, the second still longs for a "voice unheard." He feels his companion's love implicitly, despite it never being articulated. Granted, there remains a hint of tragedy to the reunion, since it is described in terms of captivity. The dove's return is said to be inevitable, the lovers' bond a "rivet" binding the two together. But evidently to Douglas, that obsessive quality is what makes the attachment true.

Here, too, it is worth recalling that Wilde did not write his poem with Douglas in mind; "Silentium Amoris" predates their first meeting by a whole decade. But Douglas was happy to invent a fiction in which "Amoris Vincula" could respond to "Silentium Amoris" as though Wilde's poem had been written about him too. By alluding to the poem, Douglas recodes it as a piece about their tumultuous affection for one another. His sonnet also presents an epilogue to the implied story of Wilde's poem, as if "Amoris Vincula" provided the actual conclusion that "Silentium Amoris" had left out. By rewriting Wilde's lines, Douglas tries to establish his own narrative of the relationship as the definitive one. Their reunion is a "victory," and it is presented as final: "And lo! what seemed a sword to cleave its chain, / Was but a link to rivet it again."

"A Song" (1894) likewise conveys the excitement that Douglas felt for Wilde during these early years. But it also betrays an immature, self-centered streak in his conception of love that no doubt contributed to the tensions in their relationship. Douglas wrote the poem for Wilfrid Scawen Blunt's Crabbet Poetry Club and claimed that the lover evoked in it was a handsome stranger. Yet the multiple allusions to Wilde's poetry indicate the poem's true subject.[14]

Steal from the meadows, rob the tall green hills,
   Ravish my orchard's blossoms, let me bind
A crown of orchard flowers and daffodils,
   Because my love is fair and white and kind.

To-day the thrush has trilled her daintiest phrases,
   Flowers with their incense have made drunk the air,
God has bent down to gild the hearts of daisies,
   Because my love is kind and white and fair.

To-day the sun has kissed the rose-tree's daughter,
   And sad Narcissus, Spring's pale acolyte,
Hangs down his head and smiles into the water,
   Because my love is kind and fair and white.[15]

Douglas's vision of the environment in the second and third stanzas contains multiple allusions to a passage from Wilde's "The Garden of Eros":

The missel-thrush has frighted from the glade,
   One pale narcissus loiters fearfully
Close to a shadowy nook, where half afraid
   Of their own loveliness some violets lie
That will not look the gold sun in the face
For fear of too much splendour,—ah! methinks it is a place

Which should be trodden by Persephone
   When wearied of the flowerless fields of Dis!
Or danced on by the lads of Arcady!
   The hidden secret of eternal bliss
Known to the Grecian here a man might find,
Ah! you and I may find it now if Love and Sleep be kind.[16]

Douglas carries over many of the elements from Wilde's landscape—the thrush, the narcissus, and the sun—but the mood associated with them is entirely different. Wilde connects all these items with terror: the thrush "has frighted from the glade," the narcissus "loiters fearfully," and the violets turn away from the sun "for fear of too much splendor." Yet their fear is described as a happy thing because it means that the birds and the flowers have cleared away, leaving space for the poet and his lover. What the speaker appreciates about the garden is its privacy, which he connects to Greek pastoral: "the hidden secret of eternal bliss / Known to the Grecian." Patricia Flanagan Behrendt has noted the homoerotic undertones of these classical references: Eros is "depicted in Greek art as a beautiful boy" and understood as "the god of love and loyalty between young men."[17] Wilde also conveys that homoeroticism to sympathetic readers through ambiguity: "here a man might find, / Ah you and I might find it now." The word *man* here might be generic (a substitute for *human beings*), or it might refer to the speaker, but the third, more interesting possibility is that it points to the addressee, so that both "you and I" are implicitly male. The poem does not affirm this directly, but queer readers would likely catch the possibility.

By contrast, there is no trace of fear in Douglas's landscape. Sheer contentment has taken its place. Rather than fleeing the scene or turning away, all the elements of nature contribute to make the environment hospitable to the poet. The thrush "has trilled her daintiest phrases," the sun "has kissed the rose," and "sad Narcissus"—which Douglas describes as "pale," like Wilde—only "hangs down his head" out of sudden happiness: he "smiles into the water, / Because my love is kind and fair and white." Even the Christian God lends a hand. Instead of punishing the gay lovers, he "has bent down to gild the hearts of daisies." Douglas's poem is far more optimistic about the prospect of realizing happiness. In "The Garden of Eros," the speaker's desire for privacy with his lover is subject to a conditional: "you and I may find it now *if* Love and Sleep be kind." The reader never learns whether Love and Sleep follow suit. "A Song" contains no "if": "*Because* my love *is* kind and white and fair." The line is stated thrice and serves as the explanation for all of nature's efforts to make the landscape accommodating for the poet.

By contrast, the speaker in Douglas's poem remains solitary. Even though it is never clear in "The Garden of Eros" if the two lovers come together in the end, the speaker does at least address his beloved, so there is an implicit contact through speech. The speaker of "A Song," on the other hand, never addresses a "you." He also never describes his love joining him in the garden or even imagines that as a possibility. If anything, the poet is content to wander the garden alone and think about his love, without the two men spending time together. His attitude bears a narcissistic streak, since he derives pleasure from luxuriating in the thought of love, rather than experiencing its reality. The references to "sad Narcissus" betray Douglas's immaturity at this point in his life. The poem is so self-involved that he borrows his love's language without understanding what it communicates or without realizing that he has radically altered its ideas.

Douglas's allusions continued well beyond the period of their initial relationship, from their first meeting in 1891 to Wilde's imprisonment in 1895.[18] After he was released from Reading Gaol on May 19, 1897, the two were reunited in Rouen. That year, Wilde published "The Ballad of Reading Gaol," in which he reflected on his time in prison through an account of a soldier's execution for the murder of his wife. The speaker accompanies the soldier as he witnesses the suffering of all the prisoners, who are vindicated to some degree by the poet's statement that, in fact, "each man kills the thing he loves" through different means: "The coward does it with a kiss, / The brave man with a sword!"[19] That rhetorical slip, conflating passion and crime, is not intended to justify murder but, rather, to defend love that is criminalized, for which the combination of kiss and sword provides a useful cover. The narrator is, as Matthew Sturgis puts it, "a thinly-veiled self-portrait," allowing him to seek sympathy for his unjust incarceration.[20]

Two years later, Douglas published his book of poetry *The City of the Soul* (1899). The second poem in the collection, "The Ballad of Saint Vitus," alludes heavily to "Reading Gaol." Although he never refers to his companion by name, Douglas attempts to honor Wilde after the shame of public scrutiny and legal judgment. The choice of Saint Vitus, the patron saint of dancers, as a stand-in for Wilde may seem curious at first. Unlike, say, Saint Sebastian, Vitus has no symbolic connection with same-sex love. Instead, he was mainly associated with neurological disorders because his relics were believed to cure Sydenham's cholera, a disease that caused involuntary movement of the limbs. The resonance of depicting Wilde as a martyr is obvious, since it presents him as the victim of an unjust society. But the selection of Vitus becomes clearer if we set Douglas's poem alongside the following stanza from "Reading Gaol," in which Wilde describes the writhing limbs of a hanging man:

> It is sweet to dance to violins
>   When Love and Life are fair:
> To dance to flutes, to dance to lutes
>   Is delicate and rare:
> But it is not sweet with nimble feet
>   To dance upon the air![21]

It is this stanza that Douglas alludes to repeatedly throughout "The Ballad of Saint Vitus":

> The lark was singing up over his head,
>   As he went by so lithe and fleet,
> And the flowers danced in white and red
>   At the treading of his nimble feet
>
> . . . .
>
> For the room was filled with a soft sweet light
>   Of ambergris and apricot,
> And round the walls were angels bright,
>   With lute and flute and angelot
>
> . . . .

And in the midst serene and sweet
　With God's light on his countenance
Was Vitus, with his gold shod feet,
　Dancing in a courtly dance.[22]

Douglas echoes a whole cluster of key words from Wilde's ballad. Of course, *dance* recurs several times, as one might expect. But in addition to that, Douglas takes the word *sweet* from "it is not sweet" and deploys it in "the midst serene and sweet." He also expands Wilde's array of instruments by taking "to dance to flutes, to dance to lutes" and transforming it into "lute and flute and angelot." Moreover, both Saint Vitus and the hanged man in "Reading Gaol" are defined by a common attribute: "nimble feet." This is a distinct approach to allusion. Instead of evoking a whole line, for instance, Douglas repurposes a sequence of words that may not be all that significant when taken in isolation but that cumulatively establish a connection between the two poems. The purpose of this method is to fully anchor the poem to its source, making clear to sympathetic readers that the entire poem should be read as a response to "Reading Gaol" and that Saint Vitus should be understood as a substitute for Wilde.

Together, these miniature allusions serve to take what is in "Reading Gaol" a scene of horror (capital punishment) into a vindication of Wilde. The last two lines of the stanza in "Reading Gaol" use a chilling euphemism to describe the man's desperate struggle as he is hanged. Wilde reimagines his feet so that they do not writhe but instead "dance upon the air," and skillfully to boot. The word *nimble* takes a chaotic, haphazard movement and turns it into an orderly ballet. By contrast, Saint Vitus's feet are not in the air but firmly on the ground, where they are seen "treading." Moreover, the beauty of his choreography inspires the flowers around him to dance as well "in white and red." There is no terror or disorder here—only peace and artfulness.

In the last stanza of "The Ballad of Saint Vitus" quoted here, Douglas uses his allusions to reestablish, albeit figuratively, Wilde's position in society. Rather than being subject to public shame, or martyrdom, Vitus receives divine approval, as "God's light" shines down upon his face. Even more important, Douglas refers to Vitus's performance as a "courtly dance"—a significant detail, considering that Wilde's position in London society had been effectively destroyed by his trial. There is no sign here of the stigma that would haunt Wilde in the years following his time in prison. The word *sweet* that Wilde had used ironically to say how unsweet it is to be hanged (something that need not be pointed out) appears in "Saint Vitus" without irony or qualification: the scene of the dance is "serene and sweet."

Douglas does not claim that a poem has the power to restore Wilde's social position, but he does take pleasure in imagining an alternative world where his companion would not suffer public judgment. The ballad has a double audience: Wilde, whom Douglas hoped to touch with his poetic exoneration, and the wider circle of readers who would have seen Wilde's imprisonment as unjust and found some pride and enjoyment in the deification of this most notorious of gay men. While Douglas's ballad may not show Vitus subject to martyrdom, his status within religious iconography does present Wilde as a queer martyr, the patron saint of men who desire other men.

Whether or not Wilde read the poem and appreciated its reference is unknown; and indeed, the two men would have little time left together. On November 25, 1900, a year after the release of *The City of the Soul,* Wilde died of meningitis in Paris. To come to terms with his loss and pay homage to his friend, Douglas turned again to poetry and allusion. Shortly after Wilde's passing, he wrote a sonnet titled "The Dead Poet" that alludes movingly to Wilde's "The Burden of Itys."[23] This might seem like an odd poem for Douglas to choose under the circumstances. "Itys" may be a tragedy, but its story is far removed from Wilde's own situation. The poet begins by praising the English Thames over classical Rome. The comparison prompts him to think about Itys, a relatively minor character from the myth of Philoméla—minor enough that a summary of the story may be useful here. After Tereus, a Thracian king, rapes his wife's sister Philoméla, he cuts off her tongue to prevent her from revealing what he has done. Unable to speak, she secretly writes to

Procne, her sister and Tereus's wife, for advice. Procne suggests that they feed Tereus's son Itys to her husband as punishment, which Philoméla agrees to. Once Tereus has unwittingly consumed some of his son's body, Procne presents Itys's head to her husband. Tereus attempts to kill both Procne and Philoméla, but the gods take pity on the women and turn all three family members into birds: Tereus becomes a hawk, Procne a nightingale, and Philoméla a swallow. Of these three, Procne retains the power of song and expression, despite her pain. It is this element of the story that captured the imagination of both Wilde and Douglas.

In the months that followed his friend's death, "The Burning of Itys" became a resource for Douglas, allowing him to work through the loss of Wilde as both a lover and a poet.[24] The passage that Douglas focused on in his allusions finds the speaker urging Procne to endure through song. The choice is appropriate since it enabled Douglas to imagine the persistence of Wilde's art beyond his own symbolic transformation in death:

> Sing on! sing on! O feathered Niobe,
>   Thou canst make sorrow beautiful, and steal
> From joy its sweetest music, not as we
>   Who by dead voiceless silence strive to heal
> Our too untended wounds, and do but keep
> Pain barricaded in our hearts, and murder pillowed sleep.[25]

Wilde urges the nightingale to keep singing as he and other mortals on earth remain bound by "dead voiceless silence," unable to express their deepest emotions. The bird's gift lies in its ability to serve as a voice for many but also to change sorrow into beauty. Human beings in pain "murder pillowed sleep," so weighed down by suffering that they cannot rest; Procne takes that grief and turns it into the "sweetest music." These phrases recur, transformed, at the end of Douglas's sonnet "The Dead Poet":

> I dreamed of him last night, I saw his face
> All radiant and unshadowed of distress,

And as of old, in music measureless,
I heard his golden voice and marked him trace
Under the common thing the hidden grace,
And conjure wonder out of emptiness,
Till mean things put on beauty like a dress
And all the world was an enchanted place.

And then methought outside a fast locked gate
I mourned the loss of unrecorded words,
Forgotten tales and mysteries half said,
Wonders that might have been articulate,
And voiceless thoughts like murdered singing birds.
And so I woke and knew that he was dead.[26]

Through allusion, Wilde becomes the figure with a "golden voice" and "measureless music," whose song displays unmatched powers. Rather than describing all of humanity silently suffering on earth as a collective, Douglas focuses on himself, a solitary "I." It is the poet who finds himself haunted by "voiceless" thoughts. The word *murder* that Wilde had used for restless sleepers returns here, this time in a metaphor evoking the speaker's silent pain: "like murdered singing birds." The simile is canny because it explicitly connects Wilde's nightingale with Douglas's "dead poet" (namely, Wilde), bringing home the idea that his own Niobe is gone. The source of the poet's suffering here is precisely Wilde's passing. Unlike "The Burden of Itys," in which the speaker could beg his "feathered Niobe" to continue singing on his behalf, "The Dead Poet" offers no such hope of expression and release. Douglas suffers a double loss, in that Wilde's death has also robbed him of his only outlet: the one who could have given voice to his suffering, transformed it into the "sweetest music," and so offered him some form of relief. The last word in the poem, *dead*, reinforces the sense of grim finality.

That Wilde's death continued to haunt the younger poet is evidenced by the fact that Douglas returned to the same passage again five years later in another sonnet titled "The Green River." The poem begins with a picturesque description of a solitary landscape that does not look especially melancholic. Tucked away, however, is a place whose silence is a symptom of loss, and the poet himself reveals that he suffers from the same desolation:

> I know a green grass path that leaves the field,
> And like a running river, winds along
> Into a leafy wood where is no throng
> Of birds at noon-day, and no soft throats yield
> Their music to the moon. The place is sealed,
> An unclaimed sovereignty of voiceless song,
> And all the unravished silences belong
> To some sweet singer lost or unrevealed.
> So is my soul become a silent place.
> Oh, may I wake from this uneasy night
> To find a voice of music manifold.
> Let it be shape of sorrow with wan face,
> Or Love that swoons on sleep, or else delight
> That is as wide-eyed as a marigold.[27]

There are multiple connections between "The Green River," "The Dead Poet," and through these "The Burden of Itys": the "voiceless song," the "unravished silences," and the "sweet singer lost." It is at the beginning of the sestet, with the line "So is my soul become a silent place," that Douglas reveals the landscape as a metaphor for his own internal suffering. But unlike in "The Dead Poet," Douglas does offer some glimpse of hope in the future. The "sweet singer" may be "lost," or he may simply be "unrevealed," suggesting that some other voice may come to reassure him. Rather than ending with the finality of death, he devotes the last five lines to a prayer. Like Wilde entreating Niobe to "sing on," Douglas hopes that he will find "a voice of music manifold" and that this voice will assume the shape of "Love." Even as he acknowledges the power that Wilde continues to exert over him, he begins to recognize the need to find some way out of his pain, to discover new loves.

Unfortunately, he would not feel so kindly toward Wilde in the ensuing years. The 1910s found Douglas publicly rejecting Wilde and renouncing homosexuality more broadly. Several factors prompted this change in attitude. First, there was his conversion to Roman Catholicism in 1911. As Douglas Murray relates, his newfound fear of sin and damnation led him to renounce all associations with his former companion, even if that meant being dishonest about his past: "The only way for him to survive was to turn completely. He would lie about his relationship with Wilde and deny any improprieties, which he had to do at the time, and he would break away from his friends of the Wilde period."[28] Another, perhaps more important factor was the influence of T. W. H. Crosland, an archconservative eager to persecute homosexuals. The two became friends when Crosland took up the editorship of the *Academy*. Crosland dragged Douglas into a series of legal disputes, few of which proved successful. Douglas later recognized that Crosland had exploited their friendship to advance his agenda, with little regard for Douglas's well-being. As he wrote in his autobiography in 1929, "Although Crosland did a lot for *The Academy* and, although its undoubted success at this time was due really more, I believe, to him than to me, he let me and the paper in for all sorts of trouble which would never have come our way but for him."[29] But it would take several years for him to acknowledge this.

Two legal disputes, in particular, implicated Wilde's legacy and prompted Douglas to break from his late friend publicly. The first involved a book by Arthur Ransome called *Wilde: A Critical Study* (1912). Ransome had been encouraged by the publisher Martin Secker to find Robbie Ross, Wilde's former lover and literary executor, because he possessed unpublished letters by Wilde that framed Douglas as the one responsible for Wilde's downfall. Douglas had long viewed Ross as a romantic rival and so already harbored some feelings of resentment toward him. Crosland egged Douglas on, urging him to sue Ransome for libel. Douglas did so in 1913 but lost the case, after pouring considerable money into the legal proceedings.[30] The second dispute implicating Wilde occurred a year later, in 1914, when Crosland wrote to Ross and accused him of homosexuality. He warned that "a letter nailing you down has been sent by Lord Alfred Douglas to Mr. Justice Darling and two other judges, the Prime Minister, the Director of Public Prosecutions, Sir George Lewis, Mr. John Lane, and others." Ross sued Crosland for criminal conspiracy and Douglas himself for libel. The case was settled out of court, with Douglas agreeing to cease libeling Ross.[31]

Douglas also spoke out against Wilde on several occasions. For example, there was the criminal libel prosecution brought forward in 1918 against Noel Pemberton Billing by dancer Maud Allen. Billing, then a member of Parliament, had argued that a production of Wilde's *Salome* would attract people with sexual proclivities vulnerable to blackmail by the German Secret Service. In his testimony, Douglas referred to Wilde as "the greatest force for evil that has appeared in Europe during the last 350 years"—a shocking departure from the adoring homages of "The Ballad of Saint Vitus" or "The Dead Poet." But the Douglas of this era was a Roman Catholic, terrified of sin and just as fearful of the legal problems he might encounter if his own sexual history came under further scrutiny.

By the end of the 1910s, Douglas had begun to recognize Crosland's manipulations for what they were, breaking with him entirely in 1921. He expressed his new attitude in a sonnet titled "The Unspeakable Englishman," which Douglas Murray notes is a reference to Crosland:

> You were a brute and more than half a knave,
> Your mind was seamed with labyrinthine tracks
> Wherein walked crazy moods bending their backs
> Under grim loads. You were an open grave
> For gold and love. Always you were the slave
> Of crooked thoughts (tortured upon the racks
> Of mean mistrust). I made myself as wax
> To your fierce seal. I clutched an ebbing wave.
>
> Fool that I was, I loved you; your harsh soul
> Was sweet to me: I gave you with both hands
> Love, service, honour, loyalty and praise;
> I would have died for you! And like a mole

You grubbed and burrowed till the shifting sands
Opened and swallowed up the dream-forged days.[32]

Of special interest here is the fact that the description of Crosland's tor-
tured mind in the first stanza (from the images of labyrinth and treading
thoughts to specific words such as *knave* and *crooked*) combines allusions
to several passages from "The Ballad of Reading Gaol." This point has
yet to be made, yet the juxtapositions are significant. From Wilde:

> Silently we went round and round,
>   And through each hollow mind
> The Memory of dreadful things
>   Rushed like a dreadful wind,
> And Horror stalked before each man,
>   And Terror crept behind.

And:

> But there is no sleep when men must weep
>   Who never yet have wept:
> So we—the fool, the fraud, the knave—
>   That endless vigil kept,
> And through each brain on hands of pain
>   Another's terror crept.

And again:

> The gray cock crew, the red cock crew,
>   But never came the day:
> And crooked shapes of Terror crouched,
>   In the corners where we lay:
> And each evil sprite that walks by night
>   Before us seemed to play.

In condemning Crosland, Douglas uses the language of the very person whom Crosland had worked so hard to get him to betray. But the allusions also reveal a profound inner conflict, between a desire to reject Crosland outright and a lingering impulse to make excuses for his former friend's cruelty. Complicating his attitude even further is newfound guilt over the role he himself played in tarnishing Wilde's reputation.

The most significant change in Douglas's allusions is his (altogether confused) emphasis on blame and responsibility. Douglas takes images that Wilde had used to describe the pain of a whole collective and repurposes them as emblems of a single individual's failing. The pronoun *we* gives way to an accusatory *you*. In "The Ballad of Reading Gaol," "we" are "the fool, the fraud, the knave," but in "The Unspeakable Englishman," "you were a brute and more than half a knave." In Wilde, sorrow binds the prisoners together: "through each brain on hands of pain / Another's terror crept." Douglas uses the same imagery to describe Crosland as a solitary figure possessed by madness:

> Your mind was seamed with labyrinthine tracks
> Wherein walked crazy moods bending their backs
> Under grim loads.

The attitude in Wilde, empathy, has given way to judgment, though only to an extent. The words *under grim loads* also present Crosland as a victim of his own vices. It is as if Douglas, right when he was about to finish the first sentence of the poem and complete his rebuke of Crosland, had retreated somewhat, realizing that he could not bring himself to place all the blame on his former associate. Ultimately, Crosland is not a willful agent of chaos and malice but "the slave / Of crooked thoughts" he did not control.

As the poem wears on, Douglas shifts more of the blame onto himself. Even as he presents Crosland as a destructive influence on him, he concedes, by using active verbs, that he bears some of the responsibility as well. This pattern is established by "I made myself as wax / To your fierce seal," and then reiterated with "I clutched," "I loved," "I gave," and "I would have." It is only in the last two lines of the poem that the actor shifts back from Douglas to Crosland: "You grubbed and burrowed till the shifting sands / Opened and swallowed up the dream-forged days." But even that concluding image describes the swallowing up as a self-destructive process, rather than a sign of intentional ill will toward Douglas. Crosland has ultimately drowned himself, and the choice of *dream* rather than *nightmare* considerably softens the portrait in its final moments.

The darkest allusion to "Reading Gaol," and the most emblematic of Douglas's conflicting attitude toward Crosland, is the description of him as "an open grave / For gold and love." Wilde's readers would connect the image to a stanza from "Reading Gaol" (in which it is made to rhyme with another word that Douglas borrows, *knave*):

> So still it lay that every day
>   Crawled like a weed-clogged wave:
> And we forgot the bitter lot
>   That waits for fool and knave,
> Till once, as we tramped in from work,
>   We passed an open grave.[33]

In Wilde, the "open grave" is a symbol of how the prospect of pain and death haunts the prisoners. In "The Unspeakable Englishman," however, Crosland himself has become the open grave. He is a black hole that consumes all the "gold and love" around him, a mindless force that destroys itself in the process. The poet's attitude is a queasy, jarring mixture of anger, judgment, and pity.

It is clear what Douglas intended to accomplish with this poem: to cleanse himself of guilt by using Wilde's own language to attack Crosland. Yet the outcome remains messy at best. Wilde's images derive their energy from sympathy for the pain surrounding him as well as pity in his own situation. Turning those images against Crosland does not acknowledge the pain felt by Wilde, let alone the other prisoners. The only victims recognized within the sonnet are Douglas and Crosland. Douglas's desire to rid himself of shame by blaming Crosland was complicated by the recognition that he bore some of the responsibility. The sonnet wavers between two different attitudes, Douglas pointing the finger at Crosland and himself.

No doubt sensing that the sonnet had not achieved what he had intended, Douglas did not leave Wilde to rest after "The Unspeakable Gentleman." He found other contexts beyond poetry to continue making amends, albeit in small steps, without quite being able to shake off the ideology of the church. In 1933, he delivered a speech to the Catholic Poetry Society in which he admitted that he had "reacted violently" against Wilde after his conversion but expressed hope that he had become "more charitable and broad-minded" than before. Seven years later, Douglas published *Oscar Wilde: A Summing Up,* in which he defended Wilde on the basis that homosexuality, while still a sin in his mind, should not be deemed a crime.[34] Neither example shows a complete embrace of Wilde, let alone his own sexual history, but they do mark a considerable shift from the litigious, homophobic campaigns that he had undertaken with Crosland.

The allusions considered in this chapter, which extend over two decades, show the range of emotions that Douglas experienced toward Wilde, both during their time together and in the years following Wilde's death, from longing to adoration to resentment and regret. Or more specifically, they show us how Douglas wanted his relationship to be perceived variously at different points in time. The poems are of biographical value in that they give us Douglas's own account of the affair. They also reveal, unwittingly, some conflicting emotions that he did not entirely control, be it the narcissistic conception of love during his early years with Wilde or the confused mix of anger and guilt after he distanced himself from Crosland. In sum, the poems give us Douglas's own record of what he felt he could make (partly) public for a queer audience, but they also grant us insight into a range of feelings that he did not fully understand himself and that poetry allowed him to articulate.

TWO

W. H. Auden *and* Stephen Spender

The relationship between W. H. Auden and Stephen Spender differed from that of Wilde and Douglas. Their bond was never romantic or sexual. When they first met as students at Oxford, they devoted much of their time together to talking about poetry, so that they connected as friends and fellow writers. Yet their dynamic off the page was hardly equal. Auden behaved as the leader of his friend group, while Spender assumed the position of a "timorous latecomer," per Justin Replogle.[1] John Sutherland notes that "from the first, Auden adopted the role of oracular master to a new and somewhat disordered disciple."[2] David Leeming concurs: "The Spender-Auden relationship was . . . a genuinely deep friendship, but from the beginning it was a mentor-pupil arrangement. Spender was shy and retiring, often self-denigrating, always seemingly anxious for constructive criticism. Auden gave the impression of supreme confidence and was more than willing to criticize. He was a born teacher and Spender was a born pupil."[3] In fact, Spender had wanted to meet Auden for some time, but his brother had deferred the introduction. Spender, always lacking in confidence, attributed this delay to a fear that "in producing me he would be playing the weakest card in his hand." His first memoir, *World Within World* (1951), contains many examples of the power imbalance between them. He deemed their introduction, arranged by mutual friend Archie Campbell, "a humiliating failure" after Auden quizzed Spender about what authors he considered "the best poets writing today" and swiftly dismissed his responses. In subsequent meetings,

Auden tried to impress upon his disciple which poets he ought to emulate or avoid. Before long, Spender brought Auden copies of his own poems for feedback. Auden's evaluative style was terse and liable to heighten Spender's desire for praise: "Occasionally he would grunt. Beyond this his comment was restrained to selecting one line for praise."[4] The inequality of their friendship is even more striking if one considers that they were less than two years apart: when they first met, Spender was nineteen years old and Auden just shy of twenty-one.

One might expect Auden to have been a major influence on the development of Spender's style, and to some extent, he did serve as a guide to him as well as to other poets of the so-called Auden Group (Louis MacNeice and Cecil Day-Lewis). A. Kingsley Weatherhead pinpoints that influence in Spender's "rhetorical techniques and attitudes," namely "his ellipses, his catalogues, metonymies and synecdoches, his symbols, his awareness, paradoxically vivid, of the boring and the dull, his brilliant treatment of quotidian things, the 'usual' things, in his own familiar terminology."[5] Spender himself admitted to Auden's importance, though always with some quiet hedging. In *World Within World*, he writes that "doubtless Auden influenced me at this time." The sentence reads as an obligatory, begrudging qualification, as though he would rather explain the ways in which Auden did *not* influence him. Later he adds that "my own work showed his influence in certain imagery, the tone of certain lines."[6] The word *certain*, which appears twice, betrays a desire not to give Auden too much credit.

It is notable, then, that Spender's poetry contains so few allusions to specific lines in Auden, but that Auden alluded repeatedly to Spender across several decades. This defies one of the principal suppositions about allusion: that the poet who alludes occupies a lower hierarchical position than the poet who is being alluded to, because such references are evidence of a poetic "debt." But, in fact, it was Auden who drew from his disciple repeatedly. There are several explanations for that reversal. Spender, always alert to the power imbalance between them, likely did not wish to yield too much to Auden. He also saw Auden's sensibility as fundamentally different from his own. To his ear, Auden's early poetry resembled "an intellectual game—a game to which the name Clinical Detachment might be given. It is a game of impartial objectivity about catastrophes, wars, revolutions, violence, hatreds, loves, and all the forces which move through human lives."[7] He also wrote that "Auden, despite his perceptiveness, lacked something in human relationships" and that he put himself in "the position of observer" rather than participant.[8] Edward Callan offers a similar picture of the poet's early work: "Auden's cast of mind from the start was scientific," so that the poems "draw their images primarily from anthropology, geology, and psychology."[9] By contrast, Spender saw his young self as ruled by emotions that he could never quite keep in check. This difference in sensibility also explains why Auden himself was so proficient in allusion. In *World Within World*, Spender writes:

> One significant difference was the use to which each put his memory. Auden, as I have described, knew much poetry by heart. I knew almost none. The difference here was not just of his good and my bad memory. It was one of our having different attitudes towards remembering. I resisted learning poems by heart, because in recollecting them I did not want to hold them word by word in my mind, in exactly the same form as when I read them. I wanted to remember not the words and the lines, but a line beyond the lines, a sensuous quality which went, as it were, into the lines before they were written by the poet and which remained after I, the reader, had forgotten them.[10]

It seems only logical, then, that Auden's influence on Spender was visible in terms of theme, mood, and general attitude, whereas Auden, always focused on textual particulars, responded to his friend via allusion. Spender's sentimentality, his love of atmosphere, and his desire to bask in "sensuous" impressions made him resistant to the memorization and specificity required for allusion. Auden, on the other hand, eager to commit poetry to heart, found it natural to engage with a poem by working through its specific language.

Auden and Spender met in the summer of 1928, and they remained friends until Auden's death in September 1973. Auden's attitude to

Spender in verse, as well as the specific poems that he gravitated toward, evolved over the course of four and a half decades, so any chapter
that tells the story of Auden's allusions must account for these changes.
During the early years of their friendship, to the end of the 1930s, Auden
repeatedly alluded to a cluster of poems about Spender's unrequited love
for a fellow student he nicknamed "Marston." Gabriel Carritt identifies
this student as John Freeman, an athletic young man known for his pro-
ficiency as a boxer, runner, and skier, who also served as a pilot in the
University Flying Club.[11] While Marston never expressed any romantic
or sexual interest in the young poet, Spender felt irresistibly drawn to
him. Part of his appeal lay in his archetypically masculine qualities. When
he later looked back on his Oxford years, Spender stressed Marston's
athleticism, his confidence, as well as his close-knit bond with a group of
strapping young friends. By contrast, Spender cast himself in a stereo-
typically feminine role, always dependent on the man's attention (which
Marston granted sparingly, if at all): "I chose every opportunity to see
Marston. I called on him in his rooms, which he shared with a friend, and
I made great efforts to interest myself in his boxing, skiing and flying. I
tried to behave like the hearties by whom he was surrounded, because a
pretense of heartiness gave me opportunities to behave demonstratively
. . . All the same, there was something fussy and old-womanish about my
pursuit of a person who met my enthusiasm with quiet politeness, and my
own behavior at times repelled me." Shame recurs here as the dominant
emotion of Spender's emotional life. As in his relationship with Auden,
Spender felt a profound sense of inferiority vis-à-vis his friend. Eventually, he wrote to Marston, confessing his affection. The two met up to talk,
and after listening to Spender relate his feelings in full, Marston delivered
a stinging response: "Do you know, old son, this is the first time you've
ever talked with me that I haven't been completely bored?" Intriguingly,
while Marston made it clear that he did not reciprocate his friend's love,
and while Spender asked that the two not speak again, they continued
to meet periodically in teashops. The pretext was that Marston needed a
confidant: they discussed "his affairs with girls, his loneliness, his failures
in his work, his fears when he boxed or flew." Spender eagerly accepted

Marston's confessions as acts of kindness and proof that he wished "to compensate me for a loss by making me a present of his hidden life."[12] It is possible, of course, that Marston may have felt more for Spender than he was willing to admit, to himself and to others, and these meetings were attempts to preserve ties with Spender while also keeping him at a distance.

Marston spurred what John Sutherland has called "the emotional crisis of Stephen's first year at Oxford."[13] He was the subject of the first poems Spender wrote at university and shared privately with Auden, before their publication in *Twenty Poems* (1930). It is these pieces that Auden alluded to in his own verse throughout the 1930s. In responding to Spender, Auden often adopted the attitude of a more mature and confident poet, seeing right through a younger poet's thinly veiled language to the secret hurt motivating his poems. The allusions display a degree of one-upmanship, as though Auden wanted his disciple to know that his methods were not quite so obfuscating as he may have assumed. At the same time, there is also a strong sense of kinship and sympathy for a fellow queer poet navigating a difficult emotional terrain in secret. Complicating Auden's response even further is his changing sense of whether he felt it appropriate to express private desires in poetry, particularly same-sex desires that were liable to damage the author's reputation. At times, Auden depersonalizes Spender's language, as though to purge the poems of embarrassing and unintended self-revelations. At other times, he coaxes the poems' buried homoeroticism further into the light (but not quite to the point of exposing it fully), signaling discreetly to Spender that he understands and that Spender need not feel shame. The reason for these shifts may have to do with Auden's complicated feelings about his own sexuality at this stage in his life.

When Auden enrolled at Oxford, in 1925, he was determined to reject the sexual repression that had been inculcated in him at Gresham's School. The students at Gresham's were bound to an honor code: smoking, swearing, and "indecency" were strictly prohibited, and any infractions among one's peers had to be reported to the schoolmaster. Auden resented this system, believing that any young person who buried their emotions and desires to such an extent was bound to "remain frozen and underdeveloped, or else . . . plunge into foolish and damaging dissipation." Evidently, he saw himself as belonging to the latter camp. Upon arriving at Oxford, he swore off love and pursued sex voraciously, describing his escapades to friends in extensive detail.[14] Spender's romantic and sexual experience was far more limited by comparison. Before enrolling at Oxford, he had only enjoyed a brief and unsatisfactory encounter with a boy named David Maclean while traveling in Lausanne in August 1927; then, at Oxford, much of his energy was taken up by his unrequited love for Marston.[15] It was only upon visiting Germany in the summer of 1929 that he began to explore sexually, meeting young men at parties, beaches, swimming pools, and gay bars. Still, Spender never felt completely at ease with the cruising culture of his gay friends.[16] Auden, by contrast, delighted in playing the role of the more experienced gay man, since he could view it as yet further proof that he had exorcised the repression inculcated by Gresham's School. Per Humphrey Carpenter, his motivation in sharing stories about his escapades was "partly to shock . . . and partly perhaps in order to demonstrate to them how free he was from guilt."[17]

Yet to some extent, Auden must have recognized himself in Spender as well. Even though he claimed to abandon love for lust, he frequently developed crushes on heterosexual men who were unattainable. He ragged on himself for repeatedly succumbing to "the pathetic thrill of devotion . . . for the loved heterosexual."[18] Nor could he entirely rid himself of the shame that he had been fed through so many years. As Richard Davenport-Hines writes, "Behind the bravura there was doubt, guilt and consternation."[19] In 1927, Auden wrote to a fellow student, "There still lingers in my mind the idea of something indecent in a mutual homosexual relation."[20] This shame was only reinforced by his reading of Freud and other psychoanalytical theorists who conceived of homosexuality as a mark of emotional immaturity.[21] Auden often blamed his inability to forge deep romantic connections on his orientation.[22] Sadly, his thinking did not much improve after his departure from Oxford. He continued to express reservations about his sexuality well into the 1930s, even as he tried to think himself out of guilt. In 1932, for example, he wrote: "The mere fact that A prefers girls and B boys is unimportant. The real cause for alarm lies in the large number of nervous and unhappy people who are incapable of any intimate faithful relationship at all, in whom sensation has remained at or regressed to the infantile level as an end in itself . . . and to whom, therefore, the object is really non-existent. It is true that nearly all homosexual relations are of this kind but so are a large proportion of heterosexual ones and there is nothing to choose between them." He was, at this point, still too quick to see same-sex relationships as lacking in intimacy and depth. But he was also starting to admit that these problems were not exclusive to queer people. The next year, he described homosexuality as "a naughty habit like thumb-sucking": a negative image but also one that shows some willingness to make light of his experience.[23] By alluding to Spender's poems in the early 1930s, then, Auden was motivated by paradoxical impulses: eagerness to portray himself as the more experienced one; fear that the disappointments Spender felt would always be his as well; and sympathy for the difficulties that Spender encountered, including the pain of unrequited love.

The first poem that Auden alluded to, "Discovered Mid-Ocean," is typical in that Spender does not speak directly of desire or love for Marston. Instead, he adopts an impersonal voice, as if he were a remote observer with no personal stake in the scene. To distance himself from the scene even further, he imagines Marston as a heroic, larger-than-life figure, if one who nevertheless displays human foibles. John Sutherland praises the poem as the earliest product of Spender's "mature voice."[24] Still, it is worth remembering that Spender wrote "Discovered in Mid-Ocean" in late 1928 or early 1929, when he was just nineteen years old.[25] The poem certainly bears the mark of its author's youth: the grand, self-important tone; the adolescent longing after idols; and the cringing flight from emotions that might otherwise expose him to embarrassment.

> He will watch the hawk with an indifferent eye
> Or pitifully;
> Nor on those eagles that so feared him, now
> Will strain his brow;
> Weapons men use, stone, sling and strong-thewed bow
> He will not know.

This aristocrat, superb of all instinct,
>With death close linked,
Had paced the enormous cloud, almost had won
>War on the sun;
Till now, like Icarus mid-ocean-drowned,
>Hands, wings are found.[26]

"Discovered Mid-Ocean" has received only limited commentary. A. Kingsley Weatherhead, one of the few critics to have written about the poem, gestures toward the difficult, personal motivations that animate it: "Spender as poet has resolved the oppression of his real personal predicament by a species of amputation—making an image of the unattainable beloved as dead."[27] Yet there is still more to unpack. Certainly, part of Spender's intent here is to soften the pain of unrequited love by imagining the beloved as deceased. Within the boundaries of the poem at least, Marston will remain cold to Spender's affection, not because of anything about Spender himself but because Marston has died. This has the added benefit of casting Marston beyond the reach of potential rivals as well: if the poet cannot win his friend's love, then nobody else will either.

At the same time, there are also darker, more vengeful impulses at play. Spender compares Marston to Icarus, a mythological figure associated with the fatal consequence of pride. The poem in its entirety underlines his arrogance and decline in tandem, as if to suggest that the young man had been punished for claiming too much. He may have once wished to fly alongside the hawk, and at one time he may have "paced the enormous cloud" and overshadowed the sun; but now that he has fallen into the ocean, he can only view the bird—and, implicitly, himself—with indifference or mere pity. Even the line "This aristocrat, superb of all instinct" expresses a critical attitude. By 1929, the term *aristocrat* would have landed with implications of unearned privilege, especially for a group of socially conscious writers in Auden's circle. *Superb*, ostensibly a word of praise, conveys the haughtiness Spender perceived in his subject. The implicit argument of the poem is that Marston had reaped what he sowed.

Spender reframes Marston's resistance to his love as a mark of his friend's arrogance, rather than a sign of Spender's own limitations.

Readers of Auden would doubtless have recognized the opening line of "Consider This and in Our Time" (1930) as an echo of the opening line in "Discovered Mid-Ocean." Here is the first stanza from Auden:

> As the hawk sees it or the helmeted airman:
> The clouds rift suddenly—look there
> At cigarette-end smouldering on a border
> At the first garden party of the year.
> Pass on, admire the view of the massif
> Through plate-glass windows of the Sport hotel;
> Join there the insufficient units
> Dangerous, easy, in furs, in uniform
> And constellated at reserved tables
> Supplied with feelings by an efficient band
> Relayed elsewhere to farmers and their dogs
> Sitting in kitchens in the stormy fens.[28]

Several critics have identified Thomas Hardy as an influence on this poem, thanks to an essay that Auden wrote for the *Southern Review* from summer 1940: "What I valued most in Hardy, then, as I still do, was his hawk's vision, his way of looking at life from a very great height, as in the stage directions of *The Dynasts*, or the opening chapter of *The Return of the Native*."[29] Still, Spender remains the more likely interlocutor, not just because the composition dates of the two poems run so close together but also because Marston was an enthusiastic member of a flight club. The "helmeted airman" in "Consider This and in Our Time" can be read as a second nod, further cementing the connection between the poems.

To understand what Auden wished to say about Spender and "Discovered Mid-Ocean," one must consider his play on perspective. Auden begins "Consider This and in Our Time" with the same figure—a hawk—but flips the original poem's vantage point. Instead of observing the bird from the ground, he assumes the hawk's own outlook from the sky. The clouds, which Spender's "superb aristocrat" had once paced and then fallen short of, are made to "rift suddenly," allowing for an unobstructed vista. The result is what might be called a god's-eye view of the happenings on Earth. Monroe K. Spears, for example, has described "the effect of detachment and of drama" in the poem as well as "the distancing and heightening function of the style."[30]

Many have argued that the ensuing observations in the poem—the "cigarette-end," the "garden party," the "Sport hotel"—amount to a critique of English society.[31] But there is little in this opening stanza to indicate what that critique might be specifically. Critics have pointed to the cigarette end as a portent of violence, yet to read the image so requires putting rather too much symbolic weight on the word *smouldering*. The closest that Auden comes to a social critique is in the description of the attendees at the Sport hotel, specifically the words *insufficient* and *dangerous*. But even these words are chosen to cancel one another out. *Insufficient* implies that the members of the group—a mix of civilians in furs and soldiers in uniform—are ill equipped for an attack and that we as readers may wish to be concerned for their safety, whereas *dangerous* positions them as a threat, a potential source of violence whom we ought to keep at bay. Whatever tension that ambiguity might generate finds itself dissipated by the next lines, which describe the band music "Relayed elsewhere to farmers and their dogs / Sitting in kitchens in the stormy fens." As with the cigarette, Auden might be luring us into a symbolic reading of the storms, but he also gives us very little on which to ground an interpretation. What ill does the poem denounce? War, as suggested by the earlier uniforms? This seems too broad an answer. Auden gives us the bait only to quickly snatch it back before it can yield anything of substance.

In other words, despite the many readings that this poem has engendered, Auden resists any tangible critique of his society and remains doggedly neutral. The word *indifferent,* which Spender had attributed to the "aristocrat" Marston, applies to the speaker's tone in "Consider This and in Our Time." As the poem continues through two additional stanzas, Auden flirts with pity rather than condemnation, as when he addresses a businessman:

Financier, leaving your little room
Where the money is made but not spent,
You'll need your typist and your boy no more.[32]

The "little room" is not presented as a fitting punishment we ought to delight in but as a spur for pathos and sympathy. Importantly, the poem does
not gather this data toward an identifiable critique of a specific institution,
government, group, or social injustice.

Recognizing "Consider This and in Our Time" as a response to
"Discovered Mid-Ocean" supplies one answer to the long-standing debate over whether Auden betrays a dictatorial sensibility by claiming
too much. Douglas Dunn certainly thought so, arguing that the "cine-
matic quickness, the masterly narrative movement of the lines, and self-
confident reaching for definitive statements" made the poet's style "authoritarian."[33] If we read Auden's poem as a response to Spender, though,
the problem of authority and authoritarianism gives way to the issue of
emotional investment. In this light, Auden's principal motivation was not
to assume an omniscient perspective of his society but to moderate the
highly personal feelings that underlie Spender's poem and demonstrate
how a poet might write dispassionately. Spender may describe Marston as
"indifferent," yet "Discovered Mid-Ocean" is anything but. In fact, it is
ruled by contrary emotions. On the one hand, Spender worships Marston
as an idol (in a way that more closely resembles the authoritarian instincts
that Auden's critics had detected in "Consider This and in Our Time").
On the other, he angrily thrills at the thought of seeing Marston punished
for his pride and his inability to return Spender's love. For Auden, at
this point in his life, the poem was too personal in its subject matter, too
adolescent in its emotional intensity, and so too transparent in its motivations. "Consider This and in Our Time" reorients Spender's focus from
the personal to the social. Auden signals that turn from the outset with
a change in perspective from the ground to the sky. The allusion is an
argument for emptying poetry of messy personal emotions and writing
impersonally about society: in sum, adopting a hawk's-eye view of the
world. For Auden, this approach was a matter of artistic responsibility. At

the same time, his rejection of personal feeling also likely had to do with the nature of Spender's desires, which mirrored his own and which he was not prepared to address in the public form of a poem. In this, Auden was guided as much by a lingering sense of shame as by aesthetic principle.

Auden took a similar approach two years later, in the sixth ode of his long poem *The Orators* (1932). There he alluded to another poem titled "Lying Awake at Night," which Spender had shown to the dean of his college after Marston's rejection, to prove that his feelings went beyond friendship and that the two should thus be kept apart:[34]

> Lying awake at night
> Shows again the difference
> Between me, and his innocence.
> I vow he was born of light
>   And that dark gradually
>   Closed each eye,
> He woke, he sleeps so naturally.
>
> So, born of nature, amongst men most divine,
> He copied, and was our sun.
>   And his mood was thunder
>   For anger,
> But mostly a calm, English one.[35]

The vengeful impulses running beneath the surface of "Discovered Mid-Ocean" are entirely absent here, but there remains the same impulse to turn Marston into a heroic figure. In the first stanza, Spender emphasizes his friend's purity by writing of his "innocence" and saying that he was "born of light." In the second stanza, the description grows more intense, with an emphasis on Marston's power, his "divine" status. For Spender, Marston *is* the weather, so that his mood affects the poet's whole environment. He is "our sun," and on his light, the "calm, English" land depends. Granted, Spender concedes that there have also been bad days when "his mood was thunder / For anger," but the poet insists that these are rare.

To emphasize both his power and his gentleness, Spender imagines him in repose. There is some lingering ambiguity whether Marston's sleep is a euphemism for death. The past tense in the second stanza certainly leaves that open as a possibility. Yet unlike in "Discovered Mid-Ocean," Spender does not imply that Marston is being punished for his arrogance. The poem is entirely praise.

Describing the beloved as the weather, capable of altering the poet's whole world at whim, is a familiar trope of love poetry. Still, this poet tries to conceal the nature of his feelings for Marston, or at least to keep these private for his own enjoyment, by resorting to the first-person plural in the second stanza. Marston was not "*my* sun" but "*our* sun." It is unclear how far that pronoun extends, but the mention of "calm, English" weather in the final line suggests that the *our* belongs to all of England. After the obvious intimacy of the first stanza, in which the poet describes himself watching Marston sleep, Spender backs away and attempts, rather awkwardly, to transform his romantic idol into a national hero. He does entirely succeed, for the shift depends on just two words: the pronoun *our* in line 9 and the evocation of England in line 12. Spender's efforts are too obvious and tardy, coming after the intimate scene of the first, longer stanza.

Auden clearly had similar feelings in the fifth ode of *The Orators* (1932), later retitled "Which Side Am I Supposed to Be On?" in *Collected Poems*. The poem was inspired by his years working as a tutor and then a schoolmaster at Larchfield Academy and the Downs School. Auden reflects on the British education system and the ideology of "English hierarchy and nationalism" that it imposes on its charges, as Bonnie Costello has put it.[36] So as to convey the strictures of this world, he transforms the school setting into an army barracks. Per John Fuller, the pupils become "recruits on the side of repression, the schoolmasters merely veteran pupils perpetuating legends."[37]

Auden evokes Spender specifically in lines in which the speaker imagines, and addresses, a young drummer caught up in a war he cannot fully understand. The soldier overhears stories of an idyllic peacetime before the conflict, but he has never lived through it and so has only experienced chaos. While eager to learn more one night, he is ordered to sleep:

> Lying awake after Lights Out a recruit may speak up:
> "Who told you all this?"
> The tent-talk pauses a little till a veteran answers
> "Go to sleep, Sonny!"

> Turning over he closes his eyes, and then in a moment
> Sees the sun at midnight bright over cornfield and pasture,
> Our hope . . . [38]

The nationalist first-person plural that Spender had adopted as a cover for the romantic undertones of his poem here reflects the national, political scope of this ode. Auden echoes several phrases from Spender. However, all these phrases are changed to convey not the power of the beloved but the powerlessness of the young recruit. This time, it is not the speaker "lying awake at night," gazing on a beautiful Marston fast asleep. Instead, it is the young recruit, distracted by stories of a time before the war. In Spender, Marston was a figural "sun" whose mood would alter the poet's entire world. In Auden, no one person carries such authority. The sun has become a symbol of the nation's hope for peace, which the recruit glimpses over an imaginary field when he closes his eyes. Granted, the young soldier may hold some small degree of power. The possessive pronoun *our*, which Auden had pinned to *sun*, attaches itself to *hope*. The syntax is ambiguous enough that *our hope* might refer to the recruit—as an emblem of England's happy future if it corrects its path—rather than an abstract peace. A reader familiar with Spender's poem and seeing the parallel between "our sun" Marston and "our hope" would be more likely to take the soldier as the referent here. But it remains far from certain that such a happy future will come to pass, let alone that any one person has the power to bring it about.

In short, Auden takes the romantic and sexual undercurrents of "Lying awake at night" that Spender had worked hard to conceal and eradicates them by altering the subject from a beloved hero to a young pupil. But queerness finds its way into the poem through different means. Tellingly, Auden goes on to relate how the young drummer was mocked by his brother for his perceived effeminacy:

> Your childish moments of awareness were all of our world,
> At five you sprang, already a tiger in the garden,
> At night your mother taught you to pray for our Daddy
> > Far away fighting,
> One morning you fell off a horse and your brother mocked you:
> > "Just like a girl!"[39]

Though it may seem like a passing detail, the brother's jeer takes on additional weight considering Auden's sexuality and the poem that he draws upon. By including the remark, the poet recognizes, sympathetically, the hostility encountered by those who deviate from expected gender norms, as he and Spender did by virtue of their sexuality. The scene enables Auden to acknowledge the queerness that had motivated Spender's poem and its obfuscations. Still, he also limits its reach by shifting the context from a love poem to a single scene of childhood bullying. The impulse behind the poem is to school Spender (albeit gently) for making Marston, or anyone, into a god. Auden communicates that by altering the theme and register. "Ode V" does not express adoration of a unique, divine entity but, instead, pity for one powerless individual among many others. The idea is that a more objective, principled view of the world will focus not on so-called gods but on frightened children—and for Auden, writing at this time, the "hawk's eye" was the most responsible vantage point that a poet could take.

By the second half of the 1930s, however, Auden's resistance to personal disclosure in verse began to wane, as did his most negative emotions about homosexuality, even if they did not entirely disappear. "Stop all the clocks" marks a change in attitude from "Ode V" of *The Orators*, if not quite a reversal. For inspiration, Auden borrowed from another Marston poem published in 1930. Like the other poems on this subject, "Hearing from its cage" does not contain a first-person singular *I*, let alone an explicit confession of love. Spender's goal is, once again, to disguise the erotic and romantic undertones of the poem by praising a heroic figure with generalizing, metaphorical language. The first three stanzas read:

> Hearing from its cage
> Lion that roars the traffic down,
> Or seeing the rash sun
> Strike out the fog, brings him.

> For he was constant April
> All times and everywhere;
> Like the straight, cherished deer
> By pride fenced from the people.

> And seeing a new god
> Dropped from the sky, no less
> Calls out on timelessness
> Than seeing where he trod.[40]

Spender repeats the fallen god imagery that he had employed in "Discovered Mid-Ocean." But like the previous example, "Lying awake at night," this poem does not frame Marston's suffering as any kind of justified punishment. Instead, Spender emphasizes the god's power. Marston is present "All times and everywhere," and even his fall "Calls out on timelessness." The final stanza affirms that power conclusively:

> And where his form passed by
> Grass would have tongues for truth,
> Stones would speak words of truth.
> And these words cannot die.

Marston is revealed to have the power of lending speech to inanimate things and ensuring that they speak the truth. But in an unusual turn, Spender grants himself considerable power as well. He is the one who immortalizes Marston in language. Several times in the poem, Spender shifts back to past tense ("he was constant April," "when his form passed by") to remind us that this god, though divine to the speaker, is not actually immortal. Since he does not have eternal life, he can only obtain that privilege from the poet. Spender likely derived some satisfaction from the thought that he, for once, could have power over his friend.

Auden's "Stop all the clocks" (later retitled "Funeral Blues") borrows much from Spender's poem, but the tone and context are largely changed. Instead of praising a divine entity, the speaker laments the death of a loved one. The extreme language Spender had used to speak of Marston's power resurfaces here to describe the drastic sights that the poet wants to see in the outer world now that their inner world has been so wracked by grief. In the first stanza, the poet orders an unknown addressee to "stop" various objects whose everyday activities are deemed inappropriate to the occasion ("Stop all the clocks, cut off the telephone," among others). These commands, cast into a void to no one in particular, highlight the mourner's powerlessness in a world that cannot mirror and affirm their pain. In the second stanza, the speaker calls out for a public display of mourning. Auden drops his first discreet allusion here: one of the mourner's pleas, "Let the traffic policemen wear black cotton gloves," echoes the opening lines in Spender, "Hearing from its cage / Lion that roars the traffic down." Marston's divine affinity with the natural world yields to the desperation of grief once again, with a plea that can never be satisfied. The parallel of traffic imagery also sets up a more substantial allusion in the third stanza, in which Auden takes Spender's high praise of Marston's power, "For he was constant April / All times and everywhere," and expands it into a full stanza on loss and grief:

> He was my North, my South, my East and West,
> My working week and my Sunday rest,

My noon, my midnight, my talk, my song;
I thought that love would last forever: I was wrong.

While Marston represented one eternal season for all, the deceased in this poem has become every day, place, and thing for the speaker. Auden narrows the beloved's impact from the entire world to the poet, yet he also deepens his importance by measuring him against not just a single season but multiple units of time, geography, and expression. As the poem winds to a close in the fourth stanza, the speaker once again demands that some natural elements be "put out," as they no longer serve a purpose for the poet's new life ("The stars are not wanted now"). In Spender, Marston's arrival was heralded by "seeing the rash sun / Strike out the fog." In Auden, the poet orders an unknown force in the universe to "dismantle the sun" (another impossible task), "For nothing now can ever come to any good."[41] The world that Marston had once dominated and conquered is of no interest to the poet in grief.

To fully understand the impulse behind these allusions, though, it is important to consider the poem's history. Auden wrote an earlier version of the poem in April 1936 for a play, *The Ascent of F6*, about a fictional climber named Michael Ransom who leads an ill-fated expedition to the top of a mountain. In that context, the lines functioned as an elegiac song marking the death of Ransom's brother James. Two years later, Auden revised the text substantially for music by Benjamin Britten. Auden removed the last three stanzas (of five) and replaced them with two new stanzas, including the one quoted here. It was at this point that he gave the piece the title "Funeral Blues." The text would later appear in *Another Time* (1940) alongside three other pieces, collected under the heading "Four Cabaret Songs for Miss Hedli Anderson," Britten's beloved soprano.[42] This history indicates that Auden, by alluding to Spender, had two paradoxical goals in mind: to preserve the secrecy of Spender's love, as he would have wished at the time, while giving his love a fuller expression.

On the one hand, Auden buries the homoerotic implications of his language. He distances himself from the poem's emotional content by assigning the lines to a specific female artist, Hedli Anderson. Had the piece first been printed as a lyric poem rather than a cabaret song designed for a particular voice, some readers may have suspected that the feelings expressed in it were founded on biography. But by ascribing the lines to a female soprano, Auden divests himself of any personal connection. It is for this reason, too, that Auden avoids describing the speaker. While the beloved's gender becomes clear thanks to the repeated use of the pronoun *he*, the text provides no clue as to the speaker's gender. At the same time, these strategies enable Auden to draw out the romantic undertones of Spender's poem more boldly. The frame of a cabaret song gives Auden license to write passionately, without fearing that the lines might be dismissed for their basis in homosexual love, since Hedli Anderson's name would mark the poem's love story as heterosexual, at least to readers who are not LGBTQ themselves and not as alert to telling signs of omission. The cabaret framework may keep Auden at a distance, but it also allows queer readers longing for evidence of same-sex love in poetry to see through the poem's obvious mechanisms for concealment.

Tracing "Stop all the clocks" back to Spender helps to understand the extremity of Auden's images, which most critics have deemed too silly to take seriously.[43] The melodramatic quality of the speaker's emotions and of the catastrophic metaphors subverts the distancing effects of the poem's framing. The subtitle "Four Cabaret Songs for Miss Hedli Anderson" seems to turn the poem into a mere "exercise in light verse," to quote Richard Bozorth.[44] Yet while the images may be viewed with irony or skepticism, the tragic severity of the speaker's attitude militates against the title's suggestion that we read the lines simply as light verse. The comedy that emerges here is camp—an aesthetic with deep connections with the LGBTQ community. The poem exhibits a complex tension between high seriousness and the failure to be serious, which is camp's principal feature. Auden extends a hand to readers, or more specifically queer readers, who are looking for clues of same-sex affection in poetry and who will likely detect the ambiguities around the speaker's gender and the carefully orchestrated melodrama as clear signals.

In sum, the allusions in "Funeral Blues" constitute an act of sympathy toward Spender, who did not feel that he could write directly about his affection for Marston. Auden maintains the secrecy of Spender's poem to some degree by framing his own piece as a cabaret song to be performed by a female soprano. But the intensity of Auden's emotional expression also presses back against that framework, signaling to the reader who may be so interested that there are other passions at play. It is fitting that the poem features in the 1994 film *Four Weddings and a Funeral,* in a scene in which a gay man mourns the death of his partner by reading the lines at his funeral. The film does not impose external information about Auden's own life onto the poem but, instead, responds to prompts within the poem itself.

By 1940, when *Another Time* first appeared, much had changed in Auden's and Spender's lives. Auden had emigrated to the United States the preceding year, and the move inevitably put some distance between them. Even though they stayed in touch and Spender did visit his friend in his new country, Auden's next significant allusion to Spender after "Funeral Blues" did not occur until "The More Loving One" in 1957. That poem is a direct response to Spender's "The Indifferent One," which he had written the year of Auden's departure for America in 1939. Auden's title, with its obvious parallel to Spender's, explicitly connects the two. The poem also marks a startling turn in Auden's attitude toward Spender in verse. His allusions there are if not an outright rejection, then at least a sharp rebuttal: a far cry from the sympathetic schooling that had marked his attitude in the earlier poems.

Some context about Spender's life is necessary to understand the force of Auden's response. By 1933, Spender had tired of cruising and longed for domestic stability. When he was introduced to Tony Hyndman, he fell for the young Welshman at once, later declaring "that was when the curtain went up, for me." Impulsively, the two men decided to travel together to Italy, and upon their return to London, they moved in together.[45] At that point, however, Spender's view of his sexuality had begun to change. He began an affair with Muriel Gardiner, an American student of nursing and psychology and medicine. The relationship prompted Spender to write that he now found "sleeping with a woman more satisfying." Then, in late 1936, he met Inez Pearn, a graduate student at Somerville College. After less than a month, Spender asked for Pearn's hand in marriage, and she accepted, bringing his relationship with Hyndman to an end.[46]

Yet Spender continued to love him and at times even regretted the decision to marry Pearn.[47] Moreover, Hyndman's involvement in the Spanish Civil War led Spender to fear intensely for his safety. Hyndman had gone to Spain to fight for the Republican faction, and in 1937, he was held captive for refusing an order to advance in the front line at Sierra de Pingarrón. Spender went searching for him, only to discover that he had been charged for desertion, insubordination, and suspicion of espionage. Spender succeeded in obtaining his release. Still, he decided not to stay by Hyndman's side after that point. Instead, he traveled back to Paris and met up with Pearn in April. John Sutherland theorizes that "The Indifferent One" was inspired by the couple's reunion.[48]

In the poem, the speaker describes himself arriving at a hotel to rejoin his beloved, feeling guilty about some unspecified mistake, his only question: "Can you forgive?" The poem does not show us the lover's response in their own words; instead, we must rely on the speaker's paraphrase: "Yes, you accept." The pair make love, and in the third and last stanza, the poet has a vision on the ceiling of the hotel room:

> Upturned to the unwritten ceiling
> My eyes there read another you,
> The naked human figure leaning
> With one hand raised towards a view
> Between whose hills are the blue spaces,
> Perspectives of my happiness!
> There on your lips the clear light lives
> Diffusing with its equable waves
> The smile's indifference which forgives.[49]

The poem ends with an apparent resolution, but some trebles of disturbance prevent the conclusion from being wholly satisfying. The fact that we do not hear from the lover directly, and that the response emerges only through paraphrase, is one sign of trouble. Another is the fact that the speaker's happiness depends on imagining "another you," as though the lover's acceptance sounded so half-hearted that the speaker needed to look to a distant future for reconciliation. The beloved does not actually forgive; only the "smile's indifference" does. That phrase makes for cold comfort and diminishes the joy that the speaker might experience when he cries out, "Perspectives of my happiness!" three lines earlier. Whatever forgiveness he receives must be partial and not quite satisfactory.

When Auden set down to write "The More Loving One," his own love life had undergone a turbulent change as well. In April 1939, Auden met a young man named Chester Kallman, a student at Brooklyn College, after a reading with Christopher Isherwood.[50] Kallman later visited Auden in his apartment, and the two became a couple after their second meeting. In July 1941, however, Auden discovered that Kallman was seeing another man. The poet felt devastated, as he was precisely the "more loving one" in the relationship. Kallman informed Auden that the two could remain friends but that they would never have sex again. Auden accepted the arrangement. And so began a long, highly asymmetrical relationship that would endure through the rest of the poet's life. Kallman would report back to Auden about his exploits with various lovers, going into considerable detail. Auden, meanwhile, remained emotionally committed to Kallman and did not seek another companion. Even as he formally accepted the arrangement, he was pained that Kallman did not reciprocate his love, let alone his sexual longing. He concealed his unhappiness from his friends, and only occasionally were his true feelings visible to others. Humphrey Carpenter relates one instance: "Stephen Spender was once sitting at an open-air café table with the two of them when Chester got up, crossed the street, and began to make advances to a young man. Spender saw that though Auden went on talking, there were tears running down his cheeks."[51]

It is no surprise that several biographers and critics—not just Carpenter but also Sherill Tippins and Alexander McCall Smith—have said that Auden based "The More Loving One" on his peculiar relationship with Kallman.[52] The allusions to Spender's poem have been ignored, though the connections between the two are readily apparent when the poems are set side by side.[53] Not only do the titles follow the same structure but Auden begins his poem by talking about *indifference*, the word that had featured in Spender's title and at the conclusion of his poem:

> Looking up at the stars, I know quite well
> That, for all they care, I can go to hell,
> But on earth indifference is the least
> We have to dread from man or beast.
>
> How should we like it were stars to burn
> With a passion for us we could not return?
> If equal affection cannot be,
> Let the more loving one be me.
>
> Admirer as I think I am
> Of stars that do not give a damn,
> I cannot, now I see them, say
> I missed one terribly all day.
>
> Were all stars to disappear or die,
> I should learn to look at an empty sky
> And feel its total dark sublime,
> Though this might take me a little time.[54]

Auden picks up on the double feeling in Spender's poem: relief at his lover's indifference, undercut by the suspicion that indifference may not be quite enough and may, in fact, be far from acceptance. In response to that late surge of anxiety, Auden retorts that there are much worse things to fear "on earth"—that is, from other people—than indifference. By this, he probably means malice, cruelty, or even violence. His argument changes considerably in the second stanza, however, in which he argues that there is an even worse fate than suffering the ill will of other people:

namely, to be indifferent ourselves and incapable of returning someone's love. To illustrate this idea, he sidesteps an example of earthly, romantic love (yet another telling evasion) and opts, instead, for an imaginary scenario in which the stars felt a devotion to humans that they could not return. This example, while ludicrous, continues to haunt the speaker throughout the rest of the poem. He recognizes the extent to which he has not cared about the stars, and although this may put them on equal footing, as the stars "do not give a damn," the thought of mutual indifference does not bring him much comfort either. The landscape of the final stanza reverses the one in Spender's poem. Whereas Spender had espied "blue spaces" offering "perspectives of my happiness," Auden sees but an "empty sky." The "clear light" has been replaced by the "total dark sublime." Granted, the last line suggests that there may be some affection there, though it may not last, as the poet admits that it will take him "a little time" to adjust to a starless sky. This final, discordant note is deeply ironic. While his temporary regret may seem to be precisely what he wants, as it would make him the more loving one, the shrinking tone suggests that he recognizes it would entail more heartache. Auden appears to give his readers a clear thesis in the second stanza—"If equal affection cannot be, / Let the more loving one be me"—but the poem as a whole is rife with mixed feelings on the virtue and pain of indifference.

The reasoning for Auden's careful evasion of human love makes sense in the context of his complicated relationship with Chester Kallman. The poem's biographical context can also help us to understand the contradictions between the stated thesis and the tone and ideas that follow it. Auden was undoubtedly the more loving one, and this poem can be understood as an attempt to tolerate Kallman's indifference by seeing his own love as the more noble position. Hence the forced coolness of "I cannot, now I see them, say / I missed one terribly all day," offset by the pinch of "this might take me a little time." Although he did believe in the nobility of being the more loving one, Auden recognized that this is a painful position to be in, and while he may have argued against indifference, part of him longed for it as a way of diminishing his pain.

Despite its nuances and paradoxes, Auden's response to Spender remains a departure from the examples surveyed previously in this chapter. Auden may not contradict Spender's longing for indifference exactly, but he does argue that his friend ought to shift focus, from what we can expect from others to what we should expect of *ourselves*. There is a touch of high-handedness to his poem, as if he were chiding Spender for being self-centered. Per Alexander McCall Smith, Auden came to view his unrequited love for Kallman as "a mature act of moral commitment."[55] "The More Loving One" is framed as the more ethical alternative to "The Indifferent One": a substantial change from the relationship implied by Auden's earlier allusions. Before, Auden had tended to position himself as a tutor responding to a promising, if imperfect, disciple. He would coolly identify the homoerotic underpinnings of Spender's poems that the younger poet had attempted—and failed—to conceal, and he would then either bury them entirely or draw them our more boldly. Still, in either case, his attitude was invariably sympathetic (if a tad scolding at times) because his recognition of Spender's half-hidden queerness was based on shared experience. "The More Loving One," however, disputes the very ethics of "The Indifferent One." The emphasis on morality registers as more scolding than sympathetic.

Auden's attitude may have partly stemmed from disappointment—even frustration—at the bond that he had lost with Spender once his friend joined the ranks of heterosexuality, and marriage to boot. While the two remained friends, one important point of connection between them was now gone. It also seems likely that Auden envied Spender for the companionship that he found in Inez Pearn. Even as Kallman conducted his affairs, Auden remained largely solitary, and the speaker of his poem (tellingly) stands alone. Auden may have felt eager to comfort himself with the thought that he, at the very least, had adopted the more ethical position.

The tensions audible in "The More Loving One" were equally evident off the page. As the two men grew older, Auden clung to the role of mentor, teasing and critiquing Spender whenever they met, even if this soured into public embarrassment. In 1969, for instance, he caused widespread discomfort among the attendees of the Poetry International Festival by making multiple patronizing comments about his friend. Behind his passivity, Spender grew resentful of Auden's condescension, refusing to write a poem for a Festschrift celebrating Auden's sixty-fifth birthday when he learned that the older poet was aware of the collection and expected Spender to pay homage. Still, for all the tensions in their relationship, Spender remained in awe of Auden. The two men cared for each other dearly and remained close until Auden's death.[56]

Auden passed away, alone in a hotel room in Vienna, after a reading, on September 28, 1973. Spender felt the loss deeply and participated in a series of events commemorating his friend's life and work. Per John Sutherland, he attended services "at Christ Church Cathedral, at the Austrian Embassy, at Westminster Abbey (where Auden was installed in Poets' Corner), a celebratory reading at the Banqueting Hall (where Alec Guinness and Peggy Ashcroft read on behalf of the Apollo Society), and a ceremony at the American Academy."[57] Touchingly, his memorial address at Christ Church on October 27 identified as the central theme of Auden's work love in the broadest sense, extending beyond romance:

> For throughout the whole development of his poetry (if one makes exception of the undergraduate work) his theme had been love: not romantic love but love as interpreter of the world, love as individual need, and love as redeeming power in the life of society and of the individual. At first there was the Lawrentian idea of unrepressed sexual fulfillment through love, then that of the social revolution which would accomplish the change of heart that would change society; then, finally, Christianity which looked more deeply into the heart than any of these, offered man the chance of redeeming himself and the society but also without illusions showed him to himself as he really was with all the limitations of his nature.[58]

The address was Spender's first public statement on Auden. Privately, it was to poetry he would turn to process his loss. He would need more than seven years to complete and publish the poem, which he titled "Auden's

Funeral." By September 10, 1980, as he noted in his journals, he felt that he had "worked through the stage of despair" and could share the elegy with a wider readership.[59]

"Auden's Funeral" is made up of four numbered sections, likely an homage to the structure of Auden's own elegy "In Memory of W. B. Yeats" (which contains three numbered sections). In the third, he directly quotes from a poem that Auden wrote while they were students at Oxford:

> (Ghost of a ghost, of you when young, you waken
> In me my ghost when young, us both at Oxford.
> You, the tow-haired undergraduate
> With jaunty liftings of the head.
> Angular forward stride, cross-questioning glance,
> A Buster Keaton–faced pale *gravitas*.
> Saying aloud your poems whose letters bit
> Ink-deep into my fingers when I set
> Them up upon my five-pound printing press:
>
> "An evening like a coloured photograph
>
> A music stultified across the water
>
> The heel upon the finishing blade of grass.")[60]

This third section is a departure from what has come before. The first two sections describe Auden's funeral and death, touchingly reimagined as a fall due to his being overwhelmed by praise from his audience. By contrast, the third relates Spender's personal memories of their early years together at university. Unlike its predecessors, the section is also set within parentheses, as if it were an aside. The punctuation effectively deepens the sense of privacy: Spender quotes little-known lines that he published for his friend on his own printing press, in an elegy designed for a broad audience, much like how funerals put private grief on public display.

The specific lines by Auden that Spender reproduces here are a fitting choice because many of the words they contain have to do with endings: *evening, stultified, finishing*. But the end has not arrived yet: the "blade of grass" is "finishing," not "finished." Moreover, there is still much beauty to be found, from art ("music"), keepsakes ("a coloured photograph"), and the environment ("water," "blade of grass"). These lines from Auden's juvenilia become an inscription, almost like a poetic tombstone: the letters "bit / Ink-deep into my fingers" when he printed them years ago on his "five-pound printing press." They also constitute the heart of this elegy, nestled within quotation marks within parentheses within one section of a long poem. This layering heightens the delicacy of the memory, as if Spender wished to tuck it away and preserve it, even as he puts it on display. In the fourth section, he returns to a description of Kallman's public mourning as Auden's body is sent away. Within these parentheses at least, Spender can preserve Auden's youth and art, and he can also safeguard a moment in time when the two friends were at their closest. The word *stultified*, which he borrows from Auden, serves as a recognition that his desire to freeze time is impractical, itself a little deadening. But Spender also accepts that he cannot stop time. *Stultified* yields to yet another word, *finishing*, which reflects the process that all must invariably go through, including Auden, and including Spender.

The allusions between Auden and Spender reflect a different relationship than that shared by Douglas and Wilde—based on poetic fellowship rather than on romantic and sexual intimacy. One might have expected to see Spender alluding to Auden and learning through imitation and homage. Certainly, Auden positioned himself as the leader of the pair, and his impersonal voice did shape Spender's own style, at least in the early years. But it was Auden who alluded to specific lines and words of Spender repeatedly over the course of his career. By writing through his disciple, Auden reflected on the differences between them. Whereas the allusions often indicate a desire to school or even dispute Spender's choices, they also forced Auden to reflect on his own approach and defend it, even as Spender eventually took a different path. At the same time, the allusions tell the story of a waning friendship and the grief that such a loss can bring. As Spender turned away from queerness, the two men lost a profound connection. The shift in their relationship, coupled with the romantic betrayal by Kallman, deepened Auden's sense of loneliness. But even as he mourned the decline of his friendship in "The More Loving One," allusion made it possible for him to sustain a point of contact with his companion. Spender, in writing his elegy to Auden, also turned to allusion as a way of coping with loss and maintaining connection. As with Douglas and Wilde, these echoes offer a record of their shared life. In allusion, Auden and Spender found a space where they could express themselves, communicate with one another, and nurture their bond virtually despite the changes and challenges that buffeted them.

II

Lineages

THREE

Christina Rossetti's
"Goblin Market"
(1862)

My first two case studies focused on authors who shared a deep and lasting connection. In both instances, allusion enabled poets to reflect on their relationship and engage in a virtual dialogue with their companion. The second part of this book considers another subgenre of queer allusion: namely, allusions to canonical authors of the past. I will consider three works from the nineteenth century that have been alluded to across the twentieth century—"Goblin Market" by Christina Rossetti," *A Shropshire Lad* by A. E. Housman, and "Song of Myself" by Walt Whitman—and trace how they have been reappropriated by LGBTQ authors variously over time.

The dynamic in these examples is different than Douglas's allusions to Wilde and Auden's allusions to Spender. What the writer seeks here is the pleasure of discovering evidence of same-sex desire in the poetry of the past and the comfort of knowing that they are not the first to have these experiences. By engaging with a prior text, the poet enjoys an imaginary connection with its author despite the historical, geographic, or cultural distance separating them. On a political level, allusions to past authors allow poets to fashion an alternative queer canon and situate themselves within that lineage through their own contribution. Notably, poets show little care if their predecessor engaged in same-sex relationships (like Walt Whitman) or not (as is the case with Christina Rossetti). When an LGBTQ poet uses allusion to reflect on their experience, they make an implicit claim about the queer potential of a prior work, if not necessarily the reality of that author's life. The source text is recoded and naturalized into the queer canon, regardless of the predecessor's biographical record. Allusion performs that work figuratively in the name of what a poem implies, inspires, or leaves open as a possibility.

Consider the following story. Two sisters, Lizzie and Laura, hear the call of goblin men urging them to "come buy" their fruit. Laura, out on her own, succumbs and offers a lock of her hair, which the goblins eagerly accept. She then feeds with complete abandon:

> She suck'd and suck'd and suck'd the more
> Fruits which that unknown orchard bore;
> She suck'd until her lips were sore.

However, she is unable to buy more after that day and begins to sicken. Desperate to save her, Lizzie seeks out the goblin men and proposes to buy fruit with a silver penny rather than a lock of hair. Offended, they attack, but Lizzie manages to withstand their blows and return to the house, drenched in the juices of the goblins' fruits. She then offers her body up to her sister in an act of sacrifice. A scene of fierce sensuality follows, as Laura rushes upon Lizzie:

> She clung about her sister,
> Kiss'd and kiss'd and kiss'd her:
> Tears once again
> Refresh'd her shrunken eyes,
> Dropping like rain
> After long sultry drouth;
> Shaking with aguish fear, and pain,
> She kiss'd and kiss'd her with a hungry mouth.

Yet Laura is repulsed by the juice, which tastes like "wormwood to her tongue."[1] The shock of this restores her to health. Each sister marries and bears children, to whom they later recount stories of goblin men.

So goes the plot of Christina Rossetti's "Goblin Market" (1862). While the poem ultimately reasserts the primacy of heterosexual marriage and childbearing, the ending simply cannot dispel what passes between Laura and Lizzie. Scholars have long noted the eroticism of their relationship. To quote three examples drawn from across a half-century: Ellen Moers in 1972 described Laura's rescue as the "most erotic moment in the poem"; Kathryn Burlinson in 1998 wrote of "same-sex, incestuous desire and activity" between the two sisters; and Kimberly Cox in 2022 read the poem as an example of "queer literary touch," whereby a female figure discovers "solace and salvation that is immanently erotic in the hands of other female characters."[2] Some critics have pushed back against the idea that the sibling relationship can be properly termed "queer" on historical grounds. Dorothy Mermin, for instance, has argued that a "conflation of spiritual and erotic intensity" was common in religious poetry before the twentieth century. For Mermin, the poem ought to be read, instead, as "a fantasy of feminine freedom, heroism, and self-sufficiency and a celebration of sisterly and maternal love."[3] Granted, Rossetti's biography contains little evidence that the author experienced same-sex desires in her own life. All her known attachments were with men: linguist Charles Cayley and painters James Collinson and John Brett.[4] Yet this cannot quite outweigh the intensity of Laura and Lizzie's contact, nor the rapturous repetition of "Kiss'd and kiss'd and kiss'd," nor the image of a devouring "hungry mouth." Adrienne Rich's theory of a "lesbian continuum" gives us one way to acknowledge the charged connection between Laura and Lizzie in the absence of same-sex affection in the record of Rossetti's life. Rich proposes to go beyond just "genital sexual experience" between women and consider "many more forms of primary intensity between and among women, including the sharing of a rich inner life, the bonding against male tyranny, the giving and receiving of practical and political support."[5] This reading makes it possible to honor the queer undercurrents of Laura and Lizzie's relationship and understand why so many LGBTQ writers have seen themselves in the poem and drawn upon its language in their own work.

The scholarship on "Goblin Market" has tended to follow a set of closely related threads. Much has been written on the poem as a commentary about capitalism, specifically women's place in the economic system.[6] Several critics have made the case that Rossetti exposes capitalism's efforts to treat women both as objects and subjects of consumption, with only sisterhood providing an escape from exploitation.[7] This, in turn, has generated ecofeminist readings that draw parallels between the exploitation of women and the exploitation of nature.[8] But little attention has been paid to the long history of how queer poets have engaged with "Goblin Market" through allusion. For these poets, the biographical facts of Rossetti's sexuality matter less than what her poem makes possible. Their understandings of "Goblin Market" are remarkably diverse, as reflected in the fact that they gravitated toward different elements in the poem, beyond even the passage of explicitly erotic same-sex contact. To capture the diversity of the responses, this chapter examines a range of poets who alluded to "Goblin Market" and reinscribed it as a queer text: A. E. Housman, Charlotte Mew, Amy Lowell, and Adrienne Rich. In their hands, Rossetti's work becomes alternatively a poem about the pain and pleasure of unrequited gay love, the relief of queer solitude, the joys of female sensuality, or the fragility of same-sex connections in a hostile world. Despite all these differences, however, three themes emerge across several poems, specifically temptation, social alienation, and the ephemerality of queer pleasure. "Goblin Market" was multivalent enough that each poet could reflect on their individual experience through Rossetti's language while also forging connections across different historical periods.

Housman deeply admired Rossetti, and his appreciation extended to her work even beyond "Goblin Market." While studying classics at Oxford, he copied passages from several of her poems in his commonplace book.[9] His brother Laurence, in a 1938 memoir, referred to Rossetti as one of "Alfred's high admirations." At the same time, some qualities in Rossetti's poetry veered too close to his experience for comfort. Laurence describes Alfred's hedging response upon first encountering "The River of Life," a poem that had previously escaped his attention: "He said, 'Yes: it's the sort of nonsense that is worth writing,' a remark which somewhat consoled me for his having described certain devotional poems of my own as 'nonsense.' Some years later he said he thought they were the 'cleverest' I had ever written; from which I gathered that with him 'nonsense' as applied to poetry was not a word of opprobrium."[10] In this context, the word *nonsense* does not refer to "nonsense verse" of the kind that Edward Lear and Lewis Carroll are known for, even though Housman wrote nonsense poems of this sort as well,[11] and Christopher Ricks has argued that even his more serious lyrics share with these the same "indirections, disparities, and emotional cross-currents."[12] Rather, the word *nonsense* betrays a keen sense of embarrassment: it is too quick to dismiss what it otherwise praises. While Housman does not elaborate further, he is likely responding to the expressiveness of Rossetti's poetry, both the specific feelings that she conveys and their perceived immediacy, which earnest devotional verse would also display. A word like *nonsense* enables Housman to claim himself too reasonable and level-headed to have truck with these feelings in his own life, even if he can find them pleasing in verse.

It is revealing, then, that the poem in which he alludes to Rossetti specifically and repeatedly bears some parallels to his experiences as a gay man but that the strongest emotions are projected onto the imagined heterosexual couple in the poem, not the speaker or poet himself. The projection suggests that Rossetti's verse felt close to home, and this proximity was a source of both comfort and embarrassment.

> When the lad for longing sighs,
>   Mute and dull of cheer and pale,
> If at death's own door he lies,
>   Maiden, you can heal his ail.

> Lovers' ills are all to buy:
>   The wan look, the hollow tone,
> The hung head, the sunken eye,
>   You can have them for your own.

> Buy them, buy them: eve and morn
> Lovers' ills are all to sell.
> Then you can lie down forlorn;
> but the lover will be well.[13]

Most critics, without noting the parallels between this poem and Rossetti's, have been troubled by the speaker urging the maiden to take on the young lad's pain. Scholars have tended to conflate the lover described *in* the poem with the speaker and the author *of* the poem, critiquing Housman for what they perceive to be a ruthless position on love.[14] However, attending to the poem's allusions reveals a more complex and deeply ironic attitude.

First, Housman draws on lines that are uttered by different speakers in "Goblin Market." The most obvious allusion is to the goblins' call, "Come buy our orchard fruits, / Come buy, come buy," which becomes

> Lovers' ills are all to buy
> . . . .
> Buy them, buy them: eve and morn
> Lovers' ills are to sell.[15]

But Housman also makes a more discreet reference to Laura's illness after tasting and missing the fruit. "Till Laura dwindling / Seem'd knocking at Death's door" makes its way into "If at death's own door he lies."[16] The moral sympathies of Rossetti's narrator shift elusively from one passage to another, reflecting Laura's excitement and pleasure in eating the fruit one moment (as in the rolling repetition of "She suck'd and suck'd and suck'd the more"),[17] only to later serve as a vector for the reader's pity in witnessing her decline, as in the lines about death's door. Housman's allusions stand out because he combines within the same voice two attitudes that in Rossetti are carefully separated out. He makes the speaker of the poem a seductive voice, instead of projecting a seductive attitude onto monsters, as in "Goblin Market," but he also weaves in lines that evoke the pity Rossetti's narrator conveys for Laura after she submits.

The poem's double claim makes it unsettling. On the one hand, Housman suggests that absorbing another person's heartache can be pleasurable when that person is also the object of one's affection. At the same time, he does not deny that this enjoyment comes with deep pain in tow. The poem itself is not so much a cruel invitation as an acknowledgment of a perverse bind that the maiden finds herself in.

The question remains what led the maiden to absorb the lad's pain. The nature of their relationship is not made explicit, and critics have tended to be silent on this point. When John Bayley refers to the speaker as a "lover," he implies that the speaker and the maiden are a couple, and the speaker is talking about himself in the third person as "the lad." But Housman never indicates that the speaker and the lover are the same. Without any evidence from the text on this subject, one might assume that the speaker is a third party entirely. Nor does Housman confirm that the maiden and the lad are, or have been, romantically involved. He refers to the lad as "the lover," never "your lover," so that his "longing sighs" may well be for another. Likewise, Housman only ever describes the maiden soothing and supporting the lad, never sharing mutual affection with him. These details give the reader good reason to believe that the lad does not return the maiden's love. Consoling him feels both pleasurable and painful because it gives her an opportunity to be close to him, even as it also reminds her of the gap between them.

In fact, Housman had a deep personal understanding of unrequited love. As a student at Oxford, he fell for his friend and roommate Moses Jackson, a handsome, athletic student of science. Sadly, Housman's affections were never reciprocated. The two had a brief falling out in the autumn of 1885, perhaps because Housman confessed his feelings. They soon made up, and Housman put considerable effort into maintaining his friendship with both Jackson and his family. While Jackson kept some distance out of caution, Housman remained steadfast in his love, so that the friendship served as a pretext for him to remain in close contact, though this doubtless proved as painful as it was soothing.[18] Per Edgar Vincent, "As long as he lived, Moses Jackson remained the central focus of Housman's feelings and fulfilled his needs for emotional attachment."[19] Similarly, Norman Page writes that "it was the love affair of his life, and his unrequited devotion was still constant when Jackson died more than forty years later after a career of useful obscurity in the service of Empire."[20] After Jackson passed away, Housman's brother Laurence recalled seeing a photograph of a grave in his possession. When asked about it, the poet replied: "That was my friend Jackson, the man who had more influence on my life than anybody else."[21] With these experiences in mind, it hardly comes as a surprise that he would take up the subject of unrequited love in verse. The relationship in his poem may be heterosexual, but this gave him adequate cover to talk about emotions that might otherwise feel too revealing, particularly for a broader readership.

"Goblin Market" proved an attractive model for three reasons. First, it contains scenes of intense same-sex contact. A queer reader alert to this facet of Rossetti's poem will not only identify the allusions in Housman but also deduce that same-sex experiences underpinned the composition of his poem as well. Second, the depiction in "Goblin Market" of pleasure and pain as intertwined matches Housman's own ideas about unrequited love as both intense joy and misery. For Housman, the lover can only feel joy when they are close to the beloved, but proximity also reminds the lover, painfully, of their relationship's limits. Third, "Goblin Market" addresses the theme of self-sacrifice, which Housman also deemed central to the experience of unrequited love, particularly in lifelong friendships. The lover strives to meet the needs of the beloved—as Housman did with Jackson and as the maiden of his poem does when she comforts the lad—but their own needs are never met, at least in full. Sometimes aiding the friend means actively working against their own happiness. The fact that "Goblin Market" ends with an assertion of heterosexuality through the sisters' marriages only reaffirms the tragic ironies of Housman's perspective, as expressed in this poem. Whoever loves a friend must deny what they long for the most and even undermine their own fulfillment.

Over a decade after A. E. Housman drew from "Goblin Market" to reflect on the pleasure and pain of unrequited love, Charlotte Mew found in Rossetti's poem the language to think about queer solitude. She took up this theme in two poems: "The Farmer's Bride" (from an eponymous collection published in 1916) and "Saturday Market" (from the 1921 expanded edition). Both speak to the security afforded by solitude in a culture hostile to people who do not fit within the confines of heterosexual marriage. At the same time, Mew acknowledges the melancholy and loneliness of standing apart from society.

Of course, it is worth noting at this juncture that very little is known about Mew's sexuality. She was intensely private about her romantic feelings. No proof has survived that she ever enjoyed an affair or partnership, nor have biographers found any record—in letter or diary form—that she ever desired another person. Although there have been persistent rumors that Mew once made a pass at her friend May Sinclair, there is no firsthand account to confirm that such a flirtation took place. It is tempting, then, to deduce that Mew was asexual. However, such a theory is complicated by the fact that her poems are replete with depictions of romantic and sexual passion. What we can be certain of is that Mew's gender expression alienated her from many of her contemporaries. Her preferred style of dress, like Amy Lowell's, was androgynous. She tended to wear clothing that was coded as masculine, such as a "tartan skirt, black velvet jacket, white blouse and soft silk tie" or "a long double-breasted top-coat of tweed with a velvet collar inset."[22] What's more, Mew refused to marry, at a time when a woman's social value was still closely tied to the institution. If there is no proof that she ever engaged in a lesbian relationship or even felt a same-sex infatuation, there is copious evidence of Mew's queerness with regards to gender and marriage.

In "The Farmer's Bride," the speaker laments that his young wife always tries to escape the house and hide in the surrounding countryside. She recoils from his touch, preferring the company of birds, rabbits, and sheep. In the last stanza, the farmer reveals that he now keeps her confined to the attic, which she cannot flee. When trying to locate Mew's own sympathies in the poem, most critics have argued that the poet identifies with the farmer. Jeredith Merrin, for example, writes that "The Farmer's Bride" speaks to "Mew's personal knowledge of frustrated sexual desire—in her case, unrequited lesbian desire."[23] In this reading, the farmer's closing exclamation ("her eyes, her hair, her hair!") echoes the author's desires for other women.[24] But the allusions to Rossetti suggest a much closer identification with the bride.

Setting "Goblin Market" alongside "The Farmer's Bride," it becomes clear why Rossetti's poem had such a profound effect on Mew. Both express a desire to escape from a masculine realm that has proven dangerous and oppressive. After being taunted by male creatures, Laura and Lizzie find safety in sisterhood. The woman in "The Farmer's Bride," meanwhile, recoils from her husband and seeks comfort in nature. As John Lucas writes, Mew's poem is memorable for "its uncovering of the woe that is in marriage, and its revelation of a woman escaping from sexual bondage . . . into a wilderness that has at its heart an implacable rejection of men."[25] Lizzie and Laura do not go so far as to reject heterosexual institutions; after all, both end up married at the end of the poem. But Mew clearly felt that she could bracket and rearrange elements in Rossetti's poem to reflect her thinking, without betraying the core sentiments of her predecessor's work. For example, the main opposition in "Goblin Market" lies between sexuality, associated with the monstrous world of goblins, and the domestic realm, associated with the security of family and marriage (even though the poem's most interesting moments occur when such lines are crossed, as when Laura must kiss Lizzie to redeem herself). In Mew, this opposition finds itself scrambled, so the chief divide appears between male heterosexual society and the natural world, where people who do not fit in this category can find solace—or so Mew hopes.

It is notable that the bride seeks comfort in the countryside rather than the company of another woman. For Mew, queerness entails profound solitude, as queer people were not granted space in the institution of marriage or in the wider heterosexual culture extending beyond it, at least in her lifetime. To Mew's mind, the person who rejects heterosexuality must live in voluntary exile, be it an exile of the mind or the body. So with the bride of her poem. When she succeeds in fleeing the farmer's house, the whole community hastens to bring the woman back: "*We* chased her, flying like a hare / Before our lanterns" (emphasis added). Once there, she opts for a state of self-exile by remaining silent ("I've hardly heard her speak at all") and refusing to smile ("Like the shut of a winter's day / Her smile went out").[26] In the end, she prefers the complete absence of human contact to the constraints she would suffer in marriage and society. Mew honors her desire for isolation through her choice of perspective. She adopts the point of view of the farmer, who sees the bride as an enigma. The reader has no access to the bride's inner thoughts and feelings, which grants her a degree of privacy. Even if she cannot physically absent herself from society, or at least not entirely, the woman can at least exist outside the structure of the lyric poem, with its expectations of disclosure and expression.

Verbal echoes of Rossetti's poem appear, first, in the structure of Mew's fourth stanza. After three stanzas in which the farmer describes the deterioration of their marriage, his wife's escape, and her grim return to domestic duties, he interrupts the forward march of his narrative with a four-line stanza made up of parallel similes:

> Shy as a leveret, swift as he,
> Straight and slight as a young larch tree,
> Sweet as the first wild violets, she,
> To her wild self. But what to me?[27]

These lines evoke a similar mechanism in "Goblin Market," whereby the narrative repeatedly pauses for a string of comparisons. The first occurs when Laura hears the goblin's call and feels tempted to join them.

> Laura stretch'd her gleaming neck
> Like a rush-imbedded swan,
> Like a lily from the beck,
> Like a moonlit poplar branch,
> Like a vessel at the launch
> When its last restraint is gone.[28]

For Mew, this structure—borrowed from Rossetti—could achieve some useful effects. She knew that there is pleasure to be had in pausing a long narrative and lingering on imagery. She also saw the power of such passages to convey emotional intensity. Rossetti uses this structure again when Laura succumbs to the goblins, when she seeks comfort from Lizzie after giving in, when Lizzie presents her body to the monsters, when Laura panics after seeing Lizzie return from the goblins, and finally when Laura falls and appears, briefly, to die. All of these are emotionally charged moments, granted more weight by a repetitive structure that slows the pace and focuses the reader's attention.

Mew makes several formal choices to draw attention to these lines even further. First, she makes this the poem's shortest stanza, at a mere four lines. The three that precede it range between eight and ten; the fifth contains eight as well; and even the final stanza extends to five. The parallel similes also stand out visually because none of the lines are indented, unlike the rest of the poem, which follows a different pattern of indentation from stanza to stanza. Musically, too, the lines draw attention by all rhyming together in one continuous sequence: "he," "tree," "she," "me." The repetitiousness of the rhyme bolsters the sense that the poet's narrative is being interrupted for an important description.

The lines do matter because they are the first to focus extensively on the woman rather than her marriage. Granted, she is still being viewed through the eyes of the farmer, who only sees her in relation to him as a "bride," but at no other point does the speaker get closer to capturing her mind and spirit. Mew reflects the importance of her personality in the structure of her similes, which stray significantly from Rossetti's model. Instead of starting each line with *like* or *as,* Mew reverts the structure of the similes to begin with adjectives that define the woman: *shy, straight and slight,* and *sweet.* All these words receive emphasis thanks to their position at the head of their respective lines, where they are capitalized. At the same time, the stanza matters because its final line captures the split in their marriage: "To her wild self. But what to me?" Because marriage feels like a prison to her, because there exists no true love between them, the woman's entire self has turned inward. The divide separating them is as concrete as the period in the middle of the line. The stanza may rhyme the words *he, she,* and *me,* but it lacks a single instance of the pronoun *we.*

Mew's engagement with Rossetti extends beyond these parallel structures. The second simile, in which the farmer compares his bride to a tree, echoes two tree similes in "Goblin Market." The first occurs when Lizzie confronts the goblins and resists their attacks:

> Lizzie stood,
>
> . . . .
>
> Like a fruit-crown'd orange tree
> White with blossoms honey-sweet
> Sore beset by wasp and bee.

Later, when Laura kisses the juices off Lizzie's body and loses consciousness, the poet writes that Laura "Spun about" "Like a wind-uprooted tree," only to collapse.[29] The images seem to reinforce the contrast between the sisters: Lizzie has the moral strength to withstand the goblins' temptations, whereas Laura has already succumbed and "fallen." But Laura enjoys a speedy recovery. After Lizzie watches over her the entire night, she wakes happily free of the goblins' influence, so that the second tree simile also connects the two sisters and foreshadows her return to the domestic sphere.

Mew enters a complicated dialogue with Rossetti's similes through her own image of the "young larch tree." The adjective *straight* captures the strength of Lizzie's "fruit-crown'd orange tree," which stands tall despite being "Sore beset by wasp and bee." The adjective *slight,* on the other hand, evokes the fragility of Laura's "wind-uprooted tree." In short, the images used to distinguish and unite two sisters in Rossetti merge here to describe a single figure. At the same time, the curious balance of strength and weakness, of resistance and submission, plays differently here. The reader can easily connect Lizzie's endurance to the bride's rejection of the farmer. Yet the word *slight,* instead of signaling a return to domesticity, only reinforces her strangeness. It is uncanny that a tree so "slight" can still stand so "straight." The word also confirms the farmer's irrelevance to her. Being slight, she can offer no aid to the farmer, but she also requires no help from him. "To her wild self. But what to me?" She stands alone and apart, purely solitary.

In sum, Mew's allusions to "Goblin Market" present a double attitude. On the one hand, Rossetti's poem appealed to Mew for passages in which the female characters resist male pressure and live outside of marriage. On the other hand, Mew was skeptical that female community or lesbian love could offer a permanent refuge from the demands of heterosexual domesticity, at least at this point in history. Even "Goblin Market" ends with both sisters marrying. To Mew's mind, solitude offered the only real solace for women, and especially queer women. When the farmer laments in the final stanza that his wife "sleeps up in the attic there, / Alone, poor maid," he does not realize that her solitude is only tragic because she is still confined to a domestic space and not allowed to escape from society as she would wish.

Mew returns to the theme of solitude in another poem that closely echoes the language and title of Rossetti's "Goblin Market": "Saturday Market." The first stanza describes the abundance of goods available for sale using a list form—"Pitchers and sugar-sticks, ribbons and laces, / Poises and whips and dicky-birds' seed"—that recalls the list of fruits in Rossetti's poem:

> Apples and quinces,
> Lemons and oranges
> Plump unpeck'd cherries.[30]

This time, though, the antagonists are not male goblins but a mixed crowd, young and old, representing the whole of society:

> What were you showing in Saturday Market
> That set it grinning from end to end

Girls and gaffers and boys of twenty—?
  Cover it close with your shawl, my friend—
Hasten you home with the laugh behind you,
  Over the down—, out of sight,
Fasten your door, though no one will find you,
  No one will look on a Market night.

At this juncture, Mew has revealed the poem's addressee as an enigmatic "you": a solitary figure who seeks refuge from society, like the woman in "The Farmer's Bride." While the "Girls and gaffers and boys of twenty" do not taunt her verbally, they do appear "grinning from end to end," in what could be mockery or menace. Critics discussing this poem have tended to focus on the mysterious "it" that she attempts to conceal from the crowd. In the third and final stanza, the poet refers to a "red dead thing" hidden beneath a "wet" shawl and offers deeply mixed reassurances:

If there is blood on the hearth who'll know it?
  Or blood on the stairs,
When a murder is over and done why show it?
  In Saturday Market nobody cares.[31]

The evocation of blood has led many critics to deduce that the "thing" is an aborted or miscarried fetus, which may or may not have further symbolic dimensions.[32] Mew herself never had children, not just because her interests lay in women but also because she feared that tragedy would repeat itself down the family line: nearly all her siblings save one had died or been committed to psychiatric hospitals. Nelljean Rice, though, has argued that the "thing" should be understood as the woman's heart "metaphorically standing for her passion."[33] The allusions to "Goblin Market" further support this reading.

The speaker's warning to "Cover it close with your shawl, my friend— / Hasten you home with the laugh behind you" harks back to Lizzie's return home after standing tall amid the goblins' taunts:

She ran and ran
As if she fear'd some goblin man
Dogg'd her with gibe or curse
Or something worse:
But not one goblin scurried after,
Nor was she prick'd by fear;
The kind heart made her windy-paced
That urged her home quite out of breath with haste
And inward laughter.[34]

When set alongside Rossetti, the laugh in Mew sounds triumphant, the "friend" having escaped the "Girls and gaffers and boys of twenty." The close parallels between the two passages also suggest the identity of the object that she conceals. In "Goblin Market," Lizzie is urged home not by the speaker but by her own "kind heart." The red thing underneath the woman's shawl in "Saturday Market" is likely her heart as well, no matter what other metaphorical possibilities may attend it. The woman, after all, longs to protect herself from an invasive society and find refuge in privacy. From the beginning, the speaker urges the woman to defend her heart: "Bury your heart in some deep green hollow / Or hide it up in a kind old tree." Later the speaker declares: "There's never a one in the town so sure of sleeping / As you, in the house on the down with a hole in your breast."[35] Because she continues to live in the home and does not escape into the natural world like the farmer's bride, she can only shield her heart by burying it apart from her.

The connections between the two poems highlight the ways in which Mew departs from Rossetti. The erotic connection between Laura and Lizzie was sufficient for Mew to establish the queerness of "Goblin Market" and for her to see herself in its lines. Still, Mew could not bring herself to imagine the possibility of erotic fulfillment between women, nor did she put stock in marriage as a cure for unruly passions. In "Goblin Market," Lizzie hastens home to rejoin Laura, with whom she engages in an intense physical exchange, before settling into the orderly domesticity of heterosexual marriage. The woman in "Saturday Market" runs home to isolate herself from the crowd, but home is not a safe place either, so she can only protect her kind heart by letting go of it. As in "The Farmer's Bride," Mew carefully selects elements from "Goblin Market"—scenes in which Laura is lured away from the home and in which Lizzie withstands the attacks of the goblin men—to reframe the text as a poem about queer solitude rather than female community. The women in both of Mew's poems feel a deep sense of alienation and a desire to live apart from society. But a total escape proves impossible, and so they are forced to remain in the home, where their solitude comes to feel like a prison.

Whereas Housman and Mew drew from Rossetti to take up the subjects of unrequited love and solitude, respectively, Amy Lowell found in "Goblin Market" the language to write about erotic desire between women and the pleasure of its fulfillment. Lowell's allusions to Rossetti are bolder about their queerness than those of Housman or Mew. This is hardly surprising if we consider the life of each poet. Granted, Lowell and Mew shared a similar gender expression, as both preferred to dress in masculine clothing. Lowell's contemporaries often commented on her appearance, even if they did not fully understand it. Her friend and fellow writer John Gould Fletcher, for instance, emphasized Lowell's rejection of traditional feminine norms, even as he was also eager to separate his male identity from her: "The old-fashioned cut of her clothes recalled the nineties; the mannish coats and stiff collars she affected emphasized her square-build masculinity; and her figure, to say the least, was constructed on principles entirely different from mine." Lowell's writing suggests that she came to identify with another gender. She referred to herself as "a great rough masculine, strong thing" and even "a kind of half man."[36]

Lowell was fortunate to enjoy a long and sustaining romance. In 1909, she met the actress Ada Dwyer Russell in Boston after her performance in *The Dawn of a Tomorrow*. The two did not meet again until 1912, when Russell came back to Boston for *The Deep Purple*. But from that moment on, the two women were inseparable. Russell accompanied Lowell to England, and after falling ill the following year, she convalesced at Sev-

enels, the poet's Brookline mansion. When Lowell tried to convince her
to move in permanently, she hesitated at first, fearing the loss of income
from theater. As a compromise, Lowell offered her a six-month position
as a personal assistant, which Russell accepted. Eventually, she agreed to
live with Lowell permanently, and, by all accounts, the women enjoyed
a deeply happy life together. According to Carl Rollyson, the poet's biographer, "to be in love with Ada Russell meant that Amy Lowell was
indeed ready to carry the world on her back." Lowell adored Russell for
"her dignity and decorum, paired with a graceful sensuality that her lover
saw in virtually religious terms."[37] Russell became the love of Lowell's
life, and the two remained inseparable until the poet's passing in 1925.

Rossetti's influence on Lowell is audible in a poem titled "In Excelsis" from *What's O'Clock* (1925), the first posthumous collection edited
by Russell. The speaker of "In Excelsis" addresses an unnamed lover,
clearly modeled after Russell. Notably, Lowell saw Rossetti's religious
feeling as an opportunity, not an impediment. For Lillian Faderman, the
love poems in *What's O'Clock* "combine metaphors of religious worship
with metaphors of Eros," so that "In Excelsis" pictures Russell as "the
Eucharist, Christ, and the beloved of the Songs of Solomon, but she is especially the beautiful woman the speaker longs to devour sexually as well
as to worship."[38] By writing through "Goblin Market," Lowell attempted
to fulfill the desires that Rossetti evokes and expresses only to suppress
in the poem's final moments. The spirit is not corrective but generous,
going where she suspects Rossetti likely wanted to go but did not dare to:

> Your words are bees about a pear-tree,
> Your fancies are the gold-and-black striped wasps buzzing among
>   red apples.
> I drink your lips,
> I eat the whiteness of your hands and feet.
> My mouth is open,
> As a new jar I am empty and open.
> Like white water are you who fill the cup of my mouth,
> Like a brook of water thronged with lilies.[39]

The most obvious reference is to Lizzie's plea, "Eat me, drink me, love me; / Laura make much of me," which finds itself transformed into the declaration: "I drink your lips, / I eat the whiteness of your hands and feet." The force of Lowell's allusion becomes clear when the reader acknowledges that these utterances have different functions in their respective poems. Lizzie's plea may sound purely erotic when taken out of context, but it is part of a self-sacrificial ritual, whereby Lizzie offers up her body for consumption and Laura gives in only to recoil and be cured of goblin-like desires. Narrative turns such as these have led critics like Lionel Stevenson to read "Goblin Market" as a "terrifying allegory of temptation and redemption," "the evil of self-indulgence, the fraudulence of sensuous beauty, and the supreme duty of renunciation."[40] Anthony H. Harrison similarly writes that the poem sets up "an equation . . . between the indulgence of female sexual desire and sickness unto death."[41] In Lowell, no redemption or renunciation lies on the horizon. The poet speaks assertively and never claims that consuming the lover's body will allow her to renege on her desires. Her goal is to find pleasure and satisfaction, not to purge herself of temptation. The poem ends by the beloved reciprocating her overtures: "As a new jar I am empty and open. / Like white water are you who fill the cup of my mouth." In these final lines, the power balance shifts in the lover's favor. This time, the speaker must stand still, and the beloved must take action; in doing so, the lover both expresses and fulfills her desires in turn.

This allusion belongs to a pattern of lines in which Lowell borrows images used by Rossetti to warn against the dangers of temptation, or to foreshadow a return to heterosexual domesticity, and then reimagines them as a vehicle for lesbian desire. At times, she accomplishes this by taking advantage of paradoxes in Rossetti's language. In "Goblin Market," for example, the wasp and the bee appear in an extended simile that describes Lizzie resisting the goblins' advances and compares her to a tree:

> Like a fruit-crown'd orange-tree
> White with blossoms honey-sweet
> Sore beset by wasp and bee.[42]

Several descriptive details in this image emphasize her innocence, specifically the words *white* and *honey-sweet*. Rossetti also frames that innocence as bounty. The tree is "fruit-crown'd" and full of "blossoms"—an implicit contrast to the sickness and decline that Laura suffers after succumbing to temptation. Yet by equating "the wasp and the bee" with the goblins, Rossetti opens up a complication that lies beyond her field of vision—certainly outside of what the poem sets out to convey. For while the poet describes the wasp and bee as attackers sorely besetting the orange tree, the literal action they are performing is pollination. The tree's bounty, which Rossetti celebrates, depends largely on the wasp and the bee. Lowell exploited this paradox in her own poem by taking the image to its logical conclusion: "Your words are bees about a pear-tree, / Your fancies are the gold-and-black striped wasps buzzing among red apples." She does not present the bees and wasps as enemies of the pear tree and apple tree. On the contrary, she implies that they should be credited for the flourishing. The pair of images culminates with fully formed fruit, in the form of "red apples." The speaker positions herself as the beneficiary, to whom the lover's "words" and "fancies" have generated a bounty of fresh desires.

This pattern continues with the final lines of Lowell's poem, which transform Rossetti's own image of lilies on a stream. In "Goblin Market," the description occurs after Laura has spent a long night recovering painfully from the juices that she has sucked off Lizzie's body.

> But when the first birds chirp'd about their eaves,
> And early reapers plodded to the place
> Of golden sheaves,
> And dew-wet grass
> Bow'd in the morning winds so brisk to pass,
> And new buds with new day
> Open'd of cup-like lilies on the stream,
> Laura awoke as from a dream,
> Laugh'd in the innocent old way,
> Hugg'd Lizzie but not twice or thrice;

Her gleaming locks show'd not one thread of grey,
Her breath was sweet as May
And light danced in her eyes.[43]

In Rossetti, the "cup-like lilies on the stream" operate as a symbol of spiritual renewal, of a return to life after a winter of sin and redemption. These are "new buds with new day," and all the mistakes that she has made can be washed away as if they never happened, resuming "the old innocent way." The hug that she shares with Lizzie, though it may express warmth and excitement ("not twice or thrice"), stands in contrast to the fierce erotic charge of their previous embrace ("kiss'd and kiss'd her with a hungry mouth"). Lowell picks up this imagery in the last two lines of her own poem but restores to it the sensuality of Laura and Lizzie's nighttime passion:

My mouth is open,
As a new jar I am empty and open.
Like white water are you who fill the cup of my mouth,
Like a brook of water thronged with lilies.

The "cup-like" shape of the flowers in Rossetti finds itself associated with the poet's mouth, which the "white water" metaphorically kisses. Far from evoking renewal and renunciation, the lilies become a symbol of sexual gratification and plenty. The brook is "thronged" with flowers, the cup "full" of white water. The poet abandons nothing. This reading of "Goblin Market," which, in fact, boldly rewrites its language and its ideas, was later echoed by Adrienne Rich, the final example in this chapter.

In 1953, Adrienne Rich published a poem in the *New Yorker* titled "Holiday," which she later collected in *The Diamond Cutters* (1955), her second book of poetry, after *A Change of World* (1950). "Holiday" belongs to the first phase of Rich's career when she still wrote in traditional forms, before her turn to free verse with *Snapshots of a Daughter-in-Law* (1963).

It has long been said that her first two books suffered from stylistic and intellectual conservativeness and that the use of traditional metrical forms, inherited from canonical male authors, showed her reluctance to deal frankly with issues of politics, gender, and sexuality.[44] Rich told this story herself in the essay "When We Dead Awaken: Writing as Re-Vision" (1972): "I know that my style was formed first by male poets: by the men I was reading as an undergraduate—Frost, Dylan Thomas, Donne, Auden, MacNiece [sic], Stevens, Yeats . . . In those years formalism was part of the strategy—like asbestos gloves, it allowed me to handle materials I couldn't pick up bare-handed."[45] In the narrative of Rich's development, *Snapshots of a Daughter-in-Law* is usually identified as the book in which she finally broke from tradition and forged a feminist voice and style, drawing from women authors rather than the male canon.[46] Yet this change, or the beginning of change, was already evident in "Holiday," which appeared a decade earlier. Even though the poem does not experiment with free verse, it does engage with a female poet, Christina Rossetti. Rich's understanding of "Goblin Market" echoes Lowell, who was also drawn to Rossetti's poem for its depiction of same-sex desire. At the same time, Rich was attentive to the fragility of what the goblin glen permits, even if she believed that the risk lay not in transgression's punishment but in its end.

Rich had not yet come out as a lesbian when she wrote "Holiday"; indeed, she had not come out to herself. All her romantic and sexual experiences up to this point had been with men, and she married Alfred Haskell Conrad, a Harvard University professor of economics, in 1953. That said, there were signs of her same-sex attraction to women long before her first lesbian love affair, in 1974, with her psychiatrist Lilly Engler. When Rich attended Radcliffe College, from 1947 to 1951, she developed an intense friendship with fellow student Eleanor Pearre. The two spent much of their time together, and soon Rich's feelings became closer to those of a lover than a friend. According to her biographer Hilary Holladay, Rich "fumed when Eleanor didn't ask to read her poems; she ached when her friend kept her feelings to herself. When Eleanor finally confessed her affection for her, Adrienne inwardly rejoiced and wrote her father about the momentous conversation."[47] Evidently, Rich did not fully understand, or allow herself to understand, the nature of her feelings for Pearre. However, "Holiday" indicates that she had some intuition of her sexuality and used poetry to safely explore what she did not yet feel ready to articulate off the page, let alone put into practice.

It is telling that Rich alludes to one of the most erotic passages in "Goblin Market," in which Laura feasts on Lizzie's body, and that she then uses Rossetti's language to imagine a picnic where two lovers can explore each other's bodies openly without fear of repercussion. While the poem does not explicitly state the gender of the lovers, the fact that Rich evokes a poem centered on two women makes the author's interest clear to the sympathetic queer reader:

> Summer was another country, where the birds
> Woke us at dawn among the dripping leaves
> And lent to all our fetes their sweet approval.
> The touch of air on flesh was lighter, keener,
> The senses flourished like a laden tree
> Whose every gesture finishes in a flower.
> In those unwardened provinces we dined
> From wicker baskets by a green canal,
> Staining our lips with peach and nectarine,
> Slapping at golden wasps. And when we kissed,
> Tasting that sunlit juice, the landscape folded
> Into our clasp, and not a breath recalled
> The long walk back to winter, leagues away.[48]

As in "Goblin Market," Rich's poem describes the consumption of fruit as a sensual act ("Staining our lips with peach and nectarine"), and the enjoyment of fruit leads to the enjoyment of another's mouth ("And when we kissed / Tasting that sunlit juice"). Laura's "hungry mouth" devouring her sister with kisses does not lie far behind. Rich also takes after Lowell by borrowing imagery that Rossetti uses to warn against temptation and transforming it into language that extolls sensuality as liberation.

While Lizzie resembles "a fruit-crown'd orange-tree / White with blossoms honey-sweet" when she resists the goblins' attacks, the speaker of Rich's poem feels her senses flourishing "like a laden tree / Whose every gesture finishes in a flower" when she is about to feast on fruit and sex.

Nature figures differently in "Holiday." The environment is not a place of temptation and danger, representative of the broader society, but "another country" that the poet can escape to when trying to abscond from the bounds of heterosexual culture. Rather than finding herself condemned to sickness and death after tasting the fruit, the poet enjoys limitless freedom in this place; these are "unwardened provinces." Inhospitality and risk have vanished from the glen, along with the goblins. Even the wasps, which in Rossetti had stood metaphorically for the goblins and "sore beset" Lizzie, can simply be "slapped" away in Rich. All of nature blesses the couple, sending as emissary birds to express their "sweet approval." The natural world is harmless because it can all be contained in miniature: the landscape can be "folded" into a "clasp." The poet and her lover feel in control of their environment, rather than being controlled by it.

By mapping this fantasy of lesbian sexual freedom onto the seasons, Rich also foreshadows its inevitable end. Winter cannot be kept at bay forever. While Rich states that "Not a breath recalled / The long walk back to winter, leagues away," this paradoxically reminds us, and the poet, that the couple will not be able to remain in summer indefinitely. Winter here likely serves as a metaphor not for mortality but for heterosexual society and marriage. This, too, marks a shift from Rossetti's own ending, in which, as Sandra M. Gilbert and Susan Gubar said, "the redeemed Eden into which Lizzie leads Laura turns out to be a heaven of domesticity."[49] The conclusion of "Goblin Market" could not much entice Rich, who even at this point in her life must have intuited that she would have preferred to remain away from society's constraints. Rich entirely reverses the geography of Rossetti's poem. The home, and the heterosexual marriage that comes to define it, cannot be a safe refuge for the speaker of "Holiday." Instead, the garden proves to be the real sanctuary because it protects the poet from heterosexual expectations. Free of male goblins, this garden can offer a safe zone for women to desire and enjoy each other's bodies.

Yet in Rich's own life, the confines of domesticity would prove difficult to escape for some time. Even as she and her husband, Conrad, grew increasingly apart, the two remained married until 1970. Before then, and certainly at the time that she was writing "Holiday," the "long walk back to winter, leagues away" must have felt inevitable. For that reason, too, "Goblin Market" likely resonated with Rich's experience, even if Rossetti remains silent on how a "traditional" home may feel like a prison.

Allusion is interpretation, and the many references to "Goblin Market" reflect the variety of ways that queer poets have understood Rossetti's poem. A. E. Housman turned to "Goblin Market" to think about unrequited love as a source of pleasure as well as pain. Charlotte Mew drew from the poem's depiction of total solitude, which she reimagined as a refuge for queer women like herself. Amy Lowell gravitated toward the poem for its sensuality and its representation of intense same-sex contact. Finally, Adrienne Rich transformed Rossetti's goblin glen into a haven where women could safely (if just temporarily) explore their desires for one another far from the confines of heterosexual marriage and domesticity.

Yet despite this diversity, some patterns do emerge if we take a long view of the allusions to "Goblin Market." First, many of the allusions deal with exclusion, be it the loneliness of the solitary lover in Housman or the self-selected isolation of the queer person in Mew and the queer couple in Rich. The isolation of the two sisters in "Goblin Market," along with the opposition between their home and the glen surrounding it, provided a useful structure through which to think variously on this topic. Second, many allusions reflect on temptation, from sexual longing in Lowell and Rich to the bitter mixture of pleasure and pain caused by unrequited love in Housman. That said, the poets had different ideas about the consequences of giving in. In Housman, the maiden who feeds on the lad's ills takes on "The wan look, the hollow tone, / The hung head, the sunken eye," sickening like Laura after she tastes the goblin fruit. But illness and death do not plague the lovers in Lowell, while in Rich the only real consequence is departure from the refuge of same-sex love. This split mirrors a paradox within "Goblin Market," which indulges in extended descriptions of desire and then asserts that indulgence can but lead to sickness and death, so the poem ends with a return to the domestic sphere. Queer poets drawn to Rossetti's frank treatment of desire had to reckon with her rebuke of indulgence, either by bracketing it out entirely or by reframing the cause of the punishment. Third, all the allusions discussed (except for Lowell's) deal with the ephemerality of queer joy. The maiden in Housman must sicken in turn. In Mew, the farmer ultimately confines the bride to his home, and the young woman traversing the marketplace has no choice but to abandon her heart. Rich's lovers must eventually take "the long walk back to winter, leagues away." In "Goblin Market," after all, the sister who tastes the goblins' fruit cannot enjoy its juices for long. This notion of pleasure's fragility resonated deeply with a queer culture in which same-sex contact, love, and self-fulfillment were often sought in passing and in secret. Ephemerality did not negate the value of queer pleasure for these writers but, instead, made it even more precious.

The poems considered in this chapter also make it possible to draw conclusions about queer allusion that turns to the poetry of the past. Notably, none of the poets felt hampered by a lack of evidence that Rossetti was herself a lesbian. The facts of Rossetti's sexuality largely did not matter. More important, "Goblin Market" contained passages that could be read as evoking queer desires and experiences and that later poets could rewrite to draw out those implications more assertively. In doing so, poets did not distort "Goblin Market" but instead fulfilled an opportunity generated by the text, regardless of Rossetti's intentions and without making implications about Rossetti's own life. In other cases of queer allusion, the sexuality of the source text's author proved central to that text's importance for later poets; we will see this with A. E. Housman's *A Shropshire Lad* and Walt Whitman's *Leaves of Grass*. But in the case of "Goblin Market," the queer potential of the text was the thing. The poem's interest lay in the fact that it depicted same-sex desire erupting and asserting itself—even in the work of an author who did not think of herself as queer and whose most famous poem warned against transgression.

FOUR

A. E. Housman's
A Shropshire Lad
(1896)

A. E. Housman's *A Shropshire Lad* proved highly popular in England throughout the twentieth century. Yet the book held a special significance for queer readers and writers in particular: a fact deserving of more attention than it has yet received. Peter Parker is one of the few critics to have considered it at all in his book *Housman Country* (2017). Parker situates Housman within an English same-sex literary tradition that had "an underground currency" but nonetheless "flourished in full view": "For every volume of privately printed 'Uranian' verse there were many more mainstream volumes that celebrated 'romantic friendships' and the beauty of boys and men. From the public-school novels of the late-Victorian and Edwardian era to the poetry and memoirs that emerged from the trenches, this literature was read and enjoyed by people who would not have thought of it as 'homosexual.' Most readers would have felt the same about *A Shropshire Lad;* but others were grateful to read a book that appeared to allude to their own particular, and more often than not secret and repressed, romantic longings."[1] What Parker, and others, do not address is how LGBTQ poets after Housman engaged with his work, specifically through allusion. The history of queer allusions to *A Shropshire Lad* is long, extending from Oscar Wilde's "The Ballad of Reading Gaol" (published just a year after *Shropshire*, in 1897), through modernism and the Harlem Renaissance with Countee Cullen's *Color* (1925), to the latter decades of the twentieth century with W. H. Auden's final poems in *Epistle to a Godson* (1972). The next several pages retrace that history.

Part of the appeal of *A Shropshire Lad* for queer poets lies in its coded nature: the fact that the poems do not explicitly present same-sex love as their subject or even as their inspiration, so that the reader has the pleasure of uncovering themes that feel like secret messages. The poems offer a range of clues for the reader to pick up, even though none are explicit. One way that Housman disguises his subject is by framing the male object of desire as a stock figure of English pastoral and patriotic verse: the shepherd, the farmer, the soldier. In doing so, Housman dresses up his fantasies in the trappings of war poetry and heterosexual romance. Norman Page has noted this figurative transfer of desire: "Most of Housman's poetry is poetry of indirection, expressing his secret feelings through metaphor: the preoccupation with soldiers going to the wars, rustics dying of love, and criminals awaiting execution allegorizes his own unuttered, unutterable anxieties and yearning."[2]

Housman also exploited linguistic and grammatical ambiguities to his advantage. In his love lyrics, he sometimes avoided disclosing the speaker's gender to leave open the possibility of a queer romance. That ambiguity is especially noticeable in the several advice poems that Housman wrote addressed to a young man. In poems that express desire for and to a "lad," Housman lets most readers assume that the speaker is female, while allowing queer readers to take note of the omission and its implications. In poems in which the speaker encourages a lad to accept love, Housman frames the advice in a way that will suggest disinterestedness to most readers, as if the speaker were simply offering counsel from one experienced man to a younger friend. But Housman also makes room for other readers—specifically, those seeking gay desire in poetry—to identify hints that the speaker may not be disinterested at all and that he may even be in love with the lad himself. For all their cleverness, these strategies also stemmed from a profound feeling of shame over his sexuality. Jeffrey Meyers picked up on this sensibility when he wrote that Housman "belongs with the sexually tormented Victorian writers" and that he was "a divided man with a buried life who hid behind a carefully constructed mask."[3]

Housman was intensely private about his same-sex attractions throughout his life. To be sure, there were good reasons for him to keep his desires quiet, considering the hostility of English society toward queer people in the nineteenth century. To engage romantically and sexually with members of the same sex could put one in grave legal jeopardy. Between 1806 and 1900, more than eight thousand men were tried on the charge of "sodomy, indecent assault, and other homosexual offences." While the death penalty for sodomy was abolished in 1861, the Labouchere Amendment of 1885 expanded the range of offenses for which individuals could face prosecution, so that "any sort of sexual transaction between men" was deemed "unmentionable" and "unnatural." Then, in 1898, the law against solicitation was revised to include "importuning" homosexual contact as a punishable offense.[4] However, these laws did not prevent all LGBTQ people from seeking companionship. Graham Robb notes that most towns in England had small coteries of gay men and lesbians who would meet at one another's houses or travel together to larger cities. Some spots, such as the Achilles statue in Hyde Park, became notorious pickup spots for men seeking other men. Some meeting places were more temporary in nature: for example, in 1880, a private club rented the Temperance Hall in Manchester for a drag ball. But other spaces, in particular universities, fostered underground queer communities across generations, like the Apostles club at Cambridge.[5]

Still, Housman did not seek out these groups at either Oxford or Cambridge, preferring to keep his orientation private.[6] Moreover, his life was marked by the pain of unrequited love, as noted in the previous chapter. Poetry gave him a medium through which to explore his desires and hurts indirectly, to maintain his privacy. It also allowed him to extend a hand to readers who might have similar experiences. In some poems, he evoked, obliquely, the frustration of concealing desires that he did not himself deem unnatural. In 1894, he wrote:

> I, a stranger and afraid
> In a world I never made
> They will be master, right or wrong;
> Though both are foolish, both are strong.

And since, my soul, we cannot fly
To Saturn nor to Mercury,
Keep we must, if keep we can,
These foreign laws of God and man.[7]

But this was as far as he would go, at least in the years that led up to the publication of *A Shropshire Lad* in 1896. It was only in the 1900s and the decades that followed, during his vacations in Paris, that he began to explore his sexuality with strangers at bathhouses or male escorts.[8] Even then, he worked hard to cordon off these experiences, always going back into the closet upon his return to England. The Continent provided an escape from the restrictive and conventional sexual morality that he associated with his home country. When he wrote the poems that would later appear in *A Shropshire Lad*, however, his only experience of love and desire was still defined by rejection, fear, and secrecy.

The queer poets who alluded to *A Shropshire Lad* acknowledged that undercurrent of secrecy and shame. To a certain extent, they were drawn to it as a reflection of their own experience. Still, they found ways to mediate Housman's feelings of disgrace without claiming to have landed on a remedy. They highlighted more boldly the ambiguities that Housman had used to conceal his desires, as if to coax the *Shropshire* poet further into the light. But they were also careful not to inadvertently expose Housman by naming their source or making explicit the meaning behind his codes. Whereas the allusions to Christina Rossetti stand out thanks to the variety of interpretations of the source text that they imply, the allusions to *A Shropshire Lad* are notable for their commonalities. Oscar Wilde, Countee Cullen, and W. H. Auden—markedly different poets with vastly disparate styles—all approached Housman's book as a model for writing about queer love indirectly and covertly in a hostile culture as well as a resource for thinking about queer shame. All three poets attempted, via allusion, to draw Housman a bit further out of the closet, not by directly naming Housman's sexuality but by revising lines from *A Shropshire Lad* to be a little clearer on the same-sex passions that inspired them, without outing Housman explicitly. The gratitude that Wilde felt for Housman specifically was deepened by the recognition that Housman himself had sympathetically evoked the trial he had suffered through and the public shaming he had faced in the process. Any discussion of Wilde's allusions to Housman must account for Housman's own allusions to Wilde, and it is there that we will begin.

It has long been said that Wilde's trial haunted Housman's imagination and played a role in the composition of his own poetry. Reviewing his brother Laurence Housman's memoir, Desmond Shawe-Taylor posed a rhetorical question: "Is it a coincidence that the greater part of *A Shropshire Lad* was written in the year, almost in the month, of the Wilde trial?"[9] Biographers and critics who have taken up this issue concur that it was not, in fact, a coincidence, though they usually insist that the events had a purely negative impact, persuading Housman to bury traces of same-sex desire in his poetry and avoid references to Wilde. George L. Watson, in *A. E. Housman: A Divided Life*, gave this hypothesis a dramatic shape:

> Housman could not have missed . . . those lyric bulletins and vicious innuendoes which accompanied day by day the excoriating public spectacle at the Old Bailey; and just while he was feverishly resurrecting his own past, the pilloried figure of Oscar Wilde gripped his imagination, and the thunder of the mob which bore down upon the prostrate author filled his ears. By what now seems more than a coincidence Housman's talent freely asserted itself only at the moment when, as he must have felt, a hostile glare focused upon the suspect moral values of literature—one further reason that may have prompted him to temper the language and obscure the implications of his poetry.[10]

Nor is this theory entirely unreasonable. The poem commonly read as a response to Wilde's arrest was not published until after the poet's death by Laurence in *Additional Poems* (1937–1939):

Oh who is that young sinner with the handcuffs on his wrists?
And what has he been after that they groan and shake their fists?
And wherefore is he wearing such a conscience-stricken air?
Oh they're taking him to prison for the colour of his hair.[11]

"The colour of his hair" stands for the capriciousness of submitting someone to public humiliation and arrest for homosexuality. The connection
allows Housman to imply that both are minor traits—innate, unalterable,
and without bearing on the person's moral character. The poem has been
widely discussed along these lines, in scholarship by Laurence Perrine and
Christopher Ricks as well as by Archie Burnett in the notes to his edition
of Housman's poetry.[12] Yet Housman also evoked Wilde in poems that
did make their way into *A Shropshire Lad* and in terms no more secretive
than "the colour of his hair." "The Carpenter's Son," composed in August
1895 (four months after Wilde's arrest), is one example:

Here hang I, and right and left
Two poor fellows hang for theft:
All the same's the luck we prove,
Though the midmost hangs for love.[13]

The final line need not be taken as a reference to homosexuality. The
poem could simply be read as part of a long tradition of ballads recounting
crimes of passion. Yet so close on the heels of Wilde's very public arrest,
Housman could hardly not have been thinking of the dangers he faced
for his same-sex desires, which are highlighted by the pairing of *love* and
theft. *Though* separates the midmost man, acknowledging his punishment
as even more unjust. While "poor fellows" conveys sympathy, "love" still
wins out over "theft," suggesting the deeper injustice that Housman saw
play out in Wilde's trial.

   These expressions of sympathy would make their way to Wilde, who
developed a profound love for Housman's poetry. While he was in jail,
his friend Robbie Ross learned some of Housman's poems by heart and

recited them for Wilde's pleasure.[14] Housman's brother Laurence was also instrumental in acquainting Wilde with the *Shropshire* poems. Later, when Wilde got out of prison, Housman sent him a personal copy of the book, which he read intently while working on "The Ballad of Reading Gaol."[15] Wilde expressed his enthusiasm to Laurence in a letter dated August 9, 1897: "I have lately been reading your brother's lovely, lyrical poems so you see you have both of you given me that rare thing happiness." Then again on August 22, defending *A Shropshire Lad* against two critics: "It is absurd of Ricketts and Shannon not to see the light lyrical beauty of your brother's work, and its grace and delicate felicity of mood and music." The same letter notes that Wilde was "occupied in finishing a poem, terribly realistic for me, and drawn from actual experience."[16] Critics soon picked up on a connection between "The Ballad of Reading Gaol" and Housman's poetry. Frank Harris, in the first biography of Wilde, stated plainly, "I believe that Wilde owed most of his inspiration to *A Shropshire Lad*."[17]

Yet most discussions of influence have been general, noting broad similarities in form and theme, so that critics have yet to attend to specific allusions in "The Ballad of Reading Gaol" and their significance.[18] Wilde turned to Housman not just for the shape and music of his stanzas, not just for his melancholic tone and how it might express the pain of incarceration, but because he detected in his poetry hints of same-sex desire and the shame associated with it. Because of their sexuality, both men faced the risk of public judgment, so Housman's poems about prisoners held a special meaning for him. Wilde also identified the *Shropshire* poet's allusions to his work and the sympathy they expressed. Through allusion, Wilde acknowledged that compassion and developed Housman's images to convey more fully his experience of jail, which Housman knew little about. He also extended a hand to his fellow poet by drawing out those coded evocations of queer desire that Housman could not express fully himself—though without going so far as to out him explicitly. In the process, Wilde connected imaginatively with a fellow queer poet across their respective isolation.

The poem that most captured Wilde's imagination was *A Shropshire Lad, IX*. "The Ballad of Reading Gaol" contains references to Housman's poem across several stanzas. Wilde does not allude to just one line but reaches instead for a cumulative effect. The chief aim in all these cases, however, is to shift points of view and bring Housman's poem closer to the immediacy of his own experience, thereby expanding the picture that Housman could only sketch out in general terms. The figure in *A Shropshire Lad, IX* might be awaiting an execution; in the third stanza, Housman writes, "They hang us now in Shrewsbury jail." But the line could be read as a generalization: *people are now hanged at Shrewsbury jail.* After that, Housman does away with the first-person plural and focuses on a "lad" who "sleeps in Shrewsbury jail to-night."[19] The wording implies that the speaker may not be in prison and that the first-person plural may have been intended as a mark of solidarity. "The Ballad of Reading Gaol" reimagines Housman's poem from the perspective of someone who lived through incarceration and felt the terror of awaiting execution.

Wilde first draws on Housman's description of the clock counting down to the hour of execution (typically eight in the morning). His re-writing is significant not just because of the shift in perspective from an external observer to a group of people suffering through incarceration but also because the passage allows Wilde to imagine community as an antidote to the isolating process of shame. Here is the passage from Housman:

> So here I'll watch the night and wait
> To see the morning shine,
> When he will hear the stroke of eight
> And not the stroke of nine;
>
> And wish my friend as sound a sleep
> As lads' I did not know,
> That shepherded the moonlit sheep
> A hundred years ago.[20]

Here is Wilde's version:

> We waited for the stroke of eight:
>   Each tongue was thick with thirst:
> For the stroke of eight is the stroke of Fate
>   That makes a man accursed,
> And Fate will use a running noose
>   For the best man and the worst.
>
> We had no other thing to do,
>   Save to wait for the sign to come:
> So, like things of stone in a valley lone,
>   Quiet we sat and dumb:
> But each man's heart beat thick and quick
>   Like a madman on a drum![21]

Both poets play on "the stroke of eight" but to different effects. Housman emphasizes disruption. The first two lines create a tense atmosphere, "watch[ing]" and "wait[ing]" for dawn. The two lines that follow bring this tension to a head by breaking a pattern: the friend is said to "hear the stroke of eight / And not the stroke of nine." The formal satisfaction of arranging two consecutive phrases—"the stroke of eight" and "the stroke of nine"—into a parallel, by placing them at the end of their lines, is undermined by the negation, which denies the very pattern that the repetition evokes. The lines leave room for a quiet yet powerful ambiguity: the friend might hear in "the stroke of eight" the absence of a ninth stroke and of all strokes beyond the one that will mark his execution. Wilde's account similarly begins with dread and suspense ("We waited"), but the poem quickens as its tensions reach a breaking point. The shift comes from the repetition of the word *stroke*. It appears once in the first line and recurs twice in the third. On its final iteration, *eight* gives way to *Fate:* one coldly sealed by the word *accursed* in the fourth line.

Wilde also changes the clock strike's aftermath. Housman's use of a semicolon instead of a period in the fourth line emphasizes the gap between the stanzas and what that gap omits. The verb that opens the second stanza connects back not to *he* (whose actions are ended) but to an earlier *I*, who was said to "watch" and "wait" and now can only "wish." Turning away from the violence of execution, the poet takes a historical view, to lads who "shepherded . . . / A hundred years ago." The scope of that activity grants the poet some solace by placing his friend's life against a panorama that has remained consistent across time. Wilde's transition is starker. His period signals the finality of Fate and the totality of its reach: "the best man and the worst." No more to say here, and the next stanza begins with a statement of helplessness as if to reinforce this point: "We had no other thing to do."

But the principal link uniting the two poems is how they imagine community—likely what captured Wilde's interest. The tension in *A Shropshire Lad, IX* stems from the separation between *I* and *he*. *Lads* offers the promise of connection through a larger plural. If the two cannot meet in the present, an imagined community of lads in the past century can serve as an alternative meeting point and a counter to the social process of shame, which seeks to isolate. Wilde, who experienced incarceration firsthand, takes Housman's desire for community and makes it real. The first-person plural pronoun *we* adopts the point of view of a group sharing the same experience in jail awaiting execution, and the generalizing language ("that makes a man accursed," "the best man and the worst") extends the poem's sympathies to all those who face the same fears or suffer from the same fate. At the same time, the allusion to Housman's "stroke of eight" superimposes an intertextual link that fulfills the desire for connection implicit in Housman.

Elsewhere, Wilde's shift in perspective affords him an opportunity to vocalize emotions that Housman, always restrained, felt the need to suppress or keep quiet. This, too, served as a rebuttal to the silencing pressure of shame with which the *Shropshire* poet was so intimately familiar. The passage in Housman:

> And naked to the hangman's noose
> The morning clocks will ring

> A neck God made for other use
>   Than strangling in a string[22]

becomes in Wilde:

> And as one sees most fearful things
>   In the crystal of a dream,
> We saw the greasy hempen rope
>   Hooked to the blackened beam,
> And heard the prayer the hangman's snare
>   Strangled into a scream.[23]

Housman's grammar is purposefully disorienting, so that the syntax only becomes clear in the third line: morning clocks will ring, and so direct, a bare neck to the hangman's noose, though the neck was made for better purposes than execution. The noose is here reimagined as a "string," whose thinness contrasts with the thickness of an actual noose and emphasizes its outsized impact. The poet never states his friend's feelings explicitly but instead conveys them through grammatical contortions and metaphor. For "string" also evokes stringed instruments (a link reinforced by the rhyme on "ring" and its implicit pun on "wring"), so that the prisoner's strangling is sublimated into music. Wilde harks back to Housman's torturous grammar in the penultimate line, with the juxtaposition of "the prayer the hangman's snare." The syntax and the internal rhyme convey the feeling of constraint they describe. As in Housman, the prisoner's speech undergoes a transformation in the final line, but rather than being silenced or sublimated, the man's prayer is distorted and heightened when it is "strangled into a *scream*." Again, Wilde could imagine the prisoner's pain more closely than Housman. At the same time, by alluding to Housman, he gives voice to an author who suppressed, tempered, or sublimated his expressions of feeling and of desire, so that the allusion serves as a mark of sympathy.

As these examples show, the poetry of Wilde and Housman presents a rich network of textual crossings. The difference in sensibility between the two writers makes the allusions even more surprising. Wilde acknowledged Housman's sympathy for his plight and returned the favor by expanding the world that Housman had sketched out for him and meeting Housman's restraint with a greater degree of expressiveness. The boldness of Wilde's revisions was a show of acceptance for a fellow queer poet who felt that he had to mask and control his expressions of feeling, both in life and in verse.

Considering Housman's self-discipline, though, it is not surprising that he downplayed his interest in Wilde's poetry and their reciprocal influence. In a letter dated June 21, 1928, to Seymour Adelman, a rare books curator, he wrote:

> Dear Mr. Adelman,
>
> *A Shropshire Lad* was published while Mr. Wilde was in prison, and when he came out I sent him a copy myself. Robert Ross told me that when he visited his friend in jail he learnt some of the poems by heart and recited them to him; so that was his first acquaintance with them . . . Parts of *The Ballad of Reading Gaol* are above Wilde's average, but I suspect they were written by Lord Alfred Douglas.
>
> Yours sincerely, A. E. Housman[24]

Housman responds factually to Adelman's inquiry about his contact with Wilde, yet the clipped tone denies that the relation is worthy of note. The cool appraisal of "The Ballad of Reading Gaol" leaves no doubt as to the profound difference in taste between the two authors, and his suspicion that the best parts "were written by Lord Alfred Douglas" reads as a snub. But it is also pure cheek, since Housman doubtless heard in Wilde's "Ballad" echoes of his own poems. While Housman felt the need to understate his connection to Wilde in this letter, allusion enabled a deeper tribute in poetry. There the two poets could think and feel through each other's verse—and enjoy a different form of companionship on the page, against the pressure of social judgment.

To speak of Countee Cullen's queerness is complicated since Cullen himself was quiet on the subject. But as Charles Molesworth points out, "While there is in his correspondence no explicit record of any homosexual relationship or encounter, or any direct acknowledgment by Cullen of his homosexuality, the circumstance surrounding his relations with a number of his male friends makes it obvious."[25] His mentor and close friend Alain Locke, himself closeted, gave Cullen reassurance and guidance with regards to his same-sex attraction. Locke introduced Cullen to *Ioläus: An Anthology of Friendship* (1902), a volume by the British radical Edward Carpenter that describes and celebrates homosexual bonds under the cover of friendship. The book allowed Cullen to view his sexuality as part of a longer history going back to ancient Greece. He wrote to Locke excitedly, stating that *Ioläus* "opened up for me soul windows which had been closed" and that it "threw a noble and evident light on what I had begun to believe, because of what the world believes, ignoble and unnatural." He also lived in New York at a time when Harlem had become a vibrant center for the LGBTQ community. There were several gay clubs between Fifth and Seventh Avenues as well as bars and speakeasies not specifically oriented toward queer customers that put on drag shows, such as the Cyril Café. Drag queens were even seen walking the streets of the neighborhood.[26] Harlem was also the site of the Hamilton Lodge Ball, an annual meeting of gay men and lesbians that was attracting seven thousand participants by the early 1930s, including celebrities and ordinary citizens who did not identify as queer. The scarcity of vice cops, who tended to focus their attention on other neighborhoods in Manhattan, helped to make Harlem a relatively tolerant environment. Still, Cullen worried about the social judgment that he would face if his sexuality became public. After all, when Cullen wrote and published the poems in *Color* (1925), the press was still mocking the attendees of the Hamilton Lodge Ball as "subnormal, or, in the language of the street, 'fairies.'"[27] In his letters, Cullen urged Locke to keep his sexuality a secret: "Sentiments expressed here would be misconstrued by others, so this letter, once read, is best destroyed."[28]

Cullen's desperation to hide his attraction to men would lead him to marry Yolande Du Bois, W. E. B. Du Bois's daughter, in 1928. The marriage did not last long, as within a year he confessed his sexual orientation to his wife. Yolande wrote to her father on May 23, 1929, not at all obliquely, about Cullen's admission: "Countée told me something about himself that just finished things. Other people told me too but I thought and hoped they were lying. If he had not told me *himself* that it was true I would not have believed it but since he did I knew that essentially I'd have to leave him . . . I knew something was wrong physically, but being very ignorant and inexperienced I couldn't be sure what. When he confessed things he'd always known that he was abnormal sexually as far as *other men were concerned* then many things became clear." Cullen would marry again a decade later, this time to Ida Mae Roberson. But throughout the early 1940s, he maintained a secret relationship with Edward Atkinson, a New York stage actor with whom he shared his longest queer relationship. The men would meet regularly by using the pretext of a night out among male friends on Friday evenings. When Atkinson enlisted in the U.S. military in 1943, and later when Cullen moved to Tuckahoe, they stayed in contact by asking Cullen's friend Harold Jackson to serve as a go-between, transmitting messages between the two lovers. This long-distance relationship lasted until Cullen's death in 1946.[29]

Throughout his life, Cullen found in Housman's poetry both a reflection of his secret queer experience and a resource through which to explore same-sex desires and challenges indirectly in his own poetry. Cullen's affection for the poet was profound and well documented. In 1923, Langston Hughes sent him an essay by "your beloved" Housman.[30] Critics have repeatedly noted the *Shropshire* poet's influence on him, but, as with Housman's influence on Wilde, the accounts are murky at best, focusing on Cullen's affinity for his predecessor's fixed forms or his pessimism.[31] There are more specific connections to be found, though, particularly in those poems that urge a lad to submit to love.

Like many other LGBTQ poets, Cullen was drawn to the genre of the advice poem for the queer aspects of its history. For example, he was also taken with Oscar Wilde's short story "The Portrait of Mr. W.H." There Wilde imagines searching for the mysterious dedicatee of Shake-

speare's sonnets, which offer advice to a young man in ways that have
been thought to imply erotic interest. (Cullen later quoted the story in an
essay he wrote at Harvard.)[32] Housman, though, was his true point of reference in composing his own advice poems. His admiration for the poet is
evident in discreet verbal allusions as well as the decision to apostrophize
a lad specifically. In Housman, he found a model for expressing queer
desire obliquely and protecting himself from the risk of hostile scrutiny.
But he also alluded to passages in which the *Shropshire* poet questioned
the shame that surrounds same-sex intimacy on the grounds of it being
"unclean." Housman gave him both a mask and the vocabulary to con-
test the need for a mask. At the same time, Cullen expanded the scope of
Housman's advice poems by using them as a vehicle to express racial pride
against a society that has repeatedly failed to value Black life. Through
Housman, Cullen addressed two interrelated aspects of his experience.

Let us now consider how these various transformations take effect.
First, Cullen actualizes through metaphor the intimacy never fulfilled in
Housman. In doing so, he gives voice to emotions that Housman did not
feel he could take so far while retaining the ambiguities and protections
of the advice poem. For instance, *A Shropshire Lad, XXIV:*

> Say, lad, have you things to do?
>   Quick then, while your day's at prime.
> Quick, and if 'tis work for two,
>   Here am I, man: now's your time.
>
> Send me now, and I shall go;
>   Call me, I shall hear you call;
> Use me ere they lay me low
>   Where a man's no use at all;
>
> Ere the wholesome flesh decay,
>   And the willing nerve be numb,
> And the lips lack breath to say,
>   "No, my lad, I cannot come."[33]

Compare this to Cullen's "Advice to Youth":

> Since little time is granted here
>   For pride in pain or play,
> Since blood soon cools before that Fear
>   That makes our prowess clay,
> If lips to kiss are freely met,
>   Lad, be not proud nor shy;
> There are no lips where men forget,
>   And undesiring lie.[34]

Jeremy Braddock argues that Cullen's poem "enables a queer reading by employing vague language that appears, in a traditional reading, to refer blandly to universal categories of life and death. But when the poem's language is read with specificity, the subjunctive third pair of verses creates a space in which same-sex desire can be expressed."[35] Much the same can be said of *A Shropshire Lad, XXIV,* which enables a queer reading to pass by identifying the addressee as male in the first stanza ("Say, lad," "Here am I, man") and allowing the reader to assume that the speaker is female, before then playing on the ambiguity of the word *man:* "Use me ere they lay me low / Where a man's no use at all." While the word could be taken as a universal marker ("where no one is of use"), readers eager for expressions of gay love could assume that *man* discloses the speaker's gender. Cullen borrows this approach in the final lines of his poem: "There are no lips where men forget, / And undesiring lie." Evidently, the first reading is of *men* as a stand-in for *everyone,* but in a poem evoking gay love, the word takes on a special resonance.

The connections between the two poems are reinforced by their common structure. Both begin with the swift passage of time and end with silent lips as a metaphor for death. Cullen notably deepens the silence by not relating what the lips will be unable to say beyond the grave. At the same time, he realizes more fully the intimacy that is never satisfied in *A Shropshire Lad, XXIV.* Although Housman does make it explicit that the lad should find love with him specifically, he also maintains a strict separation by avoiding *we*. In Cullen, by contrast, the word *our* is nestled in the fourth line, roughly in the poem's center, with no *I* or *you* in sight. Granted, the *our* could refer to all of humanity, returning to dust, but it could also be read as an invocation of the fate shared by lad and poet and of the intimacy they might enjoy before then. While Cullen never makes it clear if the lad agrees to his request, the pronoun clinches—discreetly but no less powerfully—the connection that, for many queer people in this time, was so precarious.

In addition to realizing the unfulfilled desires in Housman's poems, Cullen connects gay love with racial pride. One example is "To a Brown Boy," a defense of "Black racial pride and beauty" that alludes to several of Housman's advice poems.[36] At first glance, "To a Brown Boy" seems far from the realm of same-sex desire, as Cullen urges his addressee to enter a heterosexual relationship. But the allusions to Housman allow him to quietly evoke the pressures and longings experienced by queer people such as himself. Notably, Cullen first dedicated the poem to Hughes, another poet who kept his sexuality private. It is telling, too, that he revoked the dedication in the end:[37]

> That brown girl's swagger gives a twitch
>   To beauty like a queen;
> Lad, never dam your body's itch
>   When loveliness is seen.
>
> For there is ample room for bliss
>   In pride in clean, brown limbs,
> And lips know better how to kiss
>   Than how to raise white hymns.
>
> And when your body's death gives birth
>   To soil for spring to crown,
> Men will not ask if that rare earth
>   Was white flesh once, or brown.[38]

As in "Advice to Youth," Cullen forges a link to Housman through the apostrophe to "lad," a word that establishes Housman as an antecedent and reference point, over any other work in the tradition of the erotic advice poem. The poem also follows a downward track to the death of "flesh," though here the final image is one of rebirth ("your body's death gives birth / To soil for spring to crown"). Most important, he sets the call to love against the backdrop of racial hatred, so that an individual relationship becomes a counterpoint to negative forces in society more broadly. Cullen makes this connection as well in the second stanza, in which the word *pride* asserts self-acceptance in a hostile world. Another similar transformation occurs at the end, where Cullen repurposes the trope of death as the great equalizer that lays everyone low. Rather than persuading the lover to accept the poet's advances, the trope is put in the service of an argument about human universality beyond race: after the body's death, "men will not ask if that rare earth / Was white flesh once, or brown."

Cullen does not entirely abandon the subject of queer desire, which the initial dedication to Hughes made explicit. For the reader who recognizes the apostrophe to a lad as a link to Housman would likely pick up on another key word, *clean*, in a world where same-sex relations and feelings were condemned as unclean. Housman had turned to this word several times to work through his own conflict with queer desire. *Clean* appears grimly in *A Shropshire Lad, XXIV*, where it describes a young man's suicide. The poem is thought to have been inspired by Henry Clarkson Maclean, a cadet at the Royal Military Academy in Woolwich, who took his own life on August 6, 1895. J. M. Nosworthy notes that Housman attributed this suicide to "a recognition of irresistible homosexual tendencies,"[39] a notion that the poem evokes but never states overtly. The first stanza starts abruptly with a question meant to dispel any sentimentality:

> Shot? so quick, so clean an ending?
>   Oh that was right, lad, that was brave:
> Yours was not an ill for mending,
>   'Twas best to take it to the grave.[40]

The first line is shocking because it is itself so quick, so clean, in its grammar. Whatever shock one may be tempted to read in that question "Shot?" is swiftly dispelled by the remainder of the line, for the tone stays provokingly equable. Many ills could be envisioned here, but to those willing to pick up on such implications, *clean* conveys same-sex desire, which cannot simply be "mended." *Clean* marks the poem as being about "the ineradicable stigma of homosexuality that can only be extinguished by death."[41]

But elsewhere, Housman's use of the term is supremely ironic, contesting the notion that same-sex intimacy should be subject to change. In one poem, he insists that his love for an undetermined "you" made him "clean and brave":

> Oh, when I was in love with you,
>   Then I was clean and brave,
> And miles around the wonder grew
>   How well did I behave.
>
> And now the fancy passes by,
>   And nothing will remain,
> And miles around they'll say that I
>   Am quite myself again.[42]

If read in terms of heterosexual romance, the poem's main interest lies in the irony of its conclusion. Though to be "quite oneself again" is often used in a positive sense; for example, to signal recovery from a passing illness, the earlier point that love made him "clean and brave" suggests, amusingly, that his usual behavior is far less agreeable. But a reader alert to the queerness of Housman's poetry can find other layers of irony. If both speaker and addressee are male, then the poet was cleaner when he loved a man, refuting the notion that gay love should be deemed unclean. In turn, this enables Housman to frame the neighbors' perception as hypocritical. People from "miles around" would be unlikely to praise him if they knew the cause of his behavior. Although the neighbors will say that he is "quite himself again," the passing of his "fancy" conveys a rejection of the self. The poem's conclusion may be dour, but the skipping rhythm keeps the tone light and tongue-in-cheek.

This double emotion—the painful sense of shame over his desires and the frustration with the fact that he felt shame at all—resonated with Cullen, who had a difficult relationship with his own sexuality. When alluding to Housman's use of the word *clean,* he affirmed the *Shropshire* poet boldly through metaphor, without exposing their shared experiences in explicit terms. So with the end of "To a Brown Boy":

> Now to your grave shall friend and stranger
>   With ruth and some with envy come:
> Undishonoured, clear of danger,
>   Clean of guilt, pass hence and home.
>
> Turn safe to rest, no dreams, no waking;
>   And here, man, here's the wreath I've made:
> 'Tis not a gift that's worth the taking,
>   But wear it and it will not fade.[43]

The poet first presents an image of community, even if it is not a cheerful one. The visitors at the grave site are made up of two parties: the majority who merely regret the lad's death ("ruth") and a smaller group ("some") who feel enviously toward him. Envy may not seem a kindly emotion, but it does suggest that these visitors know why the lad took his life and that they suffer the same inner conflict. Envy, in this instance, is a mark of sympathy. The final stanza takes this idea further by establishing a personal connection between poet and lad. The gifting of a wreath is a ceremonial gesture, but it is given an intimate slant by the suggestion that the poet, too, shares the lad's desires and fears. The wreath becomes a public object containing a private message. Its intimacy is captured by the verb *wear,* which transforms the wreath from a large arrangement placed on a grave to a smaller band set on the lad's head.

"To a Brown Boy" also ends with the gifting of a wreath, though the act itself undergoes an important shift, becoming a reciprocal exchange: "And when your body's death gives birth / To soil for spring to crown." The relation is no longer between lad and poet but between lad and the natural world: he provides "soil," and nature reciprocates with a crown of flowers. The conflicted tones of Housman's ending—cynicism and uplift, loneliness and connection—give way to a far more hopeful mood. Cullen ends by turning squarely to the future with an image of rebirth, and because the wreath is eternal ("it will not fade"), there is no doubt about the value of either gift.

The reciprocal gifts frame allusion itself as a kind of gift. By alluding to Housman's advice poems, Cullen acknowledges all that the *Shropshire* poet has given him as a reader and an author and implies that he is giving back. Like the placement of a wreath in Housman's poem, Cullen's allusions are public acts containing private messages. They convey sympathy founded on common desires that both poets kept silent. Yet like the wreath, their secret can be read by those who have similar experiences and wish to find connection through poetry. The brown boy is imagined rid of shame ("clear of danger, / Clean of guilt") but without any pretense that he could have passed through the world without feeling either. In Housman, he found the language to manage, mitigate, and speak beyond the shame that social convention had imposed on him. This was Housman's gift to him, and Cullen's allusions return the favor. A. E. Housman's poetry mattered deeply to W. H. Auden from youth. In his prose, Auden described Housman not as a gay poet but as an author whose sensibility resonated with adolescents. Reviewing G. L. Watson's biography *A. E. Housman: A Divided Life* in 1957, he defended the value of such poetry into adulthood:

> It has often been said that Housman is a poet of adolescence, and this is fair enough as long as this judgment is not meant to imply, as it usually is, that nobody over the age of twenty-one can or should enjoy reading him. To grow up does not mean to outgrow either childhood or adolescence but to make use of them in an adult way. But for the child in us, we should be incapable of intellectual curiosity; but for the adolescent,

of serious feeling for other individuals. I can imagine a person who had "outgrown" both, though I have never met one; he would be a completely social official being with no personal identity. All that a mature man can give his child and adolescent in return for what they keep giving him are humility, humor, charity and hope. He will never teach them to despise any strong passion, however strange and limited, or to reject a poet, like Housman, who gives it utterance.[44]

For Auden, the force of adolescent poetry stems not simply from the fact that it expresses "strong passion" but also that it encourages "serious feeling *for other individuals.*" Housman's lyrics serve as a model for sympathy and connection (between the speaker and the addressee or between the reader and the speaker). These virtues, to his mind, do not hinder individuality. On the contrary, they make possible the development of an interior life. Someone who does not feel for other people can only become a "social official being" without a "*personal* identity": a robotic bureaucrat or a calculating politician. For Auden, identity depends on one's relation to others.

In a 1972 review of A. E. Housman's letters for the *New Yorker*, Auden returned to the notion of adolescent poetry, while qualifying his praise at least initially:

> Naturally, one cannot read Housman's letters without thinking again about this status and achievement as a poet. A minor poet, certainly, which, of course, does not mean that his poems are inferior in artistic merit to those of a major poet, only that the range of theme and emotion is narrow, and that the poems show no development over the years. On the evidence of the text alone, it would be very difficult to say whether a poem appeared in *A Shropshire Lad*, published when he was thirty-seven, or in *Last Poems*, published when he was sixty-three. I don't know how it is with the young today, but to my generation no other English poet seemed so perfectly to express the sensibility of a male adolescent. If I do not turn to him very often, I am eternally grateful to him for the joy he gave me in my youth.[45]

This time, Auden begins with some critical hedging. Housman's poems "show no development over the years," and the mention of the poet's age when *A Shropshire Lad* appeared ("thirty-seven") makes the label of adolescent poetry feel awkward. Auden even speculates that Housman's popularity may have been generational ("I don't know how it is with the young today"). Yet all these signals of moderation also permit a late rush of praise ("to my generation no other English poet seemed so perfectly to express the sensibility of a male adolescent") and personal affection ("I am eternally grateful to him for the joy he gave me in my youth").

These shifts in tone and attitude are even more notable in that the review also deals in frank terms with Housman's sexuality. The review starts with that very subject: "Mr. Henry Maas informs us that Arthur Platt's widow destroyed all Housman's 'Rabelaisian' letters to him. I am delighted to hear it. His letters to Moses Jackson have also not yet been made available. I hope they never will be. If the reader of *The Letters of A. E. Housman*, edited by Mr. Maas and published by the Harvard University Press, occasionally finds himself yawning or skipping, at least he never feels like a Peeping Tom, and if he hopes to find something titillating he will be disappointed." Auden begins with the claim that it would be indecent to dwell on Housman's sexuality and that the poet's desires and experiences ought to remain private. The reader should not be a "Peeping Tom." But Auden later proceeds to peep himself: "If Housman did feel shame and guilt, this was caused not by the Bible but by classical literature. I am pretty sure that in his sexual tastes he was an anal passive. Ancient Greece and Rome were both pederastic cultures in which the adult passive homosexual was regarded as comic and contemptible."[46]

This reaches well beyond Housman's identity to theories about specific sexual acts that Housman desired or enjoyed. The phrasing may not be "titillating," but his clinical tone ("in his sexual tastes he was an anal passive") is arguably worse. By digging into the poet's shame and its likely source, Auden runs afoul of Housman's wish for privacy. He desires to expose his predecessor, even at the risk of embarrassment, and the reference to "pederastic cultures" finding passive homosexuals like Housman "comic and contemptible" serves as another twist of the knife.

In these sentences, Auden abandons the "serious feeling for others" that he had learned from Housman.

The passages about Housman's sexuality create a strange mix of emotions in the review. Auden expresses genuine affection for Housman and an understanding for his psychology, yet at other points he manifests an impatient, aggressive desire to drag Housman's private life into the open, to the point of embarrassing him. After the *Shropshire* poet passed away in 1936, Auden published a sonnet titled "A. E. Housman" that displayed the same double attitude. On the one hand, the poem undeniably shows some degree of sympathy and understanding for Housman's interior life, particularly at the start. Auden depicts him as a man who felt a profound melancholy and who took up scholarship to bury his sadness and distract himself from it. In the first stanza, Auden writes: "Heart-injured in North London, he became / The Latin Scholar of his generation."[47] As Stephen Regan has noted, these lines express "the idea that art might begin in deprivation and assume the role of transforming what is broken and incomplete."[48] Auden shows two forms of respect: first, the professional praise of Housman as a scholar; second, the discretion of evoking the poet's heartbreak ("Heart-injured" being likely a reference to Moses Jackson in Oxford) without naming any of the particulars. As the poem wears on, however, that respectful distance begins to narrow. He writes that Housman "Kept tears like dirty postcards in a drawer"—a curious image that describes a painful desire for privacy but needlessly taints his grief with the suggestion of sexual scandal. He also flirts with the possibility of exposing Housman's sexuality when he hints at the motive behind his critical personality: "In savage foot-notes on unjust editions / He timidly attacked the life he led." To Auden's mind, Housman was motivated by shame as well as heartbreak. The charge of hypocrisy shows an eagerness to embarrass the poet by casting a light on that shame. Yet the attitude softens again as the poem draws to a close. In the final lines, Auden writes that Housman put all his feelings into

> The uncritical relations of the dead,
> Where only geographical divisions
> Parted the coarse hanged soldier from the don.[49]

Auden's point is that Housman wished for the bravery of "the coarse hanged soldier," which his timidity never permitted him. He was the don who wished to be the soldier. But the ambiguity opens a second possibility: that poetry allowed him to imagine romantic connections that he never experienced, so that in verse, at least, such divisions could vanish and the don could be *with* the soldier for the space of a lyric. The discretion of these lines does Housman a kindness while extending a hand to readers who may feel similar desires.

It would be wrong to assume that Auden was hostile towards Housman. Rather, the *Shropshire* poet drew his complicated feelings about homosexuality to the surface. In Housman, he saw a version of himself. Even as reading *A Shropshire Lad* gave him the relief of shared experiences, it also reinforced the dread that he would, like Housman, suffer in isolation throughout his life. His crushes on heterosexual students at Oxford and Chester Kallman's rejection of the poet in 1941 (discussed earlier) made him particularly sensitive to the pain of unrequited love. In 1932, he expressed concern that "nearly all homosexual relations" were marred by an incapacity to engage in "any intimate faithful relationship at all."[50] It is likely, then, as Peter Howarth has said, that "Auden privately feared that Housman's thwarted love life was inexorably to be his own fate."[51] Evidence of this crops up in his review of Laurence Housman's memoir, *My Brother, A. E. Housman* (1938). For Auden, the book prompted a reflection on—what he felt to be—the two paths that one can follow:

> Does Life only offer two alternatives: "You shall be happy, healthy, attractive, a good mixer, a good lover and parent, but on condition that you are not overcurious about life. On the other hand you shall be attentive and sensitive, conscious of what is happening round you, but in that case you must not expect to be happy, or successful in love, or at home in any company. There are two worlds and you cannot belong to them both. If you belong to the second of these worlds you will be unhappy because you will always be in love with the first, while at the same time you will despise it. The first world on the other hand will not return your love because it is in its nature to love only itself. Socrates will always fall in

love with Alcibiades; Alcibiades will only be a little flattered and rather puzzled."[52]

Richard Bozorth says of this passage that "Auden was recapitulating the binary of mind and body that had governed his thinking about homosexuality for ten years. He saw himself, like Housman, as the second type, futilely in love with the first."[53] For while life does "offer" these alternatives, there is little sense here that a person can choose which path to take. These are separate "worlds" entirely, and whether you end up in one or the other depends on your individual makeup, rather than any decision. This unpleasant prospect explains, at least in part, Auden's tendency to both sympathize with Housman and hold him at a distance—out of fear and embarrassment that his own life would turn out like Housman's.

If Auden's prose and poetry about Housman expresses a contradictory push-and-pull of feelings, his allusions to Housman tell a different story. Through these references, Auden recognizes the shame and melancholy that the *Shropshire* poet felt in his life and expressed in his verse, but he also shows a willingness to respect Housman's desire for privacy. Unlike in his titular sonnet, Auden does not seek to expose him, let alone to make assumptions about his proclivities. Instead, he gives voice to Housman's pains and disappointments while still granting him the protection of anonymity. He strikes this balance by taking poems that use the cover of patriotic song or heterosexual romance to disguise the author's homosexuality and reframes them as love poems in which the gender of one or both parties is ambiguous, so that queerness becomes a live possibility for the interested reader to detect. The covertness of allusion mattered greatly here since the source did not need to be named. Auden could engage with the buried emotions of Housman's poetry and coax out their true nature further into the light while still granting him the protection and privacy that were important to him.

Allusions to Housman hide in plain sight in some of Auden's most widely known poems. For example, "Funeral Blues" (discussed earlier) contains allusions to Housman's *A Shropshire Lad, LIII* as well as Stephen Spender's "Hearing from its cage." Tellingly, the love story in Housman's poem is explicitly heterosexual, so that Auden's allusion works to partly remove the disguise. *A Shropshire Lad, LIII* is a narrative poem in which a woman receives a visit from her lover in the middle of the night. He expresses some wariness about showing his face and ominously declares that he will never lie beside another woman, even as he travels far away. The woman then poses a series of questions, which gradually reveal the man as a ghost. Upon asking him why she cannot hear or feel his heartbeat, he replies:

> "Oh loud, my girl, it once would knock,
>   You should have felt it then;
> But since for you I stopped the clock
>   It never goes again."[54]

His reference to the stopped heart and the stopped clock is the first clear indication that he has died. Readers of Auden will recognize an echo of the last two lines in the first stanza of "Funeral Blues":

> Stop all the clocks, cut off the telephone,
> Prevent the dog from barking with a juicy bone,
> Silence the pianos and with muffled drum
> Bring out the coffin, let the mourners come.[55]

Both stopped clocks serve as declarations of love, from different sides of the threshold dividing life and death. In Housman, the lover stopped the clock in his final moments out of love; we later learn that his neck has been slit "from ear to ear," suggesting a fight (perhaps in her name) or a suicide. In Auden, the mourner demands that all the clocks be stopped now that the lover has passed away because it is intolerable to think that time would go on in his absence. That echo underscores a shift in voice. Housman's poem is a ballad containing three voices (the narrator and the two lovers), and the image appears in a bit of spoken dialogue by the ghostly lad. "Funeral Blues," on the other hand, is a lyric poem with a singular voice: that of the mourner standing alone. By carrying the image over from the dead lad to the person left behind, Auden movingly evokes the endurance of their feelings for one another. The language of their love survives even beyond death.

These changes in speaker and poetic form are meaningful, too, because they open up new possibilities as to the gender of the lovers. *A Shropshire Lad, LIII* relates the story of a heterosexual couple, of a *he* and *she*. "Funeral Blues," when encountered as a printed lyric poem, could be read as a lament for a straight or gay romance. The deceased lover is explicitly referred to as *he*, but the speaker never reveals their gender, nor does the imagery contain any implicit clues on this question. When read in the context of an allusion to Housman, and knowledge of both Housman's sexual life and Auden's feelings about it, that transition becomes especially important. By evoking the possibility of same-sex love, Auden acknowledges the private feelings that animated Housman's poetry and that (he believed) the poet concealed behind a heterosexual plot. Crucially, he also coaxes those feelings into the light, at least in part. Ambiguity is certainly more open than the disguise of a heterosexual love designed to conceal the truth of Housman's affection. By allowing the prospect of queerness into the reader's mind, he gives Housman space to breathe. In a departure from his prose, however, Auden seeks not to expose too much, let alone to out his predecessor. The queerness of "Funeral Blues" is there to be picked up on by an interested and likely sympathetic reader, but it is not presented so explicitly as to catch the attention of those who are not invested in the possibility to begin with. Auden fulfills what Housman could not, goes further than Housman felt able to, but he does not go so far as to betray the poet's wish for privacy.

While love ballads may seem to be a simple place to find buried signs of queerness, Auden also detected traces of Housman's longings in patriotic poems devoted to British soldiers. In "The Recruit," for example, the townspeople's love for a lad gone to war, and the speaker's expression of that love on the town's behalf, supplies a useful cover, allowing Housman to voice his desire for a masculine heroic figure indirectly. The speaker

begins by cheering the soldier on as he leaves the town of Ludlow, promising that luck will go with him "While Ludlow tower shall stand." The
poem then repeats and extends that reassurance:

> Oh, come you home of Sunday
> While Ludlow streets are still
> And Ludlow bells are calling
> To farm and lane and mill,
>
> Or come you home of Monday
> When Ludlow market hums
> And Ludlow chimes are playing
> "The conquering hero comes,"
>
> Come you home a hero,
> Or come not home at all,
> The lads you leave will mind you
> Till Ludlow tower shall fall.[56]

The bells of Ludlow will either celebrate the soldier's return or symbolize
the endurance of their affection for him, even beyond death. The love
of the hero outlasts all. While the collapse of Ludlow tower is evoked at
the end of the third stanza, this is presented as a remote possibility. The
final lines of the poem reinforce this notion: "Oh, town and field will mind
you / Till Ludlow tower is down." As Mihail Evans says, "There is the
promise that the recruit will live on, this time not just through his friends
but through the very landscape."[57] The soldier is granted that immortality
not just thanks to his service defending England's lands but also thanks to
the love of the people he left behind.

Auden detected in Housman's patriotic tribute hints of his desire for
the masculine figure of the soldier. This subtext was evidently on Auden's
mind when he set down to write "As I Walked Out One Evening" (1937).
The poem is written in quatrains, like Housman's, with three stresses per

line. It also shares a common theme with "The Recruit": love's endurance in the face of time. Yet Auden adopts a far more pessimistic attitude than Housman, undercutting the notion that anything can outlast time's forward march. The speaker of his poem, upon encountering a young couple by the river, overhears one of the two declare that "Love has no ending" and that they promise to love the other until an impossible future ("Till China and Africa meet," among other pledges). These vows are then swiftly undercut by the city clocks, which echo and revise (darkly) the message of the Ludlow chimes, "The conquering hero comes":

> But all the clocks in the city
> > Began to whirr and chime:
> "O let not Time deceive you,
> > You cannot conquer Time."[58]

The clocks do not concur but interrupt and contradict. They no longer declare the hero a victor over death but, instead, assert time as the ultimate conqueror. To Ben Glaser's ear, the "cloying and self-referential rhyme of 'chime' and 'time'" reinforce an uncomfortable truth, unlike the dissonant slant rhymes of the lover's discourse ("I heard a lover sing" and "Love has no ending"), which indicate an untruth.[59] While the allusion seems to perform a double shift, from patriotism to romance and from optimism to pessimism, Auden believes himself to be clarifying hidden sentiments in Housman, not quibbling with his predecessor.

Housman's love poems are haunted by time and acknowledge its destruction as inevitable. In *A Shropshire Lad, XXIV*, the speaker urges a young man to lie with him ("Say, lad, have you things to do? / Quick then, while your day's at prime") because he is painfully aware of his own mortality and the narrowing window of opportunity that he faces:

> Use me ere they lay me low,
> > Where a man's no use at all;
> Ere the wholesome flesh decay.

Housman also had a habit of using a public voice to celebrate hand-some, youthful male figures while lamenting their vulnerability to time. "To an Athlete Dying Young" is one example. There Housman speaks through a third-person plural to remember a young man's athletic prowess after his death and attempt to restore his life and youth in verse:

> And round that early-laurelled head
> Will flock to gaze the strengthless dead,
> And find unwithered on its curls
> The garland briefer than a girl's.[60]

By alluding to "The Recruit" then, Auden felt that he was drawing out the latent homoeroticism in Housman's depictions of the soldier, and the melancholy that ran through the *Shropshire* poet's thinking on desire. While "As I Walked Out One Evening" seems to contradict what "The Recruit" explicitly states, in fact, Auden remains true to the spirit of Housman's poetry. And as in "Funeral Blues," he declines to expose Housman entirely. His predecessor still retains a degree of privacy via, and in spite of, the allusion.

Considering the affection that Auden felt for Housman from youth, it is fitting that he acknowledged the *Shropshire* poet in one of his last poems, written in 1971, two years before his death. Fitting, too, that the poem he chose for his allusion was the penultimate piece in *Last Poems* (1922), the final collection that Housman released in his lifetime, so that the end point of Auden's writing career intersects with the end of Housman's own.

Auden's "Short Ode to the Cuckoo" does not name Housman explicitly, but it does evoke the poet through an allusion to the cuckoo in *Last Poems XL*. The speaker of Housman's poem is wandering through a forest when he overhears the bird sing:

> On russet floors, by waters idle,
>   The pine lets fall its cone;
> The cuckoo shouts all day at nothing
>   In leafy dells alone;

> And traveller's joy beguiles in autumn
> Hearts that have lost their own.

It is a scene of profound loneliness. Unlike the birds of Romantic poetry, the cuckoo has nothing to communicate to the poet, nor to another audience. It "shouts all day at nothing" and stands "alone." The traveler, and implicitly the poet, recognizes the bird's isolation and appreciates it as a mirror held up to their own solitude. But the cuckoo does not offer companionship or solace from melancholy. The verb *beguile* does indicate that the traveler derives joy from the cuckoo's song, but it also implies that the joy is deceptive. The final stanza elaborates why that would be the case:

> For nature, heartless, witless nature,
>   Will neither care nor know
> What stranger's feet may find the meadow
>   And trespass there and go,
> Nor ask amid the dews of morning
>   If they are mine or no.[61]

Nature cannot bring comfort because nature does not care who traverses it and for what reason. The environment, to Housman's mind, does not answer to human concerns, so the person who seeks to find a refuge from their loneliness in its midst is bound to be disappointed. As Peter E. Firchow has put it, the poem works through a series of disenchantments: "Russet floors and idle waters suggest peace, but the falling cone strikes a subtly discordant note; the cuckoo's shouting seems cheerful until we learn that it is entirely solipsistic; the traveler's joy (a flower) proffers delight, but only to those who are broken-hearted."[62] The "traveller" finds himself a "stranger" by the poem's end.

Auden's "Short Ode to the Cuckoo" begins with a stanza that echoes the language and ideas of Housman's poem:

> No one now imagines you answer idle questions
> —*How long shall I live? How long remain single?*

Will butter be cheaper?—nor does your shout make
husbands uneasy.[63]

John Fuller rightly identifies the verb *shout* as an allusion to Housman.[64]
Auden also carries over *idle*, though the word now serves to describe the
"questions" asked by passersby, rather than the waters by russet floors.
The change is appropriate, as it reinforces the idea that nature has no
truck with human concerns. As the poem continues, Auden prompts two
further transformations. The first is to turn the cuckoo into a stand-in for
Housman himself.

> Compared with arias by the great performers
> such as the merle, your two-note act is kid-stuff:
> our most hardened crooks are sincerely shocked by
> your nesting habits.

> Science, Aesthetics, Ethics, may huff and puff but they
> cannot extinguish your magic: you marvel
> the commuter as you wondered the savage.
> Hence, in my diary,

> where I normally enter nothing but social
> engagements and, lately, the death of friends, I
> scribble year after year when I first hear you,
> of a holy moment.[65]

The reader who picks up on the allusions to *shout* and *idle* is likely to find
parallels between the cuckoo's song and the description of Housman's
poetry by Auden and others.

Housman is known as the author of minor songs, "two-note acts" and
"kid-stuff"—a marked contrast to the "arias by the great performers."
Auden's language might read as a callous verdict, embarrassing Housman
for the immaturity of his style and sensibility. Moreover, these phrases
recall similar statements in Auden's prose: "a poet of adolescence," "a

minor poet," "the range of theme and emotion is narrow," "the poems show no development over the years," expressing "the sensibility of a male adolescent." But the prose also allowed for earnest praise of what Housman gave to him and other adolescents: "If I do not turn to him very often, I am eternally grateful to him for the joy he gave me in my youth." Similarly, in "Short Ode to the Cuckoo," Auden insists that the bird's performances are "magic," even as they may seem minor on a purely aesthetic scale. The poet's attachment is deeply personal in nature, beyond principle and criteria, so that the periodic reminder of the cuckoo's song becomes "a holy moment." The final phrase is solemn—a direct counter to the cringing charge of adolescence—and it matches the seriousness of the "eternal" gratitude expressed by Auden in his prose. While the cuckoo could not serve as a true friend to Housman, the *Shropshire* poet's verse can provide a form of companionship to Auden—as it did. Housman's "stranger" achieves a final transformation here into a "commuter": no longer lost or alienated but moving between two familiar places, assured of a home that he can return to in the end.

The long history of queer allusions to *A Shropshire Lad* reveals a persistent concern with issues of privacy and shame. Housman never publicly admitted the truth of his sexuality. Instead, he found in poetry a medium through which to explore desires, pains, and loves that he could not voice off the page. The figures of pastoral and romantic poetry (the soldier and the shepherd lad, among others) became vectors for these secret passions, while the ambiguities of the lyric voice supplied him with a useful disguise. Later gay poets found in Housman a host of coded queer expressions that they could take pleasure in deciphering. At the same time, they also detected in his work a profound sense of shame over his sexuality and tried to assuage that shame in their own writing. Allusion enabled these poets to reframe Housman's language and draw out the queerness that he kept buried, without discoursing on his sexuality or exposing him in terms that he would have disliked. For example, Wilde imagined a community of outsiders who could provide each other with companionship in the face of social judgment. Cullen repurposed the language of Housman's advice poems to speak of, and for, racial pride. Finally, Auden reinforced the gay subtext of his poems but without naming Housman or making explicit claims about his sexual life. All three of these examples demonstrate a deep feeling of gratitude to the *Shropshire* poet for what he gave them, a desire to give back by drawing him further out of hiding but also respect for what Housman felt he could not express.

FIVE

Walt Whitman's
Leaves of Grass
(1855–1892)

It has often been said that Walt Whitman matters in the history of queer poetry for his praise of same-sex camaraderie and his celebration of physical and emotional connection beyond the limits of heterosexual marriage. Yet the allusions that subsequent queer poets have made to *Leaves of Grass* tell a different story. For many LGBTQ writers, Whitman stood as a figure of queer loneliness in a hostile society. When these writers borrow passages from "Song of Myself" and "Calamus Poems," they typically focus on moments of alienation and unfulfilled longing. And when they apostrophize Whitman himself, he usually appears alone—at times admirably stoic, at other times strangely pitiful. By claiming him as a predecessor, LGBTQ poets have sought a temporary refuge from their own loneliness. For them, Whitman provided not the promise of a bustling American democracy but something far more personal: a shared experience of queer loneliness.

If Whitman's significance to later LGBTQ authors has been overlooked, it is likely because critics have focused so much of their attention on whether or not Whitman can even be understood as a queer writer. Some scholars and biographers, borrowing from Foucault, have framed the male bonding in Whitman's poetry not as coded depictions of gay love but as evidence of the relaxed attitude toward same-sex intimacy, permissible in a world that did not yet view sexuality in terms of identity. David S. Reynolds, for example, desexualizes Whitman's "relations with men" by describing them as a variation on the dominant culture, or "an especially intense manifestations of the kind of same-sex passion that was seen everywhere in antebellum America." For Reynolds, the early de-cades of the nineteenth century offered a paradise of platonic love among men and women: "In the free, easy social atmosphere of pre–Civil War America, overt displays of affection between people of the same sex were common. Women hugged, kissed, slept with, and proclaimed love for other women. Men did the same with other men."[1] Still, the prevalence of platonic same-sex touch cannot disprove that Whitman's affections for other men were often sexual or romantic in nature. As Jerome Loving says, even though there "existed in Whitman's day a romantic or senti-mental convention of male friendship," one that even "permitted same-sex touching and common sleeping arrangements," the poet's relations with other men went beyond those cultural boundaries. Rather, "America was still publicly naïve about, and not so fearful, of homosexuality," allowing the poet to "get away with it."[2]

Even as some tried to historicize the homosexuality out of Whitman, others got to work snooping into the history of the poet's same-sex rela-tions. The efforts to document his partners and his preferences have been exhaustive, dating back to Malcolm Cowley's article "Walt Whitman: The Secret" for the *New Republic* in 1946: "It would seem from Whitman's notebooks and letters that he played the female role in these relationships; and that he was particularly attracted by young men in the transportation industry: by ferry deck-hands, Broadway omnibus drivers, horse-car con-ductors, railway brakemen, and firemen."[3] Cowley's diagnosis is precise, clinical, even as its motivation lies within the shadowy regions of gossip. Fifty years later, in *Walt Whitman: A Gay Life* (1997), Gary Schmid-gall told a more sympathetic story of Whitman's relationships with Fred Vaughn, Peter Doyle, and Harry Stafford.[4] Jonathan Ned Katz followed Schmidgall's lead in *Love Stories: Sex Between Men Before Homosexuality* (2001), devoting several chapters to the poet's love affairs. In tandem with these biographical outings, some critics have positioned Whitman definitively as a queer author. The first was Robert K. Martin, who, in *The Homosexual Tradition in American Poetry* (1979), accused previous critics of erasing Whitman's sexuality because they could not accept the notion that such a pivotal American poet might be gay: "Although Whitman intended his work to communicate his homosexuality to his readers, and although homosexual readers have from the very beginning understood his homosexual meanings, most critics have not been willing to take Whitman at his word . . . The record of lies, half truths, and distortions is so shameful as to amount to a deliberate attempt to alter reality to suit a particular view of normality. If Whitman is to be a great poet, he must be straight."[5] The most comprehensive attempt to theorize homosexuality as integral to Whitman's writing came with Bryan Fone's *Masculine Landscapes: Walt Whitman and the Homoerotic Text* (1992). By setting aside biographical details related to Whitman's sexual encounters, Fone zeroed in on *Leaves of Grass* and what he called the "discourse of homosexual desire and identity within the confines of that text we call Whitman."[6] The shift in scholarship of the 1990s to exclude biography in favor of a total focus on "the text" (here broadly defined as the poet's entire oeuvre) proved useful for queer readings of Whitman because it allowed critics to bypass Foucault's still-influential argument that homosexuality did not exist before the end of the nineteenth century.

Central to many queer readings of *Leaves of Grass* is Whitman's notion, expressed across both poetry and prose, that there exists a direct link between male camaraderie, sexuality, and nationhood. In a footnote to *Democratic Vistas* (1871), Whitman identifies same-sex bonding as an antidote to the materialism and egotism of American society: "It is to the development, identification, and general prevalence of that fervid comradeship, (the adhesive love, at least rivaling the amative love hitherto possessing imaginative literature, if not going beyond it,) that I look for the counterbalance and offset of our materialistic and vulgar American democracy, and for the spiritualization thereof."[7] Critics have argued over the degree to which "adhesive love" can be read as a veiled reference to homosexuality. For Paul Zweig, the concept neutralizes "the drama of sexual love" by diminishing it into "the more innocuous love of comrades." More generously, M. Jimmie Killingsworth describes the notion as "Whitman's attempt to incorporate the middle-class ideal of camaraderie into a more radical vision of a democratic society based on homoerotic love." To me, the drama of this sentence lies in its peculiar shifts between directness and evasion. The term *adhesive love*, tucked away in parentheses as if it could be simply taken out, reads as bolder and yet also more timid than *fervid comradeship*. At first glance, *adhesive* lacks the passion of *fervid*. It may even sound, to quote Zweig, "strangely bloodless and philosophical."[8] But love admits to a much stronger bond than *comradeship*, which by contrast only tells part of the story. Together, the two phrases perform a delicate dance, evoking the amicable same-sex affection that was socially acceptable in Whitman's era while raising the possibility of sexual and romantic unions that go well beyond it. The double move suggests that though Whitman may have wished to push back against the conventions of his time, he also recognized the limits of his culture's tolerance for love between men. As described in *Democratic Vistas* and elsewhere, *adhesive love* was discreet enough not to raise suspicion but clear enough for sympathetic parties to recognize its full meaning and see themselves reflected in it.

Certainly, intimate same-sex friendships were common in the United States throughout the nineteenth century. Men and women could express passionate affection for their close friends of the same sex, embrace them, and even in some circumstances (such as mining towns, cowboy towns, or single-sex schools) share a bed without raising suspicion that the relationship was sexual. This would change in the 1880s, as doctors began to conceptualize *heterosexuality* and *homosexuality* and to stigmatize the latter. Yet prior to that decade, close same-sex friendships were viewed as "pure" and so actively encouraged and celebrated. At the same time, the nineteenth-century view of friendship supplied a useful cover for a range of sexual affairs. For example, there is a record from 1846 of two men who met at a church in New York City and then lived together in a boardinghouse for several months, enjoying "carnal intercourse" every night.[9] During this period, such a cohabitation would have been unlikely to raise eyebrows.

Whitman had no substantial romantic involvement with a woman in his life; all his closest connections were with men. Granted, one could frame the passionate language that he used to speak about these men, and the physical intimacy that he enjoyed with them, as evidence of friendship, not romantic or sexual partnership. When Whitman first published *Leaves of Grass* in 1855, he would not have conceived of himself as homosexual (a term yet to be invented), nor would he have thought of himself as having a distinct sexual identity founded on attraction to a specific gender. Still, the biographical record does suggest that at least some of his connections to other men likely took on a romantic and sexual dimension. When Whitman worked as a nurse at the Armory Square Hospital in 1863, he grew close to a young soldier named Lewy Bron, whom he would bathe, kiss, and call "my darling."[10] John Burroughs, after meeting the poet in 1864, reported: "He kissed me as if I were a girl . . . He bathed today while I was there—such a handsome body, and such delicate, rosy flesh I never saw before. I told him he looked good enough to eat."[11] Most touchingly, perhaps, is Peter Doyle's account in 1865 of climbing into a carriage next to Whitman: "We were familiar at once—I put my hand on his knee—we understood. He did not get out at the end of the trip—in fact went all the way back with me."[12]

For all the critical hand-wringing over Whitman's place in the history of sexuality, LGBTQ poets have not hesitated to embrace him as a precursor; many have paid homage to him through allusion. Whitman's afterlife in queer poetry is a subject that remains underexplored, particularly as the allusions to *Leaves of Grass* display a surprising pattern. One might expect gay poets (and readers) to gravitate to Whitman for his concept of adhesive love. C. K. Williams assumes as much when he writes that "Whitman devised a heartening rhetoric of acceptance and defiance for generations of gay men, and gay women."[13] Certainly, a few writers have borrowed from *Leaves of Grass* to envision the possibility of queer communities. Oscar Wilde is one example and the first case study that I will consider here. But many more have viewed Whitman as a figure of queer loneliness—feeling out of place in society, needing to hide oneself, and fearing that love will remain elusive. Poets who detected this strain in *Leaves of Grass* echoed lines that evoke longing and solitude. The pattern is evident in the most famous homages to Whitman in the twentieth century, by Hart Crane and Allen Ginsberg, even as the commentaries on these poems have largely ignored it. Fittingly, the allusions also shed new light on Whitman, who is typically discussed as a poet of universal connection and only rarely thought of as a writer of loneliness.[14] For many queer poets, alluding to *Leaves of Grass* afforded them a brief reprieve from solitude. In Whitman, they could find an antecedent to their own experience of loneliness, a transhistorical connection. This does not mean that they succumbed to the illusion that his poetry would have the power to cure their isolation entirely. The relief they enjoyed could only be transient and imaginary. But it did not lack substance.

The meeting of Oscar Wilde and Walt Whitman in 1882 has become a well-known event in literary history, retold by several critics and biographers throughout the twentieth century. The force of this story lies in the importance of each author to their respective national literatures as well as the clear differences in their style and themes. Wilde's ornate metrical verse, devoted to mythical, heroic, and pastoral subjects, diverges from Whitman's bold, loose free verse describing scenes of contemporary life and celebrating the self. The thought of their meeting seems incongruous. True, Wilde and Whitman are not entirely opposed, as several critics have pointed out. Gary Schmidgall finds in both a "constant tension and tug-of-war between self-revelation and concealment, the self-protective instinct to remain in the Closet and the self-assertive liberating urge to leave it."[15] Juan A. Hererro Brasas, while conceding that Wilde's love for the "exquisiteness of the English aristocracy" seems far removed from Whitman's ideal of "the rough, sensual American," argues that they both devoted themselves to a "rebellion against the established order."[16] Still, far more divides them than unites them in terms of style and sensibility. The differences between them have dissuaded critics from seeking out allusions, despite the admiration that they expressed for one another's work. Yet Wilde did echo Whitman in his poem "The Burden of Itys," and the references there are notable in that they represent a rare case of a poet alluding to Whitman to envision a queer community. (Later allusions by others proved far more melancholic.) It matters that Wilde published "The Burden of Itys" a year before he met Whitman, as the chronology indicates that whatever hope or optimism Whitman's poetry inspired in him dissipated after their conversation. Moreover, the biographical record suggests that his regret had something to do with a recognition of loneliness in Whitman: the feature of his life and his poetry that would preoccupy queer poets after Wilde.

First, the story as it is often told. In December 1881, Wilde embarked on an eighteen-month lecture tour through the United States. He was eager to meet Whitman, whose verse he had admired since the age of eleven, when he read passages from *Leaves of Grass* with his mother. As an adult, he had become especially drawn to Whitman's notion of male comradeship as a vector for spiritual and sensual fulfillment.[17] The publisher J. M. Stoddart proposed that the two take a carriage ride through Philadelphia. Eager to promote the encounter, Whitman suggested, instead, that the writers meet at a photographer's studio. The meeting proved sufficiently pleasant that he hosted Wilde at his Camden house for a longer conversation over elderberry wine on January 18, 1882. There Wilde expressed his deep love for *Leaves of Grass,* noting that his mother had bought him a copy when he was a young boy. As their meeting ended, Whitman gave Wilde his artistic blessing, despite their differences in style: "You are young and ardent, and the field is wide . . . I say 'go ahead.'"[18] Mindful of publicity, Wilde praised his American counterpart during interviews later that month. In the pages of the *Boston Herald* on January 29, he said of Whitman: "I spent the most charming day I have spent in America with him. He is the grandest man I have ever seen. The simplest, most natural, and strongest character I have ever met in my life. I regard him as one of those wonderful, large, entire men who might have lived in any age and is not peculiar to any one people." Then, on the same day in the *Boston Globe:* "Of all your authors, I consider Walt Whitman far the grandest and noblest. Many of his lines are like a blast fresh from Olympus. I have met him and enjoyed his society more than words can express."[19] Whitman shared his own enthusiasm for Wilde in a letter to Harry Stafford after their first meeting: "Have you read about Oscar Wilde? . . . He is a fine large handsome youngster—and had the *good sense* to take a fancy to *me!*"[20] Whitman's playful joke, aimed at his own pride, even contained the hint of a possible flirtation between the two men. Tellingly, his public commentary on the meeting showed eagerness to downplay the fellow writer's perceived effeminacy, fearful that it might taint his own perception. Speaking to a reporter for the *Philadelphia Press*, Whitman praised Wilde as "genuine, honest, manly . . . so frank and outspoken and manly." Gary Schmidgall rightly notes that "the insistence on 'manly' is suspicious," indicating that he wished to "counter the wave of American journalistic satire on the Irishman's effeminate dress, body language, and expertise in interior decoration."[21] The repeated emphasis on Wilde's masculinity betrays some anxiety about being associated with, and thus tainted by, the Irish author's disruption of gender norms.

It is unclear if Wilde read the piece in the *Philadelphia Press*. Both poets did speak more coolly of each other in the years that followed. In 1888, Whitman wrote to his biographer Horace Traubel that he regretted a lack of substance behind Wilde's style: "I never completely make Wilde out—out for good or bad. He writes exquisitely—is as lucid as a star on a clear night—but there seems to be a little substance lacking at the root—something—what is it?" Then a few weeks later: "Wilde . . . may have been some of him fraud at the same, but he was not all fraud . . . He has extraordinary brilliancy of genius with perhaps rather too little root in eternal soils. Wilde gives up too much to the extrinsic decorative values in art."[22] The following year, in an article for the *Pall Mall Gazette*, Wilde delivered a reserved verdict on Whitman's own poetry: "He stands apart, and the chief value of his work is in its prophecy, not in its performance. He has begun a prelude to larger themes. He is the herald to a new era. As a man he is the precursor of a fresh type. He is a factor in the heroic and spiritual evolution of the human being. If Poetry has passed him by, Philosophy will take note of him."[23] It may begin with praise, yet Wilde's assessment settles on a stinging criticism: in effect, the reverse of Whitman's own assessment. If Whitman felt that Wilde devoted himself too completely to style, to the detriment of philosophy, Wilde believed that Whitman put too much stock in ideas and so would be remembered as a philosopher rather than an artist. Gone, now, was the excitement that had immediately followed their meeting.

The curious thing about Wilde's critique is that his allusions to Whitman in poetry, written before the lecture tour through America, showed interest in Whitman's ideas as well as his language. He especially tended to gravitate toward "Calamus Poems," a poem that praised male comradeship in erotic terms. Whitman's language allowed Wilde, in "The Burden of Itys," to imagine a paradisical landscape where same-sex affection might express itself freely. That vision must have particularly appealed to Wilde at this stage in his self-development. When *Poems* appeared in 1881, Wilde had been conscious of his sexual inclinations for some time, though he had yet to explore them or to identify himself as a homosexual. For example, the French poet André Raffalovich reported that while at Oxford in the late 1870s, Wilde "boasted of having as much pleasure in talking about the subject of homosexuality as others in practicing it." He would not engage in his first affair with another man until Robbie Ross in 1886. The poems collected in 1881, and their revision history, show Wilde testing the degree to which he wished to be open about his same-sex attraction. At times, he seemed eager to disguise the queer inspiration for his poetry. He took lines that he had first published in *Kottabos* in 1877, describing a beautiful boy at rest:

> A fair slim boy not made for this world's pain,
>   With hair of gold thick clustering round his ears
>
> . . . .
>
> Pale cheeks whereon no kiss hath left its stain,
>   Red under-lip drawn in for fear of Love,
>   And white throat whiter than the breast of dove—

And revised these in 1881 to describe a beautiful woman, retitling the poem "Madonna Mia":

> A Lily-girl, not made for this world's pain,
>   With brown, soft hair close braided by her ears
>
> . . . .

> Pale cheeks whereon no love hath left its stain,
>> Red underlip drawn in for fear of love,
>> And white throat, whiter than the silvered dove—

But he revised other poems to draw out their homoeroticism. When "Vita Nuova" first appeared, in *Irish Monthly* in 1877, the poem described Christ in euphemistic terms commonly employed by gay men:

> When lo! a sudden brightness! and I saw
>> Christ walking on the waters! fear was past;
>> I knew that I had found my Perfect Friend.

In *Poems,* however, Christ gives way to a beautiful, male, and pagan body:

> When lo! a sudden glory! and I saw
>> The argent splendour of white limbs ascend,
>> And in that joy forget my tortured past.[24]

The allusions to Whitman were part of Wilde's self-exploration and his attempt to draw his desires further into the light, without exposing them entirely.

Fittingly, the passage that Wilde draws from in "Calamus" finds Whitman reflecting on how he will be remembered in the future and envisioning (discreetly) a queer audience:

> No labor-saving machine,
> Nor discovery have I made,
> Nor will I be able to leave behind me any wealthy bequest to found a hospital or library,
> Nor reminiscence of any deed of courage for America,
> Nor literary success nor intellect, nor book for the book-shelf,
> But a few carols vibrating through the air I leave,
> For comrades and lovers.[25]

Whitman writes that his true legacy will take the form of songs, which live in performance and can be taken up by a variety of voices. He hopes that *Leaves of Grass* will survive not as a physical book, for books must degrade over time, but as lines which can be recalled and recited for pleasure. The poet shows an unusual degree of modesty in this projection, insisting that he will not be celebrated for any inventions, discoveries, bequests, courageous acts, or literary successes. Even the word that he chooses to evoke his poems, *carols,* is notably small. His music will matter less to society and more to the individuals who find themselves moved by his lyrics. But Whitman also indicates that the songs will serve a communal purpose. By omitting the word *my* in the line "For comrades and lovers," he suggests that his songs are dedicated not to those whom he knew personally but to all who may see themselves reflected in his language. The music that he bequeaths will bring his comrades and lovers together again. The phrasing opens up the possibility that "comrades and lovers" does not refer to two distinct groups: the sympathetic listeners imagined here might be both to one another, or they may have gradually transitioned from friends to lovers. While the ambiguity is subtle, it does leave space for Whitman's poetry to have special significance for a queer audience, which will find its bonds strengthened through songs such as these.

Whitman's rolling negations—accompanied by *book, comrade,* and *lover*—make their way into the lines of Wilde's "The Burden of Itys":

> Here is no cruel Lord with murderous blade,
>   No woven web of bloody heraldries,
> But mossy dells for roving comrades made,
>   Warm valleys where the tired student lies
> With half-shut book, and many a winding walk
> Where rustic lovers stray at eve in happy simple talk.[26]

Similar to Whitman's "book for the book-shelf," forgotten to time, the only volume here remains unread, or, rather, "half-shut." To be sure, the world that surrounds it looks far too pleasant for a book to rouse much

interest. The student is content to lie, the comrades to rove, and the lovers to sleep. Even though these "roving comrades" and "rustic lovers"
do not appear together, the poet still connects them across three lines.
While the student lies alone and motionless, the comrades and lovers drift
both in groups and in motion. They also bookend the student and receive
additional emphasis from the grammar of the sentence. Importantly for
us, Wilde preserves the ambiguity of their gender. While a heterosexual
reader at this time would likely assume that the lovers are male and female, the text does not exclude the possibility that they might be of the
same sex. Wilde's queer readers, particularly those familiar with "Calamus Poems," would be alert to this option.

In sum, this stanza imagines a landscape where all might be welcome
and where queerness might possibly express itself in the open. The people
in this imaginary world enjoy total safety. The student, the lovers, and the
comrades are protected from the "bloody heraldries" of war as well as
the "cruel Lord with murderous blade." That lord could refer to someone
of a high social standing, but it could also refer to a god. If so, then the
valley offers safety from divine punishment and the religious institution
that claims to work in God's name. Two men in love would certainly find
relief in a valley far from the judgment of organized religion.

By alluding to "Calamus Poems," Wilde credits Whitman for making
this world, and its imagining, possible. The gender of the comrades and
the lovers matters so little that it need not even be noted. Wilde discovered
in *Leaves of Grass* the language to envision a place where same-sex love
might flourish openly without fear of violence. Whitman's readers are
unlikely to be surprised by what Wilde found in *Leaves of Grass*. Whitman
is traditionally thought of as a poet who celebrated human connection and
"Calamus Poems" as the sequence that advocated for homoerotic bonds as
a national good. Wilde's private remarks after meeting Whitman indicate
a shift in his understanding of Whitman's outlook and significance. As
Michèle Mendelssohn relates in her biography of Wilde:

> Meeting Whitman had stirred him deeply. When he felt Whitman's side
> and climbed into the carriage waiting outside the door at 431 Stevens

Street, the publisher J. M. Stoddart observed that he seemed a changed man. Profoundly moved by Whitman's example, Wilde sank into a meditative silence, breaking it only occasionally to speak of the old poet's grandeur, "his struggles and triumphs." Ten days later, the spell remained unbroken. His face glowed enthusiastically as he talked to an interviewer about the author of "Song of Myself." Yet his gushing ended with an ominous offhand remark. "Probably he is dreadfully misunderstood," Wilde said, "He only wants one thing, to be understood."

Before meeting Whitman, Wilde had been drawn to his work for its vision of queer community, and he had paid homage to that vision in his own poem "The Burden of Itys." Upon meeting Whitman, however, Wilde found himself struck by the poet's loneliness. Whitman was, to his mind, "dreadfully misunderstood" and only wishing "one thing, to be understood." That repeated word comes across as gently evasive: with "understanding" comes a sense of connection to others, affection, friendship, and love. By being "misunderstood," Whitman stands alone. The fact that Wilde felt so perturbed by the realization suggests that he may have seen something of himself, or of a future that he feared, in Whitman's isolation. The meeting ultimately belied what the poetry had promised, what it had meant to him.

The turn in Wilde's thinking anticipates how later gay authors responded to *Leaves of Grass*, specifically Hart Crane and Allen Ginsberg, perhaps his most well-known devotees. Far from seeing Whitman as a poet of connection, Crane and Ginsberg detected a profound sense of loneliness in his language. By alluding to *Leaves of Grass*, they sought to bring that emotion to light; to reflect on how the fear of isolation haunts the queer experience; and to test how poetry might offer a virtual point of contact for queer writers and readers.

Like Wilde, Hart Crane distinguished between Whitman's "Poetry" and his "Philosophy." But his evaluation in the essay "Modern Poetry" was far less mixed than Wilde: "The most typical and valid expression of the American psychosis seems to me still to be found in Whitman. His faults as a technician and his clumsy and indiscriminate enthusiasm are somewhat beside the point. He, better than any other, was able to coordinate those forces in America which seem most intractable, fusing them into a universal vision which takes on additional significance as time goes on. He was a revolutionist beyond the strict meaning of Coleridge's definition of genius, but his bequest is still to be realized in all its implications."[27] The flaws in Whitman's verse could be simply dismissed as minor problems of technique and mood. His achievements went far beyond what most would term "content." Whitman captured the "American psychosis" in its entirety. His brand of "revolution" made Coleridge's definition "limited" by contrast. Echoing Wilde (perhaps unknowingly), Crane looks to the future for Whitman's legacy. But Wilde described Whitman as a "herald," a "prelude," and a "precursor"—not the main event. When Crane writes that "his bequest is still to be realized in all its implications," the word *bequest* suggests that what his work did achieve was a degree of completeness and that those who came after were following his example.

Crane made no secret of Whitman's influence on his work. *The Bridge*, in particular, combines discreet allusions to Whitman with direct apostrophes, so that the poet appears, to borrow Warner Berthoff's language, "a solicited elder presence."[28] Early reviewers criticized the explicitness of his homages. Yvor Winters condemned the attitude in "Cape Hatteras" as "desperately sentimental," arguing that it revealed "the impossibility of getting anywhere with the Whitmanian inspiration." Winters deemed the book's failures so serious that Crane should serve as a warning to others: "No writer of comparable ability has struggled with [the debt to Whitman] before, and, with Mr. Crane's wreckage in view, it seems highly unlikely that any writer of comparable genius will struggle with it again."[29] Allen Tate identified the same problem in *The Bridge* and traced it back to Whitman as well: "When he philosophizes explicitly in his verse, the doctrine is a sentimental muddle of Walt Whitman and the pseudoprimitivism of Sherwood Anderson and Dr. W. C. Williams, raised to a vague and transcendental reality."[30] Granted, other names appear besides that of Whitman, but in a private letter to Crane written after the review's publication, Tate focused exclusively on the author of *Leaves of Grass:*

> I too felt that your tribute to Whitman was, while not excessive, certainly sentimental in places, particularly at the end of Cape Hatteras. But more than this I could not say except that in some larger and vaguer sense your vision of American life comes from Whitman, or from the same sources in the American consciousness as his. I am unsympathetic to this tradition, and it seems to me that you should be too. The equivalent of Whitmanism in the economic and moral aspect of America in the last sixty years is the high-powered industrialism that you, no less than I, feel is a menace to the spiritual life in this country. In the end, this is all I can see in him; though he did write some great poetry.[31]

Tate does not make it clear what aspect of Whitman's poetry struck him as an "equivalent" to "the high-powered industrialism" that he found so repulsive in America. He does, however, make it clear that Crane devoted himself too simplistically to Whitman and placed him on too high a pedestal.[32]

   This criticism stems from an aesthetic preference for irony and detachment, both hallmarks of modernist writing, and a rejection of "sentimentality," viewed as a simplistic, simpering attitude. Crane's allusions certainly express admiration and gratitude for Whitman as well as enthusiasm for his ideas about the social and spiritual force of homoerotic bonds, as Robert Martin and Catherine Davies have both pointed out.[33] Yet he hardly grovels. At most, Crane's poems betray a fear that he would eventually follow in Whitman's solitary footsteps. Paul Mariani describes the poet's "feeling of isolation, leading a double life as a gay poet: the brief encounter, the early morning departure with the other calling out the lover's name, the pain that followed each fated separation."[34] Thomas E. Yingling writes that "the ravages of time and alienation" had left Crane "bitterly and alcoholically alone by the age of thirty,"[35] a year before the

publication of *The Bridge*. Whitman functioned both as a virtual companion, whose loneliness he identified with, and an emblem of how he feared
he would end up.

Crane's experience of sexuality throughout his life was marked by
a tension between intense joy and profound loneliness. He frequently
sought out anonymous tricks in parks and docks, sailors holding a special
appeal for him. To a degree, the cruising spots of the cities he inhabited
during the 1920s (Akron, Cleveland, Washington, New York) gave him a
sense of a wider gay community. Per Clive Fisher, such places confirmed
that "those who shared his sexual interest, in his adolescence a guilty and
isolating secret, constituted a clandestine brotherhood apparently represented in every city."[36] Occasionally, Crane's hookups developed into
brief affairs for the span of several days or weeks. His longest and deepest
relationship was with Emil Opffer, a Danish merchant-marine whom he
met in 1924.[37] But Emil was so often at sea that the two saw each other
only for short periods.

In his correspondence, Crane described love and sex in Whitmanian
terms, framing deep physical pleasure as a form of spiritual ecstasy. In
1921, he wrote of a truck driver who had moved into his apartment in
religious terms: "I believe in, or have found God again . . . Of course
it is the return of devotion which astounds me . . . I have so much now
to reverence, discovering more and more beauty every day,—beauty of
character, manner, and body, that I am for the time, completely changed."
At times, pleasure proved so forceful as to become its opposite. In 1923, he
confessed that glances exchanged with a handsome stranger at a concert
provoked such a "stirring response" within him that he suffered "an hour
of agony as I supposed I was beyond feeling ever again." At its best, sex
had the power not just to connect him to others but also to expand his
own sense of self and widen his conception of love. In 1926, he wrote
after meeting a sailor in Havana, "I have learned much about love which
I did not know existed."[38]

At the same time, sex held such importance to Crane that he feared
disappointment. He saw it as inevitable that one day he would no longer
be able to reach the same highs that he had enjoyed previously. As he

wrote in 1922, following a passionate hookup: "As this happened only two nights ago, I am modest and satisfied. Still, I am uneasy. I fear for all the anti-climaxes that are surely now in store for me." Because he viewed sex as an expansion of the self, he dreaded the day that he would reach the furthest limits of physical pleasure, with no more still to discover on the horizon: "I yearn for new worlds to conquer, and I fear that there are only a few insignificant peninsulas and archipelagoes left."[39]

Importantly for our discussion of Whitman, Crane was deeply aware of the ephemerality of his romantic connections. Crane's relationships were all temporary, from the anonymous encounters at cruising spots to his passing weekend-long love affairs and to his on-and-off again romance with Emil. His penchant for sailors was doubtless a contributing factor (as Clive Fisher puts it, "To love sailors is to love those who must leave"),[40] as was the difficulty of sustaining same-sex relationships in an intolerant society. But if solitude haunted Crane, he also worked hard to capture and honor the connections that did come his way: "The climax will be all too easily reached,—But my gratitude is enduring—if only for that once, at least, something beautiful approached me and as though it were the most natural thing in the world, enclosed me in his arm and pulled me to him without my slightest bid."[41]

Crane's biography shows us why *Leaves of Grass* resonated so deeply with his experience of sexuality. Crane's language echoes many of the elder poet's key ideas and emotions: the longing for camaraderie, the desire to expand oneself by connecting to others, and the loneliness that comes from recognizing love's ephemerality. It is revealing that when Whitman appears in *The Bridge,* he is described in terms of solitude. Crane saw in Whitman both a record of the loneliness that can haunt queer life as well as a virtual companion who could provide reassurance that he was neither the first nor the last to feel these emotions.

Crane's first apostrophe to Whitman, though it builds to a climactic praise, conveys a deep sense of melancholy. While many critics have quoted the following passage, they tend to ignore how Crane uses allusion to express his sympathy for—and fear of—the loneliness that he associated with Whitman:

"—Recorders ages hence"—ah, syllables of faith!
Walt, tell me, Walt Whitman, if infinity
Be still the same as when you walked the beach
Near Paumanok—your lone patrol—and heard the wraith
Through surf, its bird note there a long time falling . . .
For you, the panoramas and this breed of towers,
Of you—the theme that's statured in the cliff,
O Saunterer on free ways still ahead![42]

Crane quotes from a "Calamus" poem in which Whitman reflects on his legacy. Much like in the passage that Wilde evokes in "The Burden of Itys," Whitman argues that his true legacy will stem from emotion—how he expressed love to others—rather than from any creative accomplishment:

Recorders ages hence,
Come, I will take you down underneath this impassive exterior, I will
    tell you what to say of me,
Publish my name and hang up my picture as that of the tenderest lover,
The friend the lover's portrait, of whom his friend his lover was
    fondest,
Who was not proud of his songs, but of the measureless ocean of love
    within him, and freely pour'd it forth,
Who often walk'd lonesome walks thinking of his dear friends, his
    lovers,
Who pensive away from one he lov'd often lay sleepless and
    dissatisfied at night,
Who knew too well the sick, sick dread lest the one he lov'd might
    secretly be indifferent to him,
Whose happiest days were far away through fields, in woods, on hills,
    he and another wandering hand in hand, they twain apart from
    other men,
Who oft as he saunter'd the streets curv'd with his arm the shoulder of
    his friend, while the arm of his friend rested upon him also.[43]

The poem concludes with the image of two male "friends," most likely lovers, walking hand in hand. But these "happiest days" are a "far away" memory that have given way to "sleepless" nights alone or dreading a lover's indifference. He whiles away the time on "lonesome walks think-ing of his dear friends, his lovers," now gone. For all the connections that the lover has enjoyed throughout life, he cannot escape the melancholy of isolation. Tellingly, Crane alludes to the word *lonesome* after quoting from Whitman: "when you walked the beach / Near Paumanok—your lone patrol—and heard the wraith." *Lone* appears in a subordinate clause, yet the dashes only serve to reinforce it.

In sum, Crane identifies loneliness as the dominant emotion of Whit-man's life and poetry. Cannily, the word *lonesome* also echoes other pas-sages from *Leaves of Grass* that dwell on solitude, in particular the "lone-some" woman of section 11 who gazes desirously at young bathers from her window:

> Twenty-eight young men bathe by the shore,
> Twenty-eight young men and all so friendly;
> Twenty-eight years of womanly life and all so lonesome . . .
> Dancing and laughing along the beach came the twenty-ninth bather,
> The rest did not see her, but she saw them and loved them . . .
> An unseen hand also pass'd over their bodies,
> It descended trembling from their temples and ribs.[44]

Critics have picked up on the homoerotic nature of this passage, whereby Whitman displaces his desire for the young men onto a female observer.[45] Crane writes from the same assumption in "Cape Hatteras." This time, Whitman walks along the beach himself, the bathers having all departed. Crane imagines music that would have accompanied the young men danc-ing there previously: "The wraith / Through the surf, its bird note there a long time falling." Sadly, the song emanates from a solitary creature, eventually drowned out by the surf. Even as he deploys allusion to con-nect with his predecessor across time, Crane recognizes that the company he provides—and receives—can only be virtual and temporary. By evoking Whitman, he reflects on how the poet might have responded to the cityscape of New York now. He dedicates the scene to Whitman ("For you") and credits him with inventing a particular way of seeing the world, which now supplies the theme of Crane's poem ("Of you—the theme that's saturated in the cliff "). But the real impetus behind this passage is to bond with a poet whose loneliness he resonated with on such a profound level and to find some fleeting comfort through that imagined connection.

Crane's handling of apostrophe reflects the compromise that he feels he must accept. In "Calamus," Whitman addresses "recorders" in the future who will speak of his legacy: not friends, lovers, or comrades but the neutral judges of history. The poet thereby looks to a time when there will be no one left on earth with whom he shared a direct personal connection. In "Cape Hatteras," Crane begins by addressing his predecessor with a friendly, intimate "Walt," before retreating to the formality of a full name, "Walt Whitman," at the end of the line. The shift signals doubt about how much he can achieve by evoking the poet as well as an acknowledgment that he should not assume too much, since any connection he makes is bound to be imaginary and unrealized.

Crane's apostrophe strays from the major theories about this poetic device. Jonathan Culler views it as an "embarrassing" show of authorial egotism, a "pure embodiment of poetic pretension of the subject's claim that in his verse he is not merely an empirical poet, a writer of verse, but the embodiment of poetic tradition and of the spirit of poesy."[46] Likewise, Barbara Johnson reads the device as a bold act of reanimation: "The absent, dead, or inanimate entity addressed is . . . made present, animate, and anthropomorphic. Apostrophe is a form of ventriloquism through which the speaker throws voice, life, and human form into the addressee."[47] Neither model fits the sensibility of Crane's call. The awkward repetition and the shift from *Walt* to *Walt Whitman* prevent the poet from connecting with "the lineage and conventions of sublime poetry" and declaring himself "the embodiment of poetic tradition." The use of a full name distances him from both Whitman and the "spirit of poesy" he could have become. He may wish to summon Whitman back into a state of "mute responsiveness," but the sudden distancing serves as a reminder that the elder poet cannot, in fact, return—that Crane is calling into a void.

This insight explains the curious stumbling that occurs at the end of "Cape Hatteras," when Crane finally seems about to make contact with the poet that he so greatly admired:

> Not soon, nor suddenly,—no, never to let go
> My hand
> in yours,
> Walt Whitman—
> so—[48]

This passage, more than any other, has been used as proof of Crane's sentimentality or, by contrast, his hostility toward an influence that grew overbearing. But neither reading captures the complex melancholy of these final lines. On the one hand, Crane fulfills the longing expressed in "Recorders Ages Hence": "Whose happiest days were far away through fields, in woods, on hills, he and another wandering hand in hand, they twain apart from other men." Whitman's memory of a lost connection becomes actualized and present again in "Cape Hatteras." At the same time, Crane reminds us that such a reprieve from loneliness is only a passing fantasy. Had the poem ended on a period, the word *so* would have conveyed finality and evoked a permanent state of intimacy: *my hand in yours, just like so.* However, the dash indicates an unfinished sentence, suggesting that the speaker had been interrupted. In this reading, what follows the dash may be a continuation of the poets' intimacy or (more likely given the empty space that lies beyond the punctuation mark) its cessation. We are quite far from the realm of sentimentality here and just as far from the anxiety of influence.

In "Cape Hatteras," Crane expresses his profound desire for a queer connection. At the same time, he recognizes the limits of what he can achieve. Any contact with Whitman is bound to be virtual and transitory, in much the same way that the real connections he made with other gay men in his life turned out to be fleeting. Throughout his life, Crane suffered from a profound sense of loneliness, as brief moments of intimacy always gave way to the blankness of solitude. I do not mean to say that he found no value in connecting with Whitman through allusion; on the contrary, the intimacy that he experienced reading and writing through Whitman provided him with genuine nourishment. But he was also not so naive as to present literature as a permanent solution. Rather, Whitman helped Crane to get by, sometimes, through the difficulties of a lonely life.

Critics have long noted the influence of Whitman on Allen Ginsberg. Early reviews of *Howl and Other Poems* by Richard Eberhart, John Hollander, and M. L. Rosenthal all cited Whitman's name,[49] and for good reason, as Ginsberg's love for the poet extends far back. He first encountered *Leaves of Grass* in high school at the suggestion of his English teacher Miss Durbin. By the age of thirty, he was referring to Whitman as his "great personal Colossus of American poetry." A year before the release of *Howl*, he listed in his diary three aesthetic principles that he wished to follow, all derived from Whitman: "1) a spontaneous method of composition, 2) a long imaginative line, 3) using the immediate consciousness of the transcriber (or writer) as the subject of the poem."[50] More than a decade later, during the trial of the Chicago Seven in 1969, Ginsberg was pressed on his poem "Love Poem on a Theme by Whitman" as he was defending the anti–Vietnam War protesters charged with conspiracy. He praised Whitman as a "spiritual teacher"—one who had taught him how to celebrate sexuality, including and especially same-sex bonds, to counter the forces of materialism and capitalism:

> He said that unless there was an infusion of feeling, of tenderness, of fearlessness, of spirituality, of natural sexuality, of natural delight in each other's bodies, into the hardened materialistic, cynical, life denying, clearly competitive, afraid, scared, armored bodies, there would

be no chance for spiritual democracy to take root in America—and he defined that tenderness between the citizens as, in his words, adhesiveness, a natural tenderness flowing between men and men as part of our democratic heritage, part of the adhesiveness which would make the democracy function: that men could work together not as competitive beasts but as tender lovers and fellows.[51]

Ginsberg may seem to stray far from the issue of political protest, but he clearly felt it relevant to defend homosexuality as an asset to the nation, particularly amid a conspiracy trial. At a time when much homophobic messaging depicted queer people as agents of anarchy, Ginsberg held up same-sex bonds as "part of our democratic heritage, part of the adhesiveness which would make the democracy function." In a clever turn, homosexuality has become synonymous with patriotism.

Scholars have identified several broad parallels between the two poets, such as Ginsberg's use of prosaic lists and catalogs or his peculiar mix of "the sacred and the profane."[52] The pages that follow will consider not broad similarities such as these but concrete allusions, in pieces that echo language directly from Whitman ("Howl"), and that at times even name the poet explicitly ("Love Poem on a Theme by Whitman," "A Supermarket in California," and "Many Loves"). Ginsberg's references focus on passages in Whitman that describe intense pleasure and profound loneliness: twin emotions that defined how he experienced his sexuality. In an interview with Allen Young, he reflected on this complex sentiment: "When I was a sensitive, little kid, hiding, not able to touch anyone or speak my feelings out, little did I realize the enormous weight of love and numbers of lovers, the enormity of the scene I'd enter into, in which I finally wound up a public spokesman for homosexuality at one point."[53] While he does find pleasure in the sheer range of loves and lovers, his tone betrays an undercurrent of pain, a sense of alienation from the faceless many who also brought him comfort. The word *enormity* suggests a burden, not boundless possibility. Ginsberg's account evokes the following lines from *Leaves of Grass:*

My lovers suffocate me,
Crowding my lips, thick in the pores of my skin,
Jostling me through streets and public halls, coming naked to me at
    night.[54]

The poems discussed in this chapter were written or published within a two-year time span, between 1954 and 1956. They reflect the paradoxes of a decade that proved deeply contradictory for queer Americans, marked both by brutal government repression and considerable advances in civil rights. On the one hand, the 1950s were marked by the surveillance and paranoia of McCarthyism, which framed homosexuality as a threat to national security. In 1950, the Investigations Committee, chaired by Senator Clyde R. Hoey, delivered to the U.S. Congress a report on the "Employment of Homosexuals and Other Sex Perverts in the U.S. Government," which Heike Bauer notes became "the motor that drove the persecution of homosexuals in the decade that followed."[55] In April 1953, shortly following his inauguration, President Eisenhower issued an executive order banning gay men and lesbians from federal employment. The FBI was ordered to investigate current or prospective members and exclude those suspected of being homosexual. This tyrannical mindset trickled down to local police forces, whose officers undertook violent crackdowns of LGBTQ bars and cruising spots across the country.[56]

At the same time, in response to this increasing government oppression, the 1950s also saw progress for queer culture and advocacy. While there had been gay or lesbian meeting places in the United States as far back as the nineteenth century, it was in the late 1940s and 1950s that LGBTQ bars truly expanded and established themselves more firmly.[57] This was certainly the case in San Francisco, where Ginsberg made his home in 1953. Queer communities could be found in a variety of places across the city, "in waterfront bars, in the theater district, along Market Street, among labor activists and communists, in Chinatown, along the old Barbary Coast, among the city's Beat artists and poets, in bohemian bars and taverns."[58] It was in San Francisco, too, that Del Martin, Phyllis

Lyon, Rosalie Bamberger, and others founded the Daughters of Bilitis, the first lesbian civil rights group in the United States, in 1955.[59] Farther south, in Los Angeles, Henry Hay had five years earlier founded the Mattachine Society, a gay rights organization that sought to foster community, educate the public, and protest discriminatory practices.[60] Beyond California, the notion of homosexuality as abnormal was being challenged by the sexology research of Alfred Kinsey. His book *Sexual Behavior in the Human Male* (1948) had stirred controversy by arguing that 10 percent of American males had declared themselves "more or less exclusively homosexual for at least three years between the ages of 16 and 55" and that 46 percent had "reacted" sexually to both men and women at some point in their lives.[61]

Ginsberg was alert to the cultural and political headwinds of the mid-1950s. But he was also caught in his own difficult journey of self-acceptance. At the time that he set down to write "Love Poem on a Theme by Whitman" in 1953, his life up to this point had been defined by a profound sense of loneliness—a feeling persistently connected to his sexuality. Ginsberg got the first inklings of his same-sex attraction at the age of seven.[62] By the age of fourteen, he was developing unrequited crushes on the athletic boys in his class, though he did not disclose his budding desires to anyone. At Columbia University, he befriended a group of students who spoke more freely about their same-sex attractions, at least among themselves. Still, Ginsberg feared the social judgment that he would doubtless face if he were to speak openly about his sexuality and so remained closeted.[63] In 1944, he met Jack Kerouac and the two became close friends—their relationship complicated by Ginsberg's secret attraction to Kerouac. Ginsberg eventually confessed his feelings to him two years later, and while Kerouac accepted his friend's sexuality, he also made it clear that his affection would not be reciprocated.[64] In the years that followed, the two hooked up on a few occasions, but there was no hope of a more serious romance developing.[65]

Ginsberg's life in New York after Columbia was marked by a series of unrequited loves and secret hookups that brought him little comfort.[66]

The most important was his friend Neal Cassady, with whom he fell deeply in love. The two occasionally slept together, but like Kerouac, Cassady considered himself straight, and so there was no possibility of a sustained connection between the two: only the occasional hookups, unbeknownst to Cassady's girlfriends or (later) wife. These brief encounters brought Ginsberg some temporary relief, but they also reminded him of the distance that lay between them. His romantic troubles made him feel profoundly alone, at times succumbing to self-pity: "I am really the lowest of the low, really, no one is as useless and unlovable as myself."[67]

He attributed his "long periods of depression" to his sexuality, writing to a psychiatrist in 1947: "My main psychic difficulty, as far as I know, is the usual oedipal entanglement. I have been homosexual for as long as I can remember, and have had a limited number of homosexual affairs, both temporary and protracted. They have been unsatisfactory to me, and I have always approached love affairs with a sort of self contradictory, conscious masochism."[68] Eventually, in 1950, Ginsberg checked into the Psychiatric Institute of Columbia Presbyterian Hospital. Ginsberg's father, Louis, had been horrified by his son's disclosure of his same-sex desires and hoped that the institute would somehow convert Allen to heterosexuality. The doctors there encouraged Ginsberg to pursue stable relationships with women. Ginsberg, uncomfortable with his sexuality and pained by his difficulty at finding mutual love, declared to Kerouac after his dismissal that he would abandon homosexuality.[69]

And indeed, in 1954, shortly after moving to San Francisco, he dated a singer named Sheila Williams Boucher. But he continued to feel deeply for Cassady and slept with him when he visited from San Jose. Boucher and Ginsberg broke up before the end of the year. That December, following their separation, he fell in love with a man named Peter Orlovsky, whom he had seen depicted in a painting at the home of Robert LaVigne.[70] This relationship would not be without its complications. In October 1955, shortly after Ginsberg's successful reading of "Howl" at the Six Gallery, he worried that Orlovsky did not love him fully back and reflected on the shame that he had felt over his sexuality throughout his life: "My grief was at not loving myself. My mind is crazed by homosexuality."[71] But the two men did commit to one another, fostering a committed, nonmonogamous relationship that lasted until Ginsberg's death in 1997.

To sum up, when Ginsberg turned to write the poems discussed in this chapter, he was still very much coming to terms with his sexuality. He had moved past the point of self-denial but had not yet accepted himself fully. The poems discussed in the following pages were part of his process of self-exploration. Ginsberg interpreted Whitman as a poet of queer loneliness because his own life as a gay man, at least up to this point, had been so haunted by alienation. When he turned thirty in 1956, the year of *Howl*'s publication, his thoughts turned fittingly to his "American colossus": "Now he thought about Matthew Brady's famous photograph of Walt Whitman, in which he detected a guarded look in poor old Whitman's eyes. Allen believed that sad look was caused by a self-imposed repression of innate queerness."[72] Like Crane, Ginsberg saw in Whitman what he did not wish to become but also a poetic model and a queer companion whose verse could bring him comfort, at least for the duration of a poem.

Ginsberg first evoked his predecessor by name in "Love Poem on a Theme by Whitman" (1954), which he wrote to reflect on his unrequited love for Neal Cassady. Carolyn, Neal's wife, knew about Ginsberg's affection but had made peace with it, writing that she trusted "what he had written some years before about having overcome his sexual desire for Neal."[73] Yet this was not actually the case. In "Love Poem," Ginsberg imagined what it would be like to enjoy a night of intimacy with Cassady by slipping between husband and wife: "I'll go into the bedroom silently and lie down between the bridegroom and the bride."[74] Tony Trigilio reads the poem as evidence of the "self-doubt" that Ginsberg felt about his homosexuality and that he saw reflected in Whitman as well: "It reflects the same impulse that urges Whitman to celebrate the male body while, in contrast, encoding desire in displacement and synecdoche."[75] Yet if the decision to imagine a ménage à trois does slant or dilute Ginsberg's longing for same-sex contact, "Love Poem" remains noticeably more explicit about the poet's desires than the passages in "Song of Myself" he alludes to by way of inspiration. Consider, for example, the following lines from Whitman:

I am a free companion, I bivouac by invading watchfires,
I turn the bridegroom out of bed and stay with the bride myself,
I tighten her all night to my thighs and lips.[76]

Ginsberg does not pretend to feel interest only in the bride rather than the bridegroom, so that his revision of Whitman's line serves to coax these desires further, if not fully, out of the closet. Strictly speaking, his attentions might be directed to either or both, though the inner rhyme on *room* and *bridegroom* places sufficient emphasis on the male party for his feelings to be clear:

> bodies locked shuddering naked, hot hips and buttocks screwed into
>   each other
> and eyes, eyes glinting and charming, widening into looks and
>   abandon,
> and moans of movement, voices, hands in air, hands between thighs,
> hands in moisture on softened hips, throbbing contraction of bellies
> till the white come flow in the swirling sheets.[77]

When set against the summary statement "I tighten her all night to my thighs and lips," Ginsberg's scene is remarkably detailed, the sentence extending to match the rhythmic intensity of the sexual encounter. Notably, however, the poet omits crucial pronouns and possessive adjectives. Whitman clearly identifies his chosen partner as "her" and the thighs and lips as his (or "my"). Ginsberg, by contrast, parades an impersonal sequence of "bodies," "hips," "buttocks," "eyes," "hands," and "bellies."

The omission could be a sign of the partners' sexual fluidity: differences of sex and gender dissolve as the three lovers come together. But it also fits the poet's implicit fantasy of sex with the bridegroom to the exclusion of the bride; at this juncture, she might feasibly just be an observer. The homoeroticism becomes more evident if one considers the other passage that Ginsberg alludes to here—the infamous eleventh section about the beautiful young bathers:

The young men float on their backs, their white bellies bulge to the
  sun, they do not ask who seizes fast to them,
They do not know who puffs and declines with pendant and bending
  arch,
They do not think whom they souse with spray.[78]

Ginsberg's lines about the "throbbing contraction of bellies" and "white
come flow in the swirling sheets" bring to completion the suppressed desire, in Whitman, for the young men whose "white bellies bulge to the
sun" as they playfully "souse" each other with spray.

Several critics have read the poem as a protest against the primacy
of heterosexuality. Trigilio has described "Love Poem" as "the politi-
cally contestatory version of Whitman's fantasy" because it undermines
"normative activity" at the moment "when the speaker enters the cultural
sanctity of the marriage bed."[79] Jonathan D. Katz, along similar lines,
argues that Ginsberg wants to question "the productive and reproductive
imperatives of monogamous heterosexuality."[80] Such readings lend the
poem a clear political agenda, but Ginsberg's motivations strike me as
far more personal, his tone melancholic rather than strident. That gloom
becomes clear in the final lines:

and the bride cry for forgiveness, and the groom be covered with tears
  of passion and compassion,
and I rise up from the bed replenished with last intimate gestures and
  kisses of farewell—
all before the mind wakes, behind shades and closed doors in a
  darkened house
where the inhabitants roam unsatisfied in the night,
nude ghosts seeking each other out in the silence.

To Ginsberg's mind, eroticism can offer a temporary refuge from loneliness, but it cannot resolve it entirely. This dilemma is a universal problem,
not limited to the queer experience. The "nude ghosts seeking each other

out in silence" have no gender; neither do the unsatisfied "inhabitants." Although the bride and groom share a line again, the poet grammatically separates them with a comma, as if to isolate their actions. The groom's "tears of passion and compassion" may not even be directed at the bride. The passion might be for the speaker, the compassion for himself in the form of self-pity. Nor does the bride's "cry for forgiveness" receive a satisfactory response. They appear in their own bubble, alien to one another. Still, Ginsberg does highlight the distinctive risk of loneliness faced by queer people such as himself. The speaker has no marital bed to stay in, so he must roam the house with no fixed place to rest. While the bride and groom may not connect, they still formally belong to one another. Ginsberg's ghost does not, and he must invariably depart to wander on his own.

Ginsberg's reflections on loneliness are consonant with the passages that he draws from in Whitman. Section 11 ends with the total erasure of the female observer: "They do not think whom they souse with spray." The quiet pain of the final line rests on the fact that the lonely woman in the window must remain unknown to the bathers, and presumably to others she secretly desires. With the word *whom*, she has effectively turned into a ghost, lacking either a name or an identity. This disappearance runs parallel to the erasure of the pronoun *I* in Ginsberg's "Love Poem," in which the speaker's individual identity finds itself dissolved into the anonymity of *inhabitants* and *ghosts*. But Ginsberg also sensed that Whitman projected that loneliness onto a female observer to disguise his own experience as a gay man. By describing his solitude through allusions to "Song of Myself," Ginsberg argues that Whitman's lines speak to his distinctively queer struggle with loneliness. The allusion draws out the issue of Whitman's sexuality and brings it to bear on his poem. It also grants Ginsberg a historical antecedent and some consolation. While he may feel isolated, Ginsberg is not the first to have confronted loneliness as a gay man. In Whitman, he found a queer poet who he felt would have understood his dilemma and sympathized with him.

In the years that followed "Love Poem on a Theme by Whitman," Ginsberg kept returning to Whitman through allusion, both as a poetic model and as a figure who allowed him to reflect on loneliness. His long poem "Howl," first performed at the Six Gallery in San Francisco in 1955 and then published in 1956, borrows considerably from "Song of Myself." Per Jonah Raskin, Ginsberg "wanted to see what Whitman had seen, but in a new way—to forge a vision about America that would reflect the realities of the twentieth century. He seemed to think that if Whitman had been alive in 1955 he might have written *Howl*."[81] Whitman supplied him with the ambition, the scope, as well as the structure of long parallel lines in free verse. But the poet also served as a useful contrast, refracting back onto America how much the country—at least to Ginsberg's mind—had declined. Through "Howl," Ginsberg argues that Whitman's optimism about the United States must darken before the destructive contemporary forces of capitalism, social inequality, and state surveillance. As Bonnie Costello puts it, "Ginsberg's America is like Dante's hell or Blake's London."[82]

While many critics have noted general thematic and stylistic connections between the two poems, little attention has been paid to specific allusions and how these reflect Ginsberg's concerns with sexuality. From Whitman, he drew, first, images of desire. There are the young men doing farmwork in "Song of Myself": "Three scythes at harvest whizzing in a row from three lusty angels with shirts bagg'd out at their waists."[83] These make their way into Ginsberg in altered form: "who hiccuped endlessly trying to giggle but wound up with a sob behind a partition in a Turkish Bath when the blond & naked angel came to pierce them with a sword."[84] Whitman may attribute the adjective *lusty* to the laborers, but the word more accurately reflects the attitude of the observer, who elevates the three men to the status of "angels." The crux of the poet's interest evidently centers on their exposed bodies, which he evoked obliquely by the "shirts bagg'd out at their waists." In Ginsberg's hands, the image becomes more explicitly sexual but also more melancholic. The angel— now singular in "Howl"—appears wholly "naked." The scythe has been swapped for a "sword" and granted a phallic metaphor, "piercing" the group gathered at the Turkish Bath. Yet these partners are overcome by sadness once they have been visited by the angel. They attempt to "giggle" but only manage "a sob." The tryst can do little to cure their sorrow, nor can their companionship, in fact. Though singular, the *sob* reinforces their separation from one another.

The word *lonesome*, which appears in Whitman's "Recorders Ages Hence" and in section 11 of "Song of Myself," recurs throughout "Howl" as a discreet undersong: "who lit cigarettes in boxcars boxcars boxcars racketing through snow toward *lonesome* farms in grandfather night"; "who *loned* it through the streets of Idaho seeking visionary indian angels who were visionary indian angels"; "who lounged hungry and *lonesome* through Houston seeking jazz or sex or soup, and followed the brilliant Spaniard to converse about America and Eternity, a hopeless task, and so took ship to Africa"[85] (emphasis added). Whitman also gave Ginsberg the language to view sexual bonds between men not only as a fleeting refuge from loneliness but more broadly as political protest and a mark of faith in American freedom, democracy, and community.

The notion of adhesiveness as an authentic form of patriotism resurfaces in lines devoted to Carl Solomon:

> I'm with you in Rockland
>> where there are twentyfive thousand mad comrades all
>> together singing the final stanzas of the Internationale
> I'm with you in Rockland
>> where we hug and kiss the United States under our bedsheets
>> the United States that coughs all night and won't let us sleep.[86]

Whitman clearly influenced the vision of comrades pressed together in a political and sexual union. But Ginsberg's allusion is also far more specific than it might appear, evoking not just Whitman's broader concept of adhesiveness but these lines from "Calamus Poems":

> I will say what I have to say by itself,
> I will sound myself and comrades only, I will never again utter a call
>> only their call,
> I will raise with it immortal reverberations through the States,

> I will give an example to lovers to take permanent shape and will
> through the States.[87]

Whitman's image effects a complex transformation of Ginsberg. In "Calamus Poems," the speaker swears that he will only sing of and to comrades;
in turn, that music becomes an act of patriotism, the comrades absorbed
into the very fabric of the United States. Whitman describes this process
as an "example to lovers," but the comparison implies that his experience
with comrades also bears an erotic charge: the call, the "reverberations,"
the "shape and will." Ginsberg borrows the trick of juxtaposition from
Whitman. When he writes that "we hug and kiss the United States," he
implies that the United States is not the only recipient of these affections;
comrades must keep each other warm. But their love for the United
States must change in this new era, for America is both sick and sick*ening*
("coughs all night and won't let us sleep"). Ginsberg finds far less to celebrate in this Cold War era, so the only healthy bond here lies between the
comrades "all together singing." It is one of the few moments in "Howl"
in which Ginsberg envisions a community, rather than the lonely, isolated
people who have become tragic figures of American decline.

Still, loneliness cannot be kept at bay forever. When "Howl" first
appeared in print in 1956, it was followed by another poem evoking Whitman as a figure of alienation, "A Supermarket in California." Ginsberg
does not just allude to lines from his poetry; he also apostrophizes Whitman and imagines his predecessor in the present day, wandering the aisles
of a supermarket. Thomas F. Merrill describes the poem as a "study of
the contrasts" between their distinct visions of America.[88] As in "Howl,"
Ginsberg uses the structure of Whitman's verse to highlight that contrast,
since for Ginsberg any poem about the United States in his era must take
the form of a lament. This time, though, his scope is narrower, confined
mainly to the walls of a supermarket. By using Whitman as a point of
comparison, Ginsberg underlines the smallness of postwar American society, in which the glut of commerce has destroyed all philosophical and
spiritual ambitions. "What peaches and what penumbras! Whole families

shopping at night! Aisles full of husbands! Wives in the avocados, babies in the tomatoes!" The exclamations sound mock-heroic, as language devolves into the jingle-jangle of advertising rather than of epic poetry. In such a setting, Whitman proves to be, as Anton Vander Zee phrases it, "humorously and often tragically out of place."[89]

Whitman's presence enables Ginsberg to think about his place as a gay man in midcentury America, at a time when the culture only valued individuals who could fit within the structure of a heterosexual nuclear family. Ginsberg underlines Whitman's sexuality from his first appearance in the second stanza: "I saw you, Walt Whitman, childless, lonely old grubber, poking among the meats in the refrigerator and eyeing the grocery boys. / I heard you asking questions of each: Who killed the pork chops? What price bananas? Are you my Angel?"[90] The question "Are you my Angel?" cheekily evokes Whitman's deification of men whom he found beautiful, like the "three lusty angels with shirts bagg'd out at their waists." The lines also contain a far more specific allusion to a particular scene in "Song of Myself": "The butcher-boy puts off his killing-clothes, or sharpens his knife at the stall in the market."[91] When Ginsberg imagines Whitman "poking among the meats in the refrigerator," "eyeing the grocery boys," and asking "Who killed the pork chops?" he reads buried desire in what might otherwise seem like an innocuous description of a butcher. But the implied association with grocery boys and meat, though queasy, is less a knock against Whitman's desires and more a reflection of how he would be perceived by others in the store as prurient. Likewise, the phrase "childless, lonely old grubber" does not represent Ginsberg's view of Whitman but how he imagines others might describe the elder poet. The melancholy of this scene comes from the suspicion that very few would extend sympathy. Whitman would find himself labeled an old creep, desirous but not himself desirable.

Ginsberg evidently feared a similar fate in his own life. He repeatedly emphasizes Whitman's solitude. The word *lonely* bookends his description of the poet, appearing at the start ("I saw you, Walt Whitman, childless, lonely old grubber") and at the end ("Ah, dear father, graybeard, lonely old courage-teacher"). Among the aisles stocked with copious amounts of wives, babies, and husbands, Whitman stands alone. And so, too, does Ginsberg. The poem begins with an unaccompanied stroll through the city in the evening: "I walked down the sidestreets under the trees with a headache self-conscious looking at the full moon." The language of loneliness recurs as Ginsberg imagines what it would be like for Whitman to join him on the walk, as the poem winds to a close:

> Will we walk all night through solitary streets? The trees add shade to shade, lights out in the houses, we'll both be lonely.
> Will we stroll dreaming of the lost America of love past blue automobiles in driveways, home to our silent cottage?
> Ah, dear father, graybeard, lonely old courage-teacher, what America did you have when Charon quit poling his ferry and you got out on a smoking bank and stood watching the boat disappear on the black waters of Lethe?[92]

These lines complicate Frank Kearful's argument that "A Supermarket in California" functions as a "fantasy of gay poetic bonding."[93] The companionship that Ginsberg envisions may be genuine, but it also has some necessary limits. Walking together—which he can only imagine—would not cure his loneliness, though it would give him a virtual companion to feel lonely with. Tellingly, he frames the last three lines as questions, so that his tone sounds tentative, perhaps a little desperate. He reaches for a connection that is only fictional and fleeting. Still, if Whitman cannot grant him a permanent solution to his woes, he can and has taught Ginsberg how to show "courage" in the face of life's challenges, especially solitude. Whitman will serve as a model for him, even as the dominant culture continues to view them as "childless, lonely old grubbers" who ought to be kept at a distance.

Whitman surfaces in some of the most personal and intimate poems from this period of Ginsberg's life, and these, too, feature the same push-and-pull between connection and loneliness. In 1956, the year that saw the publication of *Howl and Other Poems*, Ginsberg wrote a poem titled "Many Loves," reflecting on his sexual encounter with Neal Cassady in late January 1947. The two men had shared a cot in a friend's Spanish Harlem apartment after a night out on the town together. As described by Michael Schumacher: "Allen stripped to his shorts and lay in the darkness, frightened and ashamed, keeping his distance by huddling at the edge of the cot and hanging his arm and head over the edge. Sensing Allen's fear, Neal reached out to him and told him to draw near."[94] The sex proved healing for Ginsberg, who loved Cassady deeply but had convinced himself that the two would never be intimate. Yet it also reinforced his loneliness. Cassady identified as heterosexual: he had already married once, to Lu Anne Henderson in 1946, and would marry Carolyn Robinson in 1948, after an annulment. Whatever intimacy they shared would be temporary and unlikely to foster a long-term romantic bond.

In "Many Loves," Ginsberg relates their encounter in sensual detail, using Whitman's poetry as a basis and a point of reference. He begins with a direct quote from "Calamus" on adhesiveness: "Resolved to sing no songs henceforth but those of manly attachment." Most of the poem itself, though, alludes to section 11:

> I lay there trembling, and felt his great arm like a king's
> And his breasts, his heart slow thudding against my back,
> and his middle torso, narrow and made of iron, soft at my back,
> his fiery firm belly warming me while I trembled—
> His belly of fists and starvation, his belly a thousand girls kissed in
>   Colorado
> his belly of rocks thrown over Denver roofs, prowess of jumping and
>   fists, his stomach of solitudes,
> His belly of burning iron and jails affectionate to my side.[95]

The allusions are discreet, scattered throughout the stanza, but they also gain momentum as the lines progress. Ginsberg borrows "trembling" from the lines about the "unseen hand" that touched the swimmers' bodies and "descended tremblingly from their temples and ribs." At the same time, the context and implication are entirely different. Whitman describes the hesitation and embarrassment that the woman feels as she fantasizes about the men in the water, not daring to reach out to them. Ginsberg, however, uses "trembling" to evoke his anxiety before Cassady's touch brings him comfort and reassurance. This adjustment sets the tone for the rest of the poem, which actualizes the sexual healing that remains unsatisfied for Whitman's observer. Ginsberg further heightens the eroticism of Whitman's lines by taking the same features of the swimmers' physique and lavishing more attention on them through rapturous repetition. So "the young men float on their backs" becomes "his heart slow thudding against my back" and "his middle torso, narrow and made of iron, soft at my back." "Their white bellies bulge to the sun" yields "his fiery firm belly warming me," "his belly of fists and starvation, his belly a thousand girls kissed in Colorado / his belly of rocks thrown over Denver roofs," and "his belly of burning iron and jails affectionate."[96] Distant longing gives way to the pleasure of sexual discovery.

The allusions give credit to Whitman, who showed Ginsberg the language to talk about sex and sexuality. Through these references, Ginsberg returns the favor, actualizing desires that remain unsatisfied in Whitman. The allusions enable Ginsberg to make contact with Whitman, to celebrate a fleeting relief from loneliness with a poet whose writing offered him a form of companionship. Still, loneliness haunts the corners even of this poem. The opening lines of "Many Loves" frame the entirety of Ginsberg's sexual encounter as a memory: "Neal Cassady was my animal: he brought me to my knees / and taught me the love of his cock and the secrets of his mind."[97] The quiet pain of this passage stems from the implication of the past tense for Ginsberg's present. "Neal Cassady *was* my animal," not *is*. He "*taught* me the love of his cock," but the reader has no assurance that this love has been unlearned. Ginsberg can no longer enjoy Cassady's love, so he must content himself with a memory: a parallel to, if not an exact reflection of, the woman in Whitman who can only enjoy the fantasy of sexual exploration that will never come to pass.

The allusions to Whitman by such poets as Crane and Ginsberg stand out both for their commonalities and for how far they depart from standard ideas about this poet. Critics usually think of Whitman as a writer concerned with the self and its relationship to other people, the nation, and the environment. However, many queer authors detected a strain of loneliness running beneath the surface of Whitman's verse. For these poets, Whitman represented not universal connection but the solitude experienced by queer people. By drawing on "Song of Myself," Crane and Ginsberg found an antecedent to their loneliness and derived some comfort that others had felt the same way before. At the same time, they acknowledged that the connection granted by allusion was necessarily virtual and fleeting, that it could not serve as an antidote. What "Song of Myself" could offer was a helping hand in the difficult process of learning how to live with loneliness and how to find both pleasure and meaning in the connections that do present themselves, no matter how temporary.

Coda

At the beginning of this book, I stated that allusion mattered especially to queer poets for its distinctive mix of secrecy and openness—an important feature considering the hostile social climate that many of the writers inhabited. For this reason, one might assume that the importance or value of queer allusion has diminished in the twenty-first century. It is now common in the United States to marvel at how quickly LGBTQ people have gained acceptance in the past two decades and point to the majority support for same-sex marriage as well as the rise of queer representation in popular media. But allusion continues to be a central practice in queer poetry, and for good reasons. First, while LGBTQ people are generally more accepted in most parts of the United States and Europe than they were, say, during A. E. Housman's lifetime, being queer remains difficult for many people. The resurgence of anti-LGBTQ legislation—from anti-trans bills in the United States to homophobic "parental rights" laws in Italy—testifies to the persistence of bigotry in contemporary society and the speed with which progress can slide back. Second, as David Halperin argues in *How to Be Gay,* most queer children grow up in heterosexual families and so must navigate their identity alone and steep themselves in a queer culture that played little part in their upbringing.

I quoted the following passage in the introduction, but I think it useful to reiterate here: "Although much, indisputably, has changed, gay or proto-gay children still grow up, for the most part, in heterosexual families and households. A few of them may have children's books which teach them about the existence of gay people, or about families with parents of the same sex. They may watch TV sitcoms or reality shows with gay or (more rarely) lesbian characters. All of that certainly contributes significantly to the destigmatization of homosexuality. But a culture that places less stigma on homosexuality is not the same thing as a gay culture."[1]

For Halperin, "being gay" entails not just attraction to members of the same sex but knowledge of a range of cultural practices, artifacts, and references as well as a distinctive history. His argument can, and should, be extended to other identities under the LGBTQ umbrella. With Halperin's claim in mind, it makes sense that contemporary queer poets would continue turning to allusion as a way of connecting to queer history and so learning to become more fully themselves, well after the period of childhood and adolescence during which many still assume self-discovery takes place. Third, while many poets no longer feel either the need or the inclination to conceal their sexuality for a heterosexual readership, I suspect that there is still some pleasure to be had in imagining coded queer references, to be understood by a more intimate audience of kin. The private messages of queer allusion may have less to do now with self-protection—though they can still perform that function to an extent—and more to do with the joy of a shared secret: a message in a bottle that can only be deciphered by a select few. The secrecy that has often been tied to shame in LGBTQ history can also be given a more positive and productive meaning here, as a way of forging community across historical and geographic distance.

I would like to conclude this study with a contemporary poem that shows the endurance of queer allusion as a method in the new century. Danez Smith's "bare," from the 2017 collection *Don't Call Us Dead,* begins with a poignant reference to Walt Whitman's "I Sing the Body Electric." As so often in queer allusion, Smith pays tribute to their predecessor by absorbing his language, but they also meaningfully change the language to suit their purposes. The poem begins with a declaration of love and dedication:

For you I'd send my body to battle
my body, let my blood sing of tearing

itself apart, the hollowing cords
of the white knights' intravenous joist.

love, I want & barely know how
to do much else.[2]

The phrase "let my blood sing" and the surrounding battle imagery evoke
the opening stanza of Whitman's own poem:

I sing the body electric,
The armies of those I love engirth me and I engirth them,
They will not let me off till I go with them, respond to them,
And discorrupt them, and charge them full with the charge of the
soul.[3]

The object of the speaker's love shifts from one poem to the other. In
Whitman, the "armies" that he loves represent the mass of people whom
he meets. Smith's speaker, by contrast, professes their love for an individual, turning Whitman's poem on humanity into a poem about deep and
abiding romance. The military images that their predecessor had used
to reflect the fullness of the human world find themselves transformed
into images of chivalric passion. This change does not dispute Whitman
but, rather, builds on a commonality between the two poets that interested readers can perceive. While the allusion does not explicitly point
to Whitman's relationships with other men, Smith's decision to absorb
Whitman's language in their love poem is itself significant. By writing
through a queer predecessor, Smith reaches back into queer history and
pays homage to one who came before them.

At the same time, Smith is deeply conscious of how their experience
as a Black, nonbinary individual in the United States differs from their

predecessor's. Whitman assumes no separation between himself and the multitude of people surrounding him: "The armies of those I love engirth me and I engirth them." The body, in his imagination, is "electric," and so he can touch and connect with all the other bodies around him. By contrast, Danez's experience of the body must confront the risk of violence: the violence of self-sacrifice ("tearing / itself apart") but also, more disturbingly, the threat of racist violence ("the hollowing cords / of the white knights' intravenous joist"). Whitman's speaker is an individual, and yet he also meshes with everyone whom he meets. While the armies demand much of him ("They will not let me go"), their attitude remains desirous and adoring. On the other hand, Smith's speaker stands alone, always conscious of the gap between them and the hostile culture that surrounds them. The multiple "white knights" form a single unit—their "joist" is singular, not plural—and point their weapon directly at Smith, who must defend their beloved by themself.

For all the violence and division that Smith's speaker must face, "bare" does end with the hope of unity—both between the lovers and across the fragmented society that they must navigate:

> love, stay
>
> in me until our bodies forget
> what divides us, until your blood
>
> is my blood & your hands
> are my hands, until our names
>
> are the same song & our life's work
> be to lay & be, hum & die.[4]

While Smith may be clearsighted about the obstacles to their flourishing, they still end the poem by expressing confidence in the unifying power of love. Moreover, Smith may have in mind forms of love beyond the romantic and the sexual. The happier future that they envision in the

lines "until our bodies forget / what divides us" could refer not just to
the physical connection between the two lovers but to the racist violence
they have faced ("the hollowing cords / of the white knights' intravenous
joist"). In this reading, the pronoun *our* refers both to the couple and to
humanity more broadly, so the unity they envision is universal as well as
romantic. The discreet allusions to other lines in "I Sing the Body Electric" reinforce this notion by imagining bodily unity between all people.
"Until your blood / is my blood" harks back to Whitman's "Within there
runs blood, / The same old blood! the same red-running blood!" "Your
hands are my hands" evokes "negligent falling hands all diffused, mine
too diffused."[5] Whitman, too, famously used the language of love poetry to access the possibility of universal love binding all human beings.
The end of Smith's poem connects back to Whitman's original purpose,
when it seemed that their distinct experiences might always set them apart.
Smith arguably goes even further than Whitman in their optimism. For all
that Whitman writes of the oneness he feels with others, the first-person
plural never features in "I Sing the Body Electric." His speaker remains
forever an "I," no matter how deep of a connection he may form with the
people of this world. Smith, on the other hand, concludes with a litany of
first-person plurals—"*our* bodies," "*our* names," "*our* life's work"—so
that the poem actualizes what Whitman envisions.

And there is good reason to believe that allusion will remain a perennial resource for queer poets, for there will always be new generations of LGBTQ authors seeking to better understand themselves and
their history by reaching into the poetry of the past. Since the end of the
nineteenth century, when sexuality came to be understood as an integral
part of one's personhood, queer poets have turned to allusion to reflect
on their identity, to see their experiences reflected in the literature of the
past, to help create an alternative poetic canon, and to find some temporary refuge from loneliness. Queer allusion counters some of the most
deep-seated assumptions about literary influence—namely, that writers
feel the literature of the past as a burden or that they view it more cyn-
ically as competition. The authors considered in this book showed no
desire to outshine their predecessors. At the same time, neither was their

attitude obsequious. When queer poets look for analogies to their own experiences, they do not view previous writers as unmovable monoliths that must be preserved or else outmatched. In many of the examples I have discussed, the poet took the liberty of transforming the purpose and meaning of their predecessor's language through allusion. By recognizing the queerness of prior texts, writers can approach the poems with a greater sense of intimacy and immediacy. Allusion grants LGBTQ poets a sense of connection both to their history and to their own individual experiences: in sum, a sense of belonging. For this reason, allusion has been central to the development of queer poetry throughout the twentieth century, and it will remain crucially important as queer poetry continues its flourishing in the present century.

ACKNOWLEDGMENTS

I am deeply grateful to the colleagues, friends, and family members who made this book possible. *Queer Allusion* began as an article in *Modern Language Quarterly* focused on Oscar Wilde, A. E. Housman, and Countee Cullen. The two anonymous reviewers and Marshall Brown, then editor of the journal, provided meticulous feedback that helped me to refine the broader argument of the essay. At Austin Peay State University, I was fortunate to receive the support of the Languages and Literature Department chair, Beatrix Brockman, and the dean of the College of Arts and Letters, William Hoon, both of whom ensured that I had the time to complete the project. Carol Keller, the interlibrary loan assistant, was invaluable in getting me the resources that I needed—and at astonishing speed to boot. I would like to thank my friends for their kindness, support, and conversation, both in Clarksville and farther afield: Michael Chandler, Raymond Deeren, Jessica Johnston, Andrew Kostakis, Alex MacConochie, Cady Steinberg, Ben Torres, and Paula White. My parents, Laurent and Estelle, have shown constant encouragement throughout my academic career. I dedicate this book to my husband, Christopher: "having a Coke with you" is always more fun than all the rest.

⁓

NOTES

Introduction

1. Levy, *London Plane-Tree*, 18.
2. Beckman, *Amy Levy*, 18, 31, 42, 254–55.
3. Bingham, *Valentine Ackland*, 31, 65–66, 78–80.
4. Levy, *London Plane-Tree*, 18.
5. Ackland, *Journey from Winter*, 46.
6. Foucault, *History of Sexuality*, 42–43; Sedgwick, *Epistemology of the Closet*, 2.
7. Irwin, "What Is an Allusion," 287.
8. Robb, *Strangers*, 150.
9. Bate, *Burden of the Past*, 4, 10, 11.
10. Bloom, *Anxiety of Influence*, xxiii–xxiv.
11. Ricks, "Loneliness and Poetry," 261–81.
12. Auden, *W. H. Auden: Collected Poems*, 65, 217; Larkin, *Complete Poems*, 63.
13. Nealon, *Foundlings*, 1.
14. Ohi, *Dead Letters Sent*, 1.
15. Travisano, *Love Unknown*, 218–19, 224–25.
16. Faderman, "Russell in Lowell's Life and Work," 59.
17. Bishop, *Poems*, 82.
18. Lowell, *Pictures of the Floating World*, 47, 160–61.
19. Bishop, *Poems*, 43.

1. Oscar Wilde and Alfred Douglas

1. Ellmann, *Oscar Wilde*, 385.
2. Harris, *Oscar Wilde*, 88–89, 110.
3. Croft-Cooke, *Bosie*, 47, 53, 57, 191.

4. Fisher, *Oscar and Bosie*, xviii, 228, 236–37.

5. Ellmann, *Oscar Wilde*, 324, 384–86, 396, 402.

6. Sturgis, *Oscar*, 185–87.

7. Ellmann, *Oscar Wilde*, 384–85.

8. Murray, *Bosie*, 30.

9. Douglas, *Collected Poems*, 16.

10. Wilde, *Oscar Wilde: Complete Poetry*, 88.

11. Frankel, *Oscar Wilde*, 136.

12. Wilde, *Oscar Wilde: Complete Poetry*, 104.

13. Douglas, *Collected Poems*, 15.

14. Murray, *Bosie*, 61.

15. Douglas, *Collected Poems*, 36.

16. Wilde, *Oscar Wilde: Complete Poetry*, 109.

17. Behrendt, *Oscar Wilde*, 40.

18. Hyde, *Oscar Wilde*, 335.

19. Wilde, *Oscar Wilde: Complete Poetry*, 153.

20. Sturgis, *Oscar*, 637–38.

21. Wilde, *Oscar Wilde: Complete Poetry*, 156.

22. Douglas, *Collected Poems*, 74–78.

23. John Stokes notes that the poem was written in Paris in 1901 (*Oscar Wilde*, 3).

24. Critics have offered several theories as to what made this story so moving to Wilde. For Patricia Flanagan Behrendt, Wilde was drawn to Itys for erotic and tragic qualities that are hard to separate. He is "the ultimate victim whose innocent youth and beauty are sacrificed as a result of the violent heterosexual passions of others." Behrendt goes further by arguing that his "innocent youth and beauty" serve as "a metaphor for what happens when the awakening heterosexual passions in a male youth cause his homosexual lover to lose interest in him" (*Oscar Wilde*, 47). Alex Murray, meanwhile, reads the poet's relationship to this myth along purely literary terms. For him, Wilde views Itys as a symptom of "the poison of the past, a poison that should be understood as explicitly poetic." In this reading, Wilde sees Itys as proof that the serene aesthetic of English pastoral is superior to the violence and cruelty of classical mythology. While the poet may urge Procne to "sing on" after her transformation into a nightingale, the general attitude, according to Murray, is one of horror in the face of barbarity and a desire to create an alternative style (*Landscapes of Decadence*, 100). My concern here is not with the meaning of Itys to Wilde but what "The Burden of Itys" meant to Douglas.

25. Wilde, *Oscar Wilde: Complete Poetry*, 48.

26. Douglas, *Collected Poems*, 82.

27. Ibid., 89.

28. Murray, *Bosie*, 162–63.

29. Hyde, *Oscar Wilde,* 162.

30. Murray, *Bosie,* 169–72.

31. Hyde, *Oscar Wilde,* 202–17.

32. Douglas, *Collected Poems,* 161.

33. Wilde, *Oscar Wilde: Complete Poetry,* 159.

34. Murray, *Bosie,* 266, 309–10.

2. W. H. Auden and Stephen Spender

1. Replogle, *Auden's Poetry,* 18.

2. Sutherland, *Stephen Spender,* 79.

3. Leeming, *Stephen Spender,* 33.

4. Spender, *World Within World,* 49, 52.

5. Weatherhead, *Spender and the Thirties,* 23.

6. Spender, *World Within World,* 52, 139.

7. Ibid., 54.

8. Davenport-Hines, *Auden,* 57.

9. Callan, *Auden,* 43.

10. Spender, *World Within World,* 58.

11. Sutherland, *Stephen Spender,* 74.

12. Spender, *World Within World,* 64–66.

13. Sutherland, *Stephen Spender,* 74.

14. Carpenter, *Auden,* 25, 47–48.

15. Sutherland, *Stephen Spender,* 69–70.

16. Leeming, *Spender,* 46, 74.

17. Carpenter, *Auden,* 48.

18. Ibid., 49.

19. Davenport-Hines, *Auden,* 67.

20. Carpenter, *Auden,* 49.

21. Davenport-Hines, *Auden,* 67.

22. Mendelson, *Early Auden,* 220.

23. Carpenter, *Auden,* 105.

24. Sutherland, *Stephen Spender,* 379.

25. Trolley, *Poetry of the Thirties,* 53.

26. Spender, *Stephen Spender: New Collected Poems,* 3.

27. Weatherhead, *Spender and the Thirties,* 158.

28. Auden, *W. H. Auden: Selected Poems,* 14.

29. Fuller, *Auden,* 74.

30. Spears, *Poetry of W. H. Auden,* 39.

31. Richard Johnson was one of the first to make such a case: "Those who attend garden parties, wear furs, and go to places like the Sport Hotel are both 'ruined'— infected by the universal death wish that permeates any decadent society—and incapable of recognizing that they are. The smouldering cigarette-end is a portent, a kind of fuse" (*Man's Place*, 21). Subsequent critics routinely used the language of disease, as if the poem were performing a diagnosis. Edward Callan describes the poem as "an early repository of Auden's stock images for the sickness of his own class" (*Auden*, 70). Per John Lucas: "There is nothing of random observation in Auden's method, no hapless recording of social ephemera. What we are given are synecdochic details, clues by which to read society's ills" ("Auden's Politics," 156). Michael O'Neill similarly writes that the poem "implies, through images of illness and aberration, the presence of sickness in society" ("Thirties Bequest," 40).

32. Auden, *W. H. Auden: Selected Poems*, 15.

33. Dunn, "Back and Forth," 326. Likewise, Julian Symons has asked: "Were not these Fascist sentiments? Didn't Auden clearly approve of them?" (*Thirties*, 30). Valentine Cunningham also identified a fascist strain in the poet's militaristic imagery: "high-flying, swift-swooping birds of prey, kestrels, Hitlerian and Williamsonian eagles, birds reminiscent of the modern military airplane" (*British Writers of the Thirties*, 192).

34. Spender, *Temple*, 11.

35. Spender, *Stephen Spender: New Collected Poems*, 31.

36. Costello, *Plural of Us*, 57.

37. Fuller, *Auden*, 120.

38. Auden, *W. H. Auden: Collected Poems*, 71.

39. Ibid.

40. Spender, *Stephen Spender: New Collected Poems*, 30.

41. Auden, *W. H. Auden: Selected Poems*, 48.

42. Fuller, *Auden*, 280; Bozorth, *Auden's Games of Knowledge*, 174.

43. For Dennis Davison, the poem is a "sort of parody," the "brash images" part of "Auden's criticism of sentimental moods and overstated emotions" (*W. H. Auden*, 79). John Fuller describes the poem as "a fair pastiche of the stoical lament and flamboyant imagery of the traditional blues lyric" (*Auden*, 280). Richard Bozorth makes a similar point, writing that the lines amount to "a confession that grief can be a self-indulgent performance, as manipulative of oneself as it is of others" (*Auden's Games of Knowledge*, 175).

44. Bozorth, *Auden's Games of Knowledge*, 174.

45. Leeming, *Spender*, 80.

46. Sutherland, *Stephen Spender*, 166, 196–97.

47. Leeming, *Spender*, 99.

48. Sutherland, *Stephen Spender*, 213, 217–18, 220.

49. Spender, *Stephen Spender: New Collected Poems*, 111–12.

50. Davenport-Hines, *Auden*, 187.

51. Carpenter, *Auden*, 311–12, 316.

52. Ibid., 314; Tippins, *February House*, 246; McCall Smith, *What W. H. Auden Can Do for You*, 130.

53. Some, like Richard Johnson, have argued that the poem also responds to E. M. Forster, who had reviewed Auden's *The Enchafèd Flood*, a collection of lectures on romanticism and heroism, in 1951 (*Man's Place*, 167). There Forster reflects on Auden's conception of the modern hero, no longer a solitary wanderer but a "builder" with a sense of responsibility to their community. He concludes the review with some reservations about Auden's optimism, if not a complete rejection of it: "Auden's hope—reinforced in his case by Christian dogma—is the world's hope and its only hope. For some of us who are non-Christian there still remains the comfort of the non-human, the relief, when we look up at the stars, of realizing that they are uninhabitable. But not there for any of us lies our work or our home" (*Two Cheers for Democracy*, 276). Auden may have had Forster in mind when he decided that his speaker would gaze up at a neutral sky. Still, the direct parallels between "The Indifferent One" and "The More Loving One" suggest that Auden responded more directly to Spender than to Forster.

54. Auden, *W. H. Auden: Selected Poems*, 246.

55. McCall Smith, *What W. H. Auden Can Do for You*, 130.

56. Leeming, *Spender*, 195, 222–23, 227.

57. Sutherland, *Stephen Spender*, 479.

58. Spender, "W. H. Auden Memorial Address," 232.

59. Spender, *Stephen Spender: New Selected Journals*, 557.

60. Spender, *Stephen Spender: New Collected Poems*, 326.

3. Christina Rossetti's "Goblin Market"

1. Rossetti, *Christina Rossetti: Complete Poems*, 8, 18.

2. Moers, *Literary Women*, 157; Burlinson, *Christina Rossetti*, 45; Cox, *Touch, Sexuality, and Hands in British Literature*, 173.

3. Mermin, "Heroic Sisterhood," 108.

4. Marsh, *Christina Rossetti*, 89–97, 202–8, 287–91.

5. Rich, "Compulsory Heterosexuality and Lesbian Existence," 648–49.

6. Holt, "Exchange in *Goblin Market*," 51–67; Campbell, "Of Mothers and Merchants," 393–410; Stern, "Food and Fraud," 477–511; Mendoza, "Crossing of Sexual and Consumer Desire," 913–47; Tarr, "Covent Goblin Market," 297–316; Coulson, "Redemption and Representation," 423–50.

7. Carpenter, "Consumable Female Body," 414–34; Helsinger, "Consumer Power and the Utopia of Desire," 903–33; Rappoport, "Price of Redemption," 853–75.

8. Anderson and Thullbery, "Ecofeminism in Christina Rossetti's 'Goblin Market,'" 63–87; Miller, "Ripeness and Waste," 194–203.

9. Graves, *A. E. Housman*, 40.

10. Housman, *My Brother, A. E. Housman*, 86.

11. Graves, *Housman*, 23, 142, 184.

12. Ricks, *Force of Poetry*, 173.

13. Housman, *Poems of A. E. Housman*, 9–10.

14. Terence Allan Hoagwood writes that the "the plot of the poem involves a confusion of love and malice or arm" (*A. E. Housman Revisited*, 51). John Bayley says of the "lad" who "for longing sighs" that he "wants from the girl what will transfer to her the pains of love and leave him free of them," which suggests that—to Bayley's mind, at least—the speaker refers to himself when he describes the lad's pain to the maiden (*Housman's Poems*, 112). Donna Richardson goes a step further by arguing that Housman "loses any broader perspective" in this poem, as if he were standing by, and behind, the speaker's words ("A. E. Housman's Moral Irony," 272).

15. Rossetti, *Complete Poems*, 5 (for the reference to the goblins' call).

16. Ibid., 13 ("Till Laura dwindling").

17. Ibid., 8.

18. Graves, *Housman*, 65–66.

19. Vincent, *A. E. Housman*, 365.

20. Page, *A. E. Housman*, 41.

21. Graves, *Housman*, 190.

22. Copus, *This Rare Spirit*, 3, 109–12, 243, 248.

23. Merrin, "Ballad of Charlotte Mew," 206.

24. Mew, *Charlotte Mew: Collected Poems and Selected Prose*, 3.

25. Lucas, *Radical Twenties*, 73.

26. Ibid., 2.

27. Ibid.

28. Rossetti, *Christina Rossetti: Complete Poems*, 7.

29. Ibid., 16, 18.

30. Mew, *Charlotte Mew: Collected Poems and Selected Prose*, 37; Rossetti, *Christina Rossetti: Complete Poems*, 5.

31. Mew, *Charlotte Mew: Collected Poems and Selected Prose*, 37.

32. Suzanne Raitt reads the "abortion or miscarriage" as a metaphor for "the shame of her desire": "the children that would never be born both because of her family history and because of her lesbianism" ("Charlotte Mew and May Sinclair," 12). Jessica Walsh goes into further specifics, arguing that "this red object can also be seen as the remains of a figurative, self-imposed hysterectomy," which was at the time performed under the guise of curing "women's mental illness" ("Corporeality and Fear of Insanity," 231).

33. Rice, *New Matrix for Modernism*, 71.

34. Rossetti, *Christina Rossetti: Complete Poems*, 17.

35. Mew, *Charlotte Mew: Collected Poems and Selected Prose*, 37.

36. Rollyson, *Amy Lowell Anew*, 10, 13, 42.

37. Ibid., 38, 48–49, 111, 197.

38. Faderman, "Ada Dwyer Russell in Amy Lowell's Life and Work," 71.

39. Lowell, *Selected Poems of Amy Lowell*, 86.

40. Stevenson, *Pre-Raphaelite Poets*, 105.

41. Harrison, "Christina Rossetti," 416.

42. Rossetti, *Christina Rossetti: Complete Poems*, 16.

43. Ibid., 19.

44. As Judith McDaniel puts it: "To fill the role of poet, to win the approval of those whom she imitated, Rich had nearly crafted herself out of feeling . . . These early poems seem nearly suffocated by self-control" (*Reading Adrienne Rich*, 4).

45. Rich, "When We Dead Awaken," 21.

46. Wendy Martin, for instance, has called it her "first volume of poems written from a feminist perspective" ("Consciousness and Community, 176). Likewise, Liz Yorke writes: "Recognizing that she had to seek out for herself the work of Sappho, Christina Rossetti, Emily Dickinson, Elinor Wylie, Edna Millay and H.D., Rich spoke passionately for the necessity for women to create an alternative to the male-stream canon, thus contributing to a major and energetic debate around the reclamation of 'lost' women authors in history and literature" (*Adrienne Rich*, 7).

47. Holladay, *Power of Adrienne Rich*, 26, 44.

48. Rich, *Collected Poems*, 100.

49. Gilbert and Gubar, *Madwoman in the Attic*, 567.

4. A. E. Housman's *A Shropshire Lad*

1. Parker, *Housman Country*, 125–26.

2. Page, *A. E. Housman*, 199.

3. Meyers, "Tormented Housman," 19.

4. Cocks, *Nameless Offences*, 24, 30–31.

5. Robb, *Strangers*, 159, 166–67.

6. Graves, *A. E. Housman*, 168.

7. Housman, *Poems*, 81–82.

8. Graves, *Housman*, 155, 159.

9. Shawe-Taylor, review of *My Brother*, 19.

10. Watson, *A. E. Housman*, 153.

11. Housman, *Poems*, 157.

12. Perrine, "Others, I Am Not the First," 135–38; Ricks, "Colour of His Hair," 240–55.

13. Housman, *Poems*, 50.

14. Parker, *Housman Country*, 126.

15. Bristow, "How Decadent Poems Die," 34.

16. Wilde, *Complete Letters*, 923, 928.

17. Harris, *Oscar Wilde*, 389.

18. Donald H. Ericksen writes that Wilde "had been reading *A Shropshire Lad* . . . and to some extent the meter he adopted, as well as the subject, was inspired by Housman's poem" (*Oscar Wilde*, 172). Peter Parker argues for a stylistic influence on "The Ballad of Reading Gaol," though he is careful to qualify that position: "For the most part, the poem is, like *A Shropshire Lad*, written in a direct and modern voice, largely purged of the decadent and grandiloquent flourishes that characterize much of Wilde's earlier poetry, though whether Housman or two years' hard labour was responsible for this new linguistic austerity is impossible to know" (*Housman Country*, 126). Joseph Bristow briefly mentions "resonances" in Wilde's poem before returning to subject matter: "Resonances of several lyrics in Housman's volume can be heard in Wilde's stanzas, which reflect in part on the indefensible hanging, in July 1896, of Charles Thomas Wooldridge: a trooper in the Royal Horse Guards who had taken his spouse's life in what appears to have been a frenzy of sexual jealousy" ("How Decadent Poems Die," 34).

19. Housman, *Poems*, 13.

20. Ibid., 13–14.

21. Wilde, *Oscar Wilde: Complete Poetry*, 163.

22. Housman, *Poems*, 13.

23. Wilde, *Oscar Wilde: Complete Poetry*, 164.

24. Housman, *Letters*, 77–78.

25. Molesworth, *And Bid Him Sing*, 4.

26. Schwarz, *Gay Voices of the Harlem Renaissance*, 50, 244, 249.

27. Chauncey, *Gay New York*, 157–59, 259.

28. Schwarz, *Gay Voices of the Harlem Renaissance*, 50–51.

29. Molesworth, *And Bid Him Sing*, 141, 225.

30. Rampersad, *Life of Langston Hughes*, 64.

31. Most critics, like James Emmanuel and Theodore Gross, speak of sensibility: "Cullen's deepest response as a poet was to the lyric beauty of John Keats and Edna St. Vincent Millay and to the more pessimistic view of A. E. Housman" (*Dark Symphony*, 174n). Others focus on Cullen's use of traditional forms in an era of radical formal experimentation, including the Harlem Renaissance, with which Cullen was closely associated. A. B. Christa Schwarz writes about "Cullen's adherence to strict measures and

rhymes, his following of writers like John Keats, Alfred Tennyson, and A. E. Housman" (*Gay Voices of the Harlem Renaissance*, 48).

32. Braddock, "Poetics of Conjecture," 1259.

33. Housman, *Poems*, 26.

34. Cullen, *Countee Cullen: Collected Poems*, 44.

35. Braddock, "Poetics of Conjecture," 1261.

36. Davis, *Beyond the White Negro*, 201.

37. Rampersad, *Life of Langston Hughes*, 116.

38. Housman, *Poems*, 8.

39. Nosworthy, "A. E. Housman and the Woolwich Cadet," 352.

40. Housman, *Poems*, 47.

41. Meyers, "Tormented Housman," 24.

42. Housman, *Poems*, 19–20.

43. Cullen, *Countee Cullen: Collected Poems*, 48.

44. Auden, *W. H. Auden: Complete Works*, 4:92.

45. Ibid., 6:500.

46. Ibid., 6:495, 6:497.

47. Auden, *W. H. Auden: Collected Poems*, 182.

48. Regan, *Sonnet*, 325.

49. Auden, *W. H. Auden: Collected Poems*, 182.

50. Carpenter, *W. H. Auden*, 105.

51. Howarth, "Housman's Dirty Postcards," 765.

52. Auden, *W. H. Auden: Complete Works*, 1:437–38.

53. Bozorth, *Auden's Games of Knowledge*, 197.

54. Housman, *Poems*, 24.

55. Auden, *W. H. Auden: Selected Poems*, 48.

56. Housman, *Poems*, 57.

57. Evans, "Housman's Spectral Shropshire," 868.

58. Auden, *W. H. Auden: Selected Poems*, 66.

59. Glaser, "Poet Stung," 526.

60. Housman, *Poems*, 21, 24.

61. Ibid., 107.

62. Firchow, "Land of Lost Content," 111.

63. Auden, *W. H. Auden: Collected Poems*, 862.

64. Fuller, *W. H. Auden*, 538.

65. Auden, *W. H. Auden: Collected Poems*, 862.

5. Walt Whitman's *Leaves of Grass*

1. Reynolds, *Walt Whitman in America*, 198.

2. Loving, *Walt Whitman*, 252.

3. Cowley, "Walt Whitman," 482.

4. Schmidgall, *Walt Whitman*, 193–98, 206–13, 214–19.

5. Martin, *Homosexual Tradition*, 3.

6. Fone, *Masculine Landscapes*, 3.

7. Whitman, *Leaves of Grass*, 770.

8. Zweig, *Walt Whitman*, 92.

9. D'Emilio and Freedman, *Intimate Matters*, 121–22.

10. Kaplan, *Walt Whitman*, 284.

11. Callow, *From Noon to Starry Night*, 257.

12. Kaplan, *Whitman*, 312–13.

13. Williams, *On Whitman*, 128.

14. Jerome Loving is one of the few to have made this observation in passing, as he discusses the poem "A Sketch": "It reveals—perhaps for the first time in the poetry—the loneliness found in parts of 'Song of Myself,' the 'Calamus' poems, and of course the 'Sea-Drift' series, not only 'Out of the Cradle,' but 'As I Ebb'd with the Ocean of Life.' Whitman's narrator seems lonely even in the midst of lovers" (*Walt Whitman*, 85).

15. Schmidgall, *Containing Multitudes*, 81.

16. Brasas, *Whitman's Mystical Ethics of Comradeship*, 81.

17. Mendelssohn, *Making Oscar Wilde*, 126–27.

18. Schmidgall, *Containing Multitudes*, 280–81.

19. Wilde, *Oscar Wilde in America*, 43, 49.

20. Reynolds, *Walt Whitman's America*, 540.

21. Schmidgall, *Containing Multitudes*, 280–81.

22. Ibid.

23. Wilde, *Complete Works: Reviews*, 4:401.

24. Ellmann, *Oscar Wilde*, 61–62, 76, 275–76.

25. Whitman, *Walt Whitman: The Complete Poems*, 163.

26. Wilde, *Oscar Wilde: Complete Poetry*, 50.

27. Crane, *Complete Poems and Selected Letters and Prose*, 263.

28. Berthoff, *Hart Crane*, 91.

29. Winters, *Crane*, 31.

30. Tate, *Poetry Reviews*, 103.

31. Unterecker, *Voyager*, 621.

32. Many critics, following on Bloom's theory of influence, later detected some uneasiness in Crane's relationship with Whitman. In Lee Edelman's reading, *The Bridge* is animated by the realization that Crane "can never be free of, never shake off the Whitman

in whose tracks he must follow, even as he knows that he must hold on for dear life to the older poet's hand" (*Transmemberment of Song*, 227). Langdon Hammer likewise describes Crane as "pulled down by his massive and embarrassing predecessor" (*Hart Crane and Allen Tate*, 176). Yet the charge of sentimentality has endured through the ensuing decades. Brian Reed's critique of *The Bridge* dovetails neatly with that of Winters and Tate: the conclusion to "Cape Hatteras," to him, "reads like the schmaltzy finale of a B-movie romance, down to the breathlessness of the final lines" (*Hart Crane*, 226).

33. Robert K. Martin reads the poem "Episode of Hands" as "a strong statement of social and political unity founded on sexual bonds" inspired by Whitman (*Homosexual Tradition in American Poetry*, 139). For Catherine A. Davies, too, "Whitman's concepts of adhesiveness and 'manly attachments' clearly inform Crane's own sense of the sustaining and redemptive quality of male bonding" (*Whitman's Queer Children*, 53–54).

34. Mariani, *Broken Tower*, 138.

35. Yingling, *Hart Crane and the Homosexual Text*, 210.

36. Fisher, *Hart Crane*, 111.

37. Mariani, *Broken Tower*, 153.

38. Crane, *O My Land, My Friends*, 55, 127, 274.

39. Ibid., 94.

40. Fisher, *Hart Crane*, 344.

41. Crane, *O My Land, My Friends*, 133.

42. Crane, *Complete Poems*, 78.

43. Whitman, *Walt Whitman: The Complete Poems*, 154–55.

44. Ibid., 73.

45. Erkkila, *Whitman and the Political Poet*, 101.

46. Culler, *Pursuit of Signs*, 143.

47. Johnson, "Apostrophe, Animation, and Abortion," 30.

48. Crane, *Complete Poems*, 84.

49. Lewis, *On the Poetry of Allen Ginsberg*, 24, 27, 30.

50. Morgan, *I Celebrate Myself*, 210.

51. Schultz, *Chicago Conspiracy Trial*, 192.

52. Thomas F. Merrill traces back to Whitman "the concept of the poet as a diarist" and "the technique of the catalogue" (*Allen Ginsberg*, 43, 50). Jonah Raskin finds biographical, thematic, and stylistic connections in Ginsberg: "Like Whitman, he wrote long poems with long, prose-like lines and long catalogues of things and people and events. Like Whitman, he wrote for America and about America, and like Whitman he sang about himself in the first person. Neither Whitman nor Ginsberg extinguished his personality in his poetry" (*American Scream*, 20). Bonnie Costello, meanwhile, contends that Ginsberg is "the closest we have to a modern Whitman," for his "expansiveness," his peculiar mix of "the sacred and the profane," and his transcendental defiance of space and time." Per

Costello, Ginsberg departs from his predecessor mainly in his dark view of the United States: "Whitman's optimistic vision has been severely tested by contemporary American realities" ("Poetry of Walt Whitman and Allen Ginsberg," 21).

53. Ginsberg, *Gay Sunshine Interviews*, 103.

54. Whitman, *Walt Whitman: The Complete Poems*, 116.

55. Bauer, "Sexology Backward," 143.

56. D'Emilio and Freedman, *Intimate Matters*, 293–94.

57. Ibid., 290–91.

58. Boyd, *Wide Open Town*, 5.

59. Tobin and Wicker, *Gay Crusaders*, 50.

60. For a thorough account of this story, see Cervini, *Deviant's War.*

61. Kinsey, *Sexual Behavior in the Human Male*, 651, 656.

62. Schumacher, *Dharma Lion*, 10, 15.

63. Morgan, *I Celebrate Myself*, 30, 36–37.

64. Schumacher, *Dharma Lion*, 43, 49.

65. Morgan, *I Celebrate Myself*, 71–72.

66. Schumacher, *Dharma Lion*, 55–56.

67. Morgan, *I Celebrate Myself*, 85.

68. Ibid.

69. Schumacher, *Dharma Lion*, 118–19.

70. Ibid., 183, 186–87.

71. Morgan, *I Celebrate Myself*, 209.

72. Ibid., 222.

73. Schumacher, *Dharma Lion*, 180.

74. Ginsberg, *Allen Ginsberg: Collected Poems*, 115.

75. Trigilio, *Allen Ginsberg's Buddhist Poetics*, 48.

76. Whitman, *Walt Whitman: The Complete Poems*, 99.

77. Ginsberg, *Allen Ginsberg: Collected Poems*, 115.

78. Whitman, *Walt Whitman: The Complete Poems*, 73.

79. Trigilio, *Allen Ginsberg's Buddhist Poetics*, 49.

80. Katz, "Naked Politics," 74.

81. Raskin, *American Scream*, 22–23.

82. Costello, "Poetry of Walt Whitman and Allen Ginsberg," 21.

83. Whitman, *Walt Whitman: The Complete Poems*, 109.

84. Ginsberg, *Allen Ginsberg: Collected Poems*, 128.

85. Ibid., 127.

86. Ibid., 133.

87. Whitman, *Walt Whitman: The Complete Poems*, 147.

88. Merrill, *Allen Ginsberg*, 103.

89. Zee, "Whitman, Lately," 98.

90. Ginsberg, *Allen Ginsberg: Collected Poems*, 136.

91. Whitman, *Walt Whitman: The Complete Poems*, 72.

92. Ginsberg, *Allen Ginsberg: Collected Poems*, 136.

93. Kearful, "Alimentary Poetics," 93.

94. Schumacher, *Dharma Lion*, 75.

95. Ginsberg, *Allen Ginsberg: Collected Poems*, 156.

96. Whitman, *Walt Whitman: The Complete Poems*, 73.

97. Ginsberg, *Allen Ginsberg: Collected Poems*, 156.

Coda

1. Halperin, *How to Be Gay*, 119.

2. Smith, *Don't Call Us Dead*, 37.

3. Whitman, *Walt Whitman: The Complete Poems*, 127.

4. Smith, *Don't Call Us Dead*, 37.

5. Whitman, *Walt Whitman: The Complete Poems*, 130, 133.

BIBLIOGRAPHY

Ackland, Valentine. *Journey from Winter: Selected Poems*. Edited by Frances Bingham. Manchester, UK: Carcanet Press, 2008.

Anderson, Kathleen, and Hannah Thullbery. "Ecofeminism in Christina Rossetti's 'Goblin Market.'" *Victorians: A Journal of Culture and Literature* 126 (2014): 63–87.

Auden, W. H. *The Complete Works of W. H. Auden: Prose, Volume 1: And Travel Books in Prose and Verse, 1926–1938*. Edited by Edward Mendelson. Princeton, NJ: Princeton University Press, 1997.

———. *The Complete Works of W. H. Auden: Prose, Volume 4: 1956–1962*. Edited by Edward Mendelson. Princeton, NJ: Princeton University Press, 2002.

———. *The Complete Works of W. H. Auden: Prose, Volume 6: 1969–1973*. Edited by Edward Mendelson. Princeton, NJ: Princeton University Press, 2015.

———. *W. H. Auden: Collected Poems*. Edited by Edward Mendelson. New York: Vintage, 1991.

———. *W. H. Auden: Selected Poems*. Edited by Edward Mendelson. New York: Vintage, 2007.

Bate, Walter Jackson. *The Burden of the Pats and the English Poet*. Cambridge: Harvard University Press, 1972.

Bauer, Heike, and Matt Cook, eds. *Queer 1950s: Rethinking Sexuality in the Postwar Years*. London: Palgrave Macmillan, 2012.

———. "Sexology Backward: Hirschfeld, Kinsey and the Reshaping of Sex Research in the 1950s." In *Queer 1950s: Rethinking Sexuality in the Postwar Years*, edited by Heike Bauer and Matt Cook, 133–49. London: Palgrave Macmillan, 2012.

Bayley, John. *Housman's Poems*. London: Clarendon Press, 1992.

Beckman, Linda Hunt. *Amy Levy: Her Life and Letters*. Athens: Ohio University Press, 2000.

Behrendt, Patricia Flanagan. *Oscar Wilde: Eros and Aesthetics*. London: Palgrave Macmillan, 2016.

Belford, Barbara. *Oscar Wilde: A Certain Genius*. New York: Random House, 2000.

Berthoff, Warner. *Hart Crane: A Re-Introduction*. Minneapolis: University of Minnesota Press, 1985.

Bingham, Frances. *Valentine Ackland: A Transgressive Life*. Bath, UK: Handheld Press, 2021.

Bishop, Elizabeth. *Poems: Elizabeth Bishop*. Edited by Saskia Hamilton. New York: Farrar, Straus and Giroux, 2011.

Bloom, Harold. *The Anxiety of Influence: A Theory of Poetry*. 2nd ed. London: Oxford University Press, 1997.

Boyd, Nan Alamilla. *Wide Open Town: A History of Queer San Francisco to 1965*. Berkeley: University of California Press, 2003.

Bozorth, Richard R. *Auden's Games of Knowledge: Poetry and the Meanings of Homosexuality*. New York: Columbia University Press, 2001.

Braddock, Jeremy. "The Poetics of Conjecture: Countee Cullen's Subversive Exemplarity." *Callaloo* 25, no. 4 (2002): 1250–71.

Bristow, Joseph. "How Decadent Poems Die." In *Decadent Poetics: Literature and Form at the British Fin de Siècle*, edited by Jason David Hall and Alex Murray, 26–45. New York: Palgrave, 2013.

Burlinson, Kathryn. *Christina Rossetti*. Plymouth, UK: Northcote House, 1998.

Callan, Edward. *Auden: A Carnival of Intellect*. New York: Oxford University Press, 1983.

Callow, Philip. *From Noon to Starry Night: A Life of Walt Whitman*. Chicago: Ivan R. Dee, 1992.

Campbell, Elizabeth. "Of Mothers and Merchants: Female Economics in Christina Rossetti's 'Goblin Market.'" *Victorian Studies* 33, no. 3 (1990): 393–410.

Carpenter, Humphrey. *W. H. Auden: A Biography*. Boston: Houghton Mifflin, 1981.

Carpenter, Mary Wilson. "'Eat Me, Drink Me, Love Me': The Consumable Female Body in Christina Rossetti's *Goblin Market*." *Victorian Poetry* 29, no. 4 (1991): 414–34.

Cervini, Eric. *The Deviant's War: The Homosexual vs. the United States of America*. New York: Farrar, Straus and Giroux, 2020.

Chauncey, George. *Gay New York: Gender, Urban Culture, and the Making of the Gay Male World, 1890–1940*. New York: Basic Books, 1994.

Cocks, H. G. *Nameless Offences: Homosexual Desire in the Nineteenth Century*. London: I. B. Tauris, 2003.

Cooper, Jane Roberta, ed. *Reading Adrienne Rich: Reviews and Re-Visions, 1951–81*. Ann Arbor: University of Michigan Press, 1984.

Copus, Julia. *This Rare Spirit: A Life of Charlotte Mew*. London: Faber and Faber, 2022.

Costello, Bonnie. *The Plural of Us: Poetry and Community in Auden and Others*. Princeton, NJ: Princeton University Press, 2020.

———. "The Poetry of Walt Whitman and Allen Ginsberg." *Bulletin of the American Academy of Arts and Sciences* 69, no. 4 (2016): 20–22.

Coulson, Victoria. "Redemption and Representation in *Goblin Market:* Christina Rossetti and the Salvic Signifier." *Victorian Poetry* 55, no. 4 (2017): 423–50.

Cowley, Malcolm. "Walt Whitman: The Secret." *New Republic,* April 1946, 481–84.

Cox, Kimberly. *Touch, Sexuality, and Hands in British Literature, 1740–1901*. New York: Routledge, 2022.

Crane, Hart. *Complete Poems and Selected Letters and Prose of Hart Crane*. Edited by Brom Weber. New York: Liveright, 1966.

———. *The Complete Poems of Hart Crane*. Edited by Marc Simon. New York: Liveright, 2000.

———. *O My Land, My Friends: The Selected Letters of Hart Crane*. Edited by Langdon Hammer and Brom Weber. New York: Four Walls Eight Windows, 1997.

Croft-Cooke, Rupert. *Bosie: The Story of Lord Alfred Douglas, His Friends and Enemies*. London: W. H. Allen, 1963.

Cullen, Countee. *Countee Cullen: Collected Poems*. Edited by Major Jackson. New York: Library of America, 2013.

Culler, Jonathan. *The Pursuit of Signs: Semiotics, Literature, Deconstruction*. Ithaca, NY: Cornell University Press, 1981.

Cunningham, Valentine. *British Writers of the Thirties*. Oxford: Oxford University Press, 1988.

Davenport-Hines, Richard. *Auden*. New York: Pantheon Books, 1995.

Davies, Catherine A. *Whitman's Queer Children: America's Homosexual Epics.* London: Continuum, 2012.

Davis, Kimberly Chabot. *Beyond the White Negro: Empathy and Anti-Racist Reading.* Urbana: University of Illinois Press, 2014.

Davison, Dennis. *W. H. Auden.* London: Evans Brothers, 1970.

D'Emilio, John, and Estelle B. Freedman. *Intimate Matters: A History of Sexuality in America.* Chicago: University of Chicago Press, 2012.

Douglas, Alfred. *The City of the Soul.* London: Grant Richards, 1899.

———. *The Collected Poems of Lord Alfred Douglas.* London: Martin Secker, 1919.

Dunn, Douglas. "Back and Forth: Auden and Political Poetry." *Critical Survey* 6, no. 3 (1994): 325–35.

Edelman, Lee. *Transmemberment of Song: Hart Crane's Anatomies of Rhetoric and Desire.* Stanford: Stanford University Press, 1987.

Ellmann, Richard. *Oscar Wilde.* New York: Vintage, 1988.

Emmanuel, James A., and Theodore L. Gross, eds. *Dark Symphony: Negro Literature in America.* New York: Free Press, 1968.

Ericksen, Donald H. *Oscar Wilde.* Boston: Twayne, 1977.

Erkkila, Betsy. *Whitman and the Political Poet.* New York: Oxford University Press, 1989.

Evans, Mihail. "Housman's Spectral Shropshire." *Victorian Literature and Culture* 43, no. 4 (2015): 857–73.

Faderman, Lillian. "'Which, Being Interpreted, Is as May Be, or Otherwise': Ada Dwyer Russell in Amy Lowell's Life and Work." In *Amy Lowell, American Modern,* edited by Adrianne Munich and Melissa Bradshaw, 59–76. New Brunswick, NJ: Rutgers University Press, 2004.

Firchow, Peter E. "The Land of Lost Content: Housman's Shropshire." *Mosaic: An Interdisciplinary Critical Journal* 13, no. 2 (1980): 103–21.

Fisher, Clive. *Hart Crane: A Life.* New Haven, CT: Yale University Press, 2002.

Fisher, Trevor. *Oscar and Bosie: A Fatal Passion.* Thrupp, Stroud, Gloucestershire: Sutton, 2002.

Fone, Bryan. *Masculine Landscapes: Walt Whitman and the Homoerotic Text.* Carbondale: Southern Illinois University Press, 1992.

Forster, E. M. *Two Cheers for Democracy.* London: Arnold, 1951.

Foucault, Michel. *The History of Sexuality.* Vol. 1. Translated by Robert Hurley. New York: Random House, 1990.

Frankel, Nicholas. *Oscar Wilde: The Unrepentant Years*. Cambridge: Harvard University Press, 2017.

Fuller, John. *W. H. Auden: A Commentary*. Princeton, NJ: Princeton University Press, 1998.

Gilbert, Sandra, and Susan Gubar. *The Madwoman in the Attic: The Woman Writer and the Nineteenth-Century Literary Imagination*. New Haven, CT: Yale University Press, 1979.

Ginsberg, Allen. *Allen Ginsberg: Collected Poems, 1947–1997*. New York: Harper Perennial Modern Classics, 2007.

———. *Howl and Other Poems*. San Francisco: City Lights Books, 1956.

Glaser, Ben. "The Poet Stung: Verse Drama, Modern Rhythm, and the Politics of W. H. Auden's Metrical Stammer." *Modernism/modernity* 28, no. 3 (September 2021): 511–34.

Graves, Richard Perceval. *A. E. Housman: The Scholar-Poet*. London: Faber and Faber, 2014.

Hall, Jason David, and Alex Murray, eds. *Decadent Poetics: Literature and Form at the British Fin de Siècle*. New York: Palgrave, 2013.

Halperin, David M. *How to Be Gay*. Cambridge: Harvard University Press, 2012.

Hammer, Langdon. *Hart Crane and Allen Tate: Janus-Faced Modernism*. Princeton, NJ: Princeton University Press, 1992.

Harris, Frank. *Oscar Wilde: His Life and Confessions*. New York: Carroll & Graf, 1916.

Harrison, Anthony H. "Christina Rossetti: Illness and Ideology." *Victorian Poetry* 45, no. 4 (2007): 415–28.

Helsinger, Elizabeth. "Consumer Power and the Utopia of Desire: Christina Rossetti's 'Goblin Market.'" *ELH* 58, no. 4 (1991): 903–33.

Hererro Brasas, Juan A. *Whitman's Mystical Ethics of Comradeship: Homosexuality and the Marginality of Friendship at the Crossroads of Modernity*. Albany: State University of New York Press, 2010.

Hoagwood, Terence Allan. *A. E. Housman Revisited*. Boston: Twayne, 1995.

Holladay, Hilary. *The Power of Adrienne Rich: A Biography*. New York: Doubleday, 2020.

Holt, Terrence. "'Men Sell Not Such in Any Town': Exchange in *Goblin Market*." *Victorian Poetry* 28, no. 1 (1990): 51–67.

Housman, A. E. *The Letters of A. E. Housman*. Edited by Archie Burnett. London: Clarendon Press, 2007.

————. *The Poems of A. E. Housman*. Edited by Archie Burnett. London: Clarendon Press, 1997.

Housman, Laurence. *My Brother, A. E. Housman: Personal Recollections, Together with Thirty Hitherto Unpublished Poems*. New York: Scribner's Sons, 1938.

Howarth, Peter. "Housman's Dirty Postcards: Poetry, Modernism, and Masochism." *PMLA* 124, no. 3 (May 2009): 764–89.

Hyde, H. Montgomery. *Oscar Wilde*. Farrar, Straus and Giroux, 1975.

Hyde, Lewis, ed. *On the Poetry of Allen Ginsberg*. Ann Arbor: University of Michigan Press, 1984.

Irwin, William. "What Is an Allusion?" *Journal of Aesthetics and Art Criticism* 59, no. 3 (2001): 387–97.

Johnson, Barbara. "Apostrophe, Animation, and Abortion." *Diacritics* 16, no. 1 (1986): 28–47.

Johnson, Richard. *Man's Place: An Essay on Auden*. Ithaca, NY: Cornell University Press, 1973.

Kaplan, Justin. *Walt Whitman: A Life*. New York: Simon and Schuster, 1980.

Katz, Jonathan D. "Naked Politics: The Art of Eros, 1955–1975." In *Queer Difficulty in Art and Poetry: Rethinking the Sexed Body in Verse and Visual Culture*, edited by Jongwoo Jeremy Kim and Christopher Reed, 74–86. London: Taylor & Francis, 2017.

Kearful, Frank. "Alimentary Poetics: Robert Lowell and Allen Ginsberg." *Partial Answers: Journal of Literature and the History of Ideas* 11, no. 1 (January 2013): 87–108.

Kim, Jongwoo Jeremy, and Christopher Reed, eds. *Queer Difficulty in Art and Poetry: Rethinking the Sexed Body in Verse and Visual Culture*. London: Taylor & Francis, 2017.

Kinsey, Alfred C., Wardell B. Pomeroy, and Clyde E. Martin. *Sexual Behavior in the Human Male*. Philadelphia: W. B. Saunders, 1948.

Larkin, Philip. *The Complete Poems of Philip Larkin*. Edited by Archie Burnett. New York: Farrar, Straus and Giroux, 2012.

Leeming, David. *Stephen Spender: A Life in Modernism*. New York: Henry Holt, 2011.

Levy, Amy. *A London Plane-Tree, and Other Verse*. London: T. Fisher Unwin, 1889.

Leyland, Winston, ed. *Gay Sunshine Interviews*. Vol. 1. San Francisco: Gay Sunshine, 1978.

Loving, Jerome. *Walt Whitman: The Song of Himself*. Berkeley: University of California Press, 2000.

Lowell, Amy. *Pictures of the Floating World*. New York: Macmillan, 1919.

———. *Selected Poems of Amy Lowell*. Edited by Melissa Bradshaw and Adrienne Munich. New Brunswick, NJ: Rutgers University Press, 2002.

Lucas, John. "Auden's Politics: Power, Authority, and the Individual." In *The Cambridge Companion to W. H. Auden*, edited by Stan Smith, 152–64. Cambridge: Cambridge University Press, 2004.

———. *The Radical Twenties: Writing, Politics, and Culture*. New Brunswick, NJ: Rutgers University Press, 1999.

Mariani, Paul. *The Broken Tower: A Life of Hart Crane*. Norton, 1999.

Marsh, Jan. *Christina Rossetti: A Writer's Life*. New York: Viking, 1995.

Martin, Robert K. *The Homosexual Tradition in American Poetry*. Austin: University of Texas Press, 1979.

Martin, Wendy. "'To Study Our Lives': Consciousness and Community in Adrienne Rich's *The Dream of a Common Language: Poems 1974–77*." *Ploughshares* 5, no. 1 (1979): 172–77.

McCall Smith, Alexander. *What W. H. Auden Can Do for You*. Princeton, NJ: Princeton University Press, 2013.

McDaniel, Judith. "'Reconstituting the World': The Poetry and Vision of Adrienne Rich." In *Reading Adrienne Rich: Reviews and Re-Visions, 1951–81*, edited by Jane Roberta Cooper, 3–29. Ann Arbor: University of Michigan Press, 1984.

Mendelson, Edward. *Early Auden*. New York: Viking, 1981.

Mendelssohn, Michèle. *Making Oscar Wilde*. Oxford: Oxford University Press, 2018.

Mendoza, Victor Roman. "'Come Buy': The Crossing of Sexual and Consumer Desire in Christina Rossetti's 'Goblin Market.'" *ELH* 73, no. 4 (2006): 913–47.

Mermin, Dorothy. "Heroic Sisterhood in 'Goblin Market.'" *Victorian Poetry* 21, no. 2 (1983): 107–18.

Merrill, Thomas F. *Allen Ginsberg*. Boston: Twayne, 1969.

Merrin, Jeredith. "The Ballad of Charlotte Mew." *Modern Philology* 95, no. 2 (November 1997): 200–217.

Mew, Charlotte. *Charlotte Mew: Collected Poems and Selected Prose*. Edited by Val Warner. New York: Routledge, 2003.

Meyers, Jeffrey. "Tormented Housman." *Style* 50, no. 1 (2016): 19–36.

Miller, Ashley. "Ripeness and Waste: Christina Rossetti's Botanical Women." *Victorian Studies* 61, no. 2 (2019): 194–203.

Moers, Ellen. *Literary Women*. Garden City, NY: Doubleday, 1972.

Molesworth, Charles. *And Bid Him Sing: A Biography of Countée Cullen*. Chicago: University of Chicago Press, 2012.

Morgan, Bill. *I Celebrate Myself: The Somewhat Private Life of Allen Ginsberg*. New York: Viking, 2006.

Munich, Adrianne, and Melissa Bradshaw, eds. *Amy Lowell, American Modern*. New Brunswick, NJ: Rutgers University Press, 2004.

Murray, Alex. *Landscapes of Decadence: Literature and Place at the Fin de Siècle*. Cambridge: Cambridge University Press, 2016.

Murray, Douglas. *Bosie: A Biography of Lord Alfred Douglas*. New York: Hyperion, 2000.

Nealon, Christopher S. *Foundlings: Lesbian and Gay Historical Emotion before Stonewall*. Durham, NC: Duke University Press, 2001.

Nosworthy, J. M. "A. E. Housman and the Woolwich Cadet." *Notes and Queries* 17, no. 9 (1970): 351–53.

Ohi, Kevin. *Dead Letters Sent: Queer Literary Transmission*. Minneapolis: University of Minnesota Press, 2015.

O'Neill, Michael. "The Thirties Bequest." In *The Oxford Handbook of Contemporary British and Irish Poetry*, edited by Peter Robinson, 38–56. Oxford: Oxford University Press, 2013.

Page, Norman. *A. E. Housman: A Critical Biography*. Houndmills, Basingstoke, Hampshire: Palgrave, 1996.

Parker, Peter. *Housman Country: Into the Heart of England*. New York: Farrar, Straus and Giroux, 2017.

Perrine, Laurence. "Housman's 'Others, I Am Not the First.'" *Victorian Poetry* 28, nos. 3–4 (1990): 135–38.

Raitt, Suzanne. "Charlotte Mew and May Sinclair: A Love-Song." *Critical Quarterly* 37, no. 3 (1995): 3–17.

Rampersad, Arnold. *The Life of Langston Hughes*. Vol. 1. Oxford: Oxford University Press, 1986.

Rappoport, Jill. "The Price of Redemption in 'Goblin Market.'" *Studies in English Literature, 1500–1900* 50, no. 4 (Fall 2010): 853–75.

Raskin, Jonah. *American Scream: Allen Ginsberg's Howl and the Making of the Beat Generation*. Berkeley: University of California Press, 2004.

Reed, Brian M. *Hart Crane: After His Lights*. Tuscaloosa: University of Alabama Press, 2006.

Regan, Stephen. *The Sonnet*. Oxford: Oxford University Press, 2019.

Replogle, Justin. *Auden's Poetry*. Seattle: University of Washington Press, 1969.

Reynolds, David S. *Walt Whitman in America: A Cultural Biography*. New York: Knopf, 1995.

Rice, Nelljean McConeghey. *A New Matrix for Modernism: A Study of the Lives and Poetry of Charlotte mew and Anna Wickham*. New York: Routledge, 2013.

Rich, Adrienne. *Collected Poems, 1950–2012*. Norton, 2016.

———. "Compulsory Heterosexuality and Lesbian Existence." *Signs* 5, no. 4 (1980): 631–60.

———. "When We Dead Awaken: Writing as Re-Vision." *College Literature* 34, no. 1 (1972): 18–30.

Richardson, Donna. "The Can of Ail: A. E. Housman's Moral Irony." *Victorian Poetry* 48, no. 2 (2010): 267–85.

Ricks, Christopher. "A. E. Housman and 'the Colour of His Hair.'" *Essays in Criticism* 47, no. 3 (1997): 240–55.

———. *The Force of Poetry*. Oxford: Clarendon Press, 1995.

———. "Loneliness and Poetry." In *Allusion to the Poets*, 261–81. Oxford: Oxford University Press, 2002.

Robb, Graham. *Strangers: Homosexual Love in the Nineteenth Century*. New York: Norton, 2005.

Robinson, Peter, ed. *The Oxford Handbook of Contemporary British and Irish Poetry*. Oxford: Oxford University Press, 2013.

Rollyson, Carl. *Amy Lowell Anew: A Biography*. Lanham, MD: Rowman & Littlefield, 2013.

Rossetti, Christina. *Christina Rossetti: The Complete Poems*. Edited by Betty S. Flowers. London: Penguin, 2005.

Schmidgall, Gary. *Containing Multitudes: Walt Whitman and the British Literary Tradition*. Oxford: Oxford University Press, 2014.

———. *Walt Whitman: A Gay Life*. New York: Dutton, 1997.

Schultz, John. *The Chicago Conspiracy Trial*. Rev. ed. Chicago: University of Chicago Press, 2009.

Schumacher, Michael. *Dharma Lion: A Biography of Allen Ginsberg*. New York: St. Martin's Press, 1992.

Schwarz, A. B. Christa. *Gay Voices of the Harlem Renaissance*. Bloomington: Indiana University Press, 2003.

Sedgwick, Eve Kosofsky. *Epistemology of the Closet*. Berkeley: University of California Press, 1990.

Shawe-Taylor, Desmond. Review of *My Brother, A. E. Housman*, by Laurence Housman. *New Statesman*, January 1, 1938, 19.

Smith, Danez. *Don't Call Us Dead*. Minneapolis: Graywolf, 2017.

Smith, Stan, ed. *The Cambridge Companion to W. H. Auden*. Cambridge: Cambridge University Press, 2004.

Spears, Monroe K. *The Poetry of W. H. Auden: The Disenchanted Island*. Oxford: Oxford University Press, 1963.

Spender, Stephen. *Stephen Spender: New Collected Poems*. Edited by Michael Brett. London: Faber and Faber, 2004.

———. *Stephen Spender: New Selected Journals, 1939–1995*. London: Faber and Faber, 2012.

———. *The Temple*. New York: Grove Press, 1988.

———. "W. H. Auden Memorial Address." In *The Thirties and After: Poetry, Politics, People, 1933–1970*, edited by Stephen Spender, 227–33. New York: Random House, 1978.

———. *World Within World: The Autobiography of Stephen Spender*. Berkeley: University of California Press, 1966.

———, ed. *The Thirties and After: Poetry, Politics, People, 1933–1970*. New York: Random House, 1978.

Stern, Rebecca F. "'Adulterations Detected': Food and Fraud in Christina Rossetti's 'Goblin Market.'" *Nineteenth-Century Literature* 57, no. 4 (March 2003): 477–511.

Stevenson, Lionel. *The Pre-Raphaelite Poets*. Chapel Hill: University of North Carolina Press, 1972.

Stokes, John. *Oscar Wilde: Myths, Miracles and Imitations*. Cambridge: Cambridge University Press, 1996.

Sturgis, Matthew. *Oscar: A Life*. London: Apollo, 2018.

Sutherland, John. *Stephen Spender: A Literary Life*. Oxford: Oxford University Press, 2005.

Symons, Julian. *The Thirties: A Dream Revolved*. London: Cresset Press, 1960.

Tarr, Clayton Carlyle. "Covent Goblin Market." *Victorian Poetry* 50, no. 3 (2012): 297–316.

Tate, Allen. *The Poetry Reviews of Allen Tate, 1924–1944.* Edited by Ashley Brown and Frances Neel Cheney. Baton Rouge: Louisiana State University Press, 1983.

Tippins, Sherill. *February House.* Boston: Houghton Mifflin Harcourt, 2016.

Tobin, Kay, and Randy Wicker. *The Gay Crusaders.* New York: Arno Press, 1975.

Trachtenberg, Alan, ed. *Hart Crane: A Collection of Critical Essays.* Englewood Cliffs, NJ: Prentice-Hall, 1982.

Travisano, Thomas. *Love Unknown: The Life and Worlds of Elizabeth Bishop.* New York: Viking, 2019.

Trigilio, Tony. *Allen Ginsberg's Buddhist Poetics.* Carbondale: Southern Illinois University Press, 2007.

Trolley, A. Trevor. *The Poetry of the Thirties.* New York: St. Martin's Press, 1975.

Unterecker, John. *Voyager: A Life of Hart Crane.* New York: Farrar, Straus and Giroux, 1969.

Vincent, Edgar. *A. E. Housman: Hero of the Hidden Life.* Rochester, NY: Boydell Press, 2018.

Walsh, Jessica. "'The Strangest Pain to Bear': Corporeality and Fear of Insanity in Charlotte Mew's Poetry." *Victorian Poetry* 40, no. 3 (2022): 217–40.

Watson, George L. *A. E. Housman: A Divided Life.* Boston: Beacon, 1958.

Weatherhead, A. Kingsley. *Stephen Spender and the Thirties.* Lewisburg, PA: Bucknell University Press, 1975.

Whitman, Walt. *Leaves of Grass and Other Writings.* Edited by Michael Moon. New York: Norton, 2002.

———. *Walt Whitman: The Complete Poems.* Edited by Francis Murphy. London: Penguin, 2005.

Wilde, Oscar. *The Complete Letters of Oscar Wilde.* Edited by Merlin Holland and Rupert Hart-Davis. London: Fourth Estate, 2000.

———. *The Complete Works of Oscar Wilde: Reviews.* Vol. 4. New York: National Library Company, 1909.

———. *Oscar Wilde: Complete Poetry.* Edited by Isobel Murray. Oxford: Oxford University Press, 1997.

———. *Oscar Wilde in America: The Interviews.* Edited by Gary Scharnhorst and Matthew Hofer. Urbana: University of Illinois Press, 2010.

Williams, C. K. *On Whitman.* Princeton, NJ: Princeton University Press, 2010.

Williams, Keith. *British Writers and the Media, 1930–1945.* Houndmills, Basingstoke, Hampshire, UK: Palgrave, 1996.

Winters, Yvor. "The Progress of Hart Crane." In *Hart Crane: A Collection of Critical Essays,* edited by Alan Trachtenberg, 23–31. Prentice-Hall, 1982.

Yingling, Thomas E. *Hart Crane and the Homosexual Text: New Thresholds, New Anatomies.* Chicago: University of Chicago Press, 1990.

Yorke, Liz. *Adrienne Rich: Passion, Politics, and the Body.* London: Sage, 1997.

Zee, Anton Vander. "Whitman, Lately." *Agni* 72 (2010): 97–112.

Zweig, Paul. *Walt Whitman: The Making of the Poet.* New York: Basic Books, 1984.

INDEX

For You I Write

"Today, I've decided to use my gifts for You."

For You I Write

KB

KOBALT BOOKS

© Kobalt Books LLC
www.**kobaltbooks**.com